I0740352

Life Symbols as Related to Sex Symbolism

Life Symbols as Related to Sex Symbolism

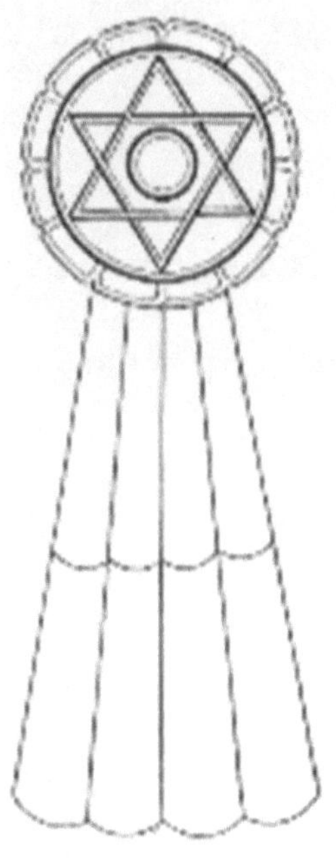

By

Elizabeth E. Goldsmith

Athens ‡ Manchester

Life Symbols as Related to Sex Symbolism

Published by: Old Book Publishing Ltd

Book Cover Design: Old Book Publishing Ltd

Title of original: Life Symbols as Related to Sex Symbolism

Originally Published in 1924 by G.P. Putnam's Sons Longmans, Green & Company

ISBN–10: 1–78107–188–8
ISBN–13: 978–1–78107–188–5

EDITOR'S NOTE

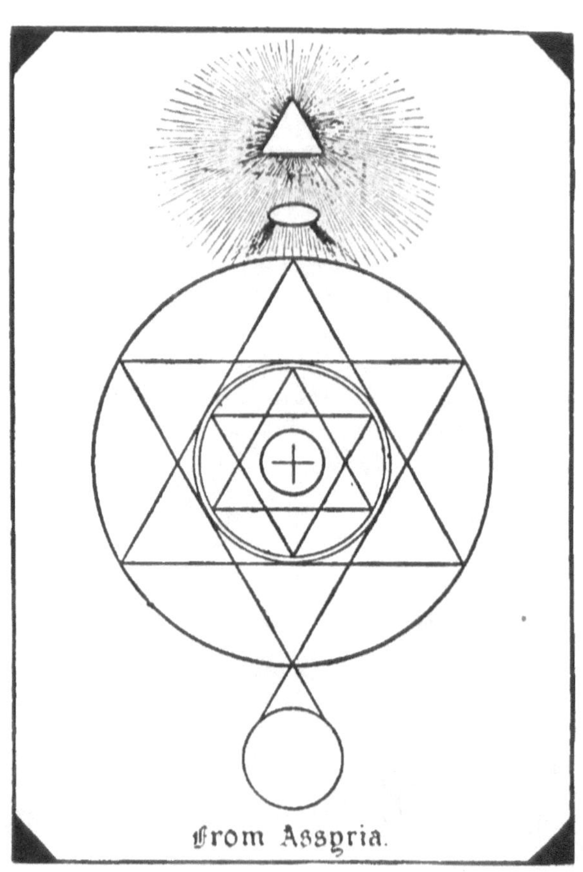

From Assyria.

Life Symbols as Related to Sex Symbolism

Photo. Alinari

Adam and Eve Driven out of Paradise.—Masaccio

(Brancacci Chapel, Santa Maria del Carmine, Florence)

Life Symbols as Related to Sex Symbolism

A brief study into the origin and significance of certain symbols which have been found in all civilisations, such as the cross, the circle, the serpent, the triangle, the tree of life, the swastika, and other solar emblems, showing the unity and simplicity of thought underlying their use as religious symbols

By

Elizabeth E. Goldsmith

Author of "Sacred Symbols in Art," "Toby: the Story of a Dog"

With more than 100 Illustrations

G. P. Putnam's Sons
New York & London
The Knickerbocker Press
1924

Made in the United States of America

To

THE FIRE WORSHIPPER

PREFACE

WHENEVER I find myself becoming depressed over world conditions I turn to symbolism for re-assurance. These old, old symbols of the profound mystery of life which, as Bergson puts it, is "continually making and unmaking" have an extraordinary effect. You follow them back and back—only to discover that you have made a step forward into a more extensive reality. Having gone thus far, it is possible that your conclusions may offend the orthodox and dismay the visionary, nevertheless I venture to affirm that whoever makes the excursion boldly yet reverently will return with vision clarified, faith heartened and belief in the Eternal Verities joyously renewed. He will have perspective; feel the brevity yet measurelessness of time, the immensity of the ages, the tremendous force of Life. He will see, too, that however many times mankind has failed, the bent of man's nature is toward the higher, and if there is a long road behind strewn with his defeats, there is still a longer road ahead and the future is ever young.

In preparing this book I am under greater obligations than I can express to the friends who have loyally sustained and encouraged me; my grateful acknowledgments are also due to George Haven Putnam for his charming courtesy and interest, to Louise Wallace Hackney for sharing with me some of her notes on China and the Chinese, to Ralph Adams Cram for permission to use at my own discretion portions of a private letter and to Harold Bayley for having written *The Lost Language of Symbolism*—a book that is a constant joy.

E. E. G.

Sorrento, Italy,
September, 1924.

"Love in which some have seen the great mystery of life, may possibly deliver us life's secret. It shows us each generation leaning over the generation that shall follow. It allows us a glimpse of the fact that the living being is above all a thorough-fare and that the essence of life is in the movement by which life is transmitted."

Creative Evolution—Bergson.

"The *traditio*, the handing down of the intellectual acquisitions of the human race from one generation to another, the constant selection of thoughts and discoveries and feelings and events so precious that they must be made into books, and then of books so precious that they must be copied and re-copied and not allowed to die—the *traditio* itself is a wonderful and august process, full, no doubt, of abysmal gaps and faults, like all things human, but full also of that strange, half-baffled and yet not wholly baffled splendour which makes all the characteristic works of man. I think the *grammaticus*, while not sacrificing his judgment, should accept it and rejoice in it—rejoice to be the intellectual child of his great fore-fathers, to catch at their spirit, to carry on their work, to live and die for the great unknown purpose which the eternal spirit of man seems to be working out upon the earth. . . . The Philistine, the vulgarian, the great sophist, the passer of base coin for true, he is all about us, and, worse, he has his outposts inside us, persecuting our peace, spoiling our sight, confusing our values, making a man's self seem greater than the race and the present thing more important than the eternal. From him and his influence we find our escape by means of the *grammata* into that calm world of theirs, where stridency and clamour are forgotten in the ancient stillness, where the strong iron is long since rusted and the rocks of granite broken into dust, but the great things of the human spirit still shine like stars pointing man's way onward to the great triumph or the great tragedy."

Religio Grammatici—Gilbert Murray.

INTRODUCTION

A WOMAN of my acquaintance averred the other day that she was perfectly sure that life to her young daughter aged sixteen meant a low, high power, rakish looking, bright yellow runabout, gas full on, daughter at the wheel, car going eighty miles an hour. And one must admit that this is a wholly convincing and delightful picture of youth, motion, life, the present age. It is a little too obvious, too circumscribed, however, to be a symbol.

Stretching across the horizon of man's beginnings, their origin lost in remotest antiquity, there are certain symbols that for thousands of years have bored the materialist, piqued the curious, enchanted the mystic, fascinated the student, bothered the Church and delighted the wise. Possibly simple and uncomplicated in their inception, adopted by every religion, they have added, taken on and lost until they seem to hold the magical essence of everything that has gone before without altering or losing their original meaning which has been invariably associated with Life.

Few in number, it is their persistence, their vitality, the way they have been interwoven with everything that we think, feel, do—that puzzles and amazes. You follow them back. They lead like a torch through much that you would rather not see and can never hope to explain. You tread gingerly looking askance at taboos, magic, animism, totemism, fetiches. If on the way you linger under the shade of Frazer's *Golden Bough*—especially when you come to taboos—you may lose some pre-conceived notion that we had gone very far beyond the savage. You are willing to leave it to Frazer, however, whether the recent colossal taboo is an advance in civilisation or a reversion to savagery. Fetiches, too! You can't resist feeling that although we may not make fetiches of stones and shells—which even in primitive times were worshipped not for themselves but as the dwelling places of spirits supposed to inhabit them—yet we do things equally amusing. We encase an idea in a word or phrase and then believe quite as naïvely as the savage that the ideal state or god or goddess resides within the word.

You begin to wonder a little uneasily, as you make your way through an incoherent maze of outworn and discarded religious forms that at one time or another represented men's thoughts on life, if the instinct for taboos and fetich worship so long indulged in has not become ineradicable. It is with a sensation of release that you finally reach the place where interpretations vanish—where nothing remains but the old and potent symbols of life.

Whether even now you are at the beginning of things, or have merely reached some clear open space that stands between us and some lost civilisation possibly higher than our own, none can say. The tradition of the lapse of mankind from a Golden Age and the destruction of the world by water is current in all races. Geologists have assumed that in the tertiary epoch there was a land connection between the two continents. This may have been the lost island of Atlantis which was said to have been overwhelmed by the sea about 9600 B.C. The theory has been advanced that the submersion of Atlantis may account, too, for the universal legend of the Great Flood and that the "lost cradle of civilisation was not in Asia but in Atlantis." The fact that these life symbols are found on both continents, also the similarity of superstitions, folk lore and fairy tales among all ancient peoples would indicate that mankind had a common cradle—but where?—We can only speculate. Nor do we know except as we are haunted by dreams of a world like a garden—very beautiful, very fair—whether civilisations in the long processes of time have lost or gained. As the sublimer portions of the Egyptian religion are the oldest, Bayley infers that "the remoter the time the simpler and purer was Humanity." And it is in some such spirit of belief that one approaches these ancient symbols. None know how they came into being nor what further portal of past or future life they guard. They take one beyond the farthest reach of thought—so far back that men and women cease to be individuals. Their idiosyncrasies, their tragi-comic aspects that give pith and point to meditation are swallowed up in the resistless flow of the life current. And men and women are merely the active and passive principles through which the life current flows—peacefully when its appointed channels are kept strong and fit, and destructively, wastefully, breaking down all barriers when the channels have become weakened and unfit.

Our glorious and inglorious past would be of little moment however unless we could link it up with our glorious and inglorious present. Nor would the study of these symbols of life be anything but sheer waste of time, or at most the gratification of intellectual curiosity if, in trying to discover what the ancients were through their religious customs and beliefs, we were not seeking the answer to the even more difficult question of what we ourselves are.

Reinach, while admitting that he does not like it, calls religion "a sum of scruples which impede the free exercise of the faculties." Max Müller defines it as "a faculty of mind which enables man to grasp the infinite independently of sense or reason."

I am inclined to suggest something less recondite, if only to see how far it carries us. It seems simpler and perhaps nearer the truth to say that Religion is Life—and that all religions have as their fundamental basis reverence for life.

Worship of this mysterious, impersonal, quickening power would easily explain man's changing beliefs which at one time or another have exalted nearly every phase of life. In his long history man has had many gods—war-like, merciful, stern, just, compassionate—evoked in response to some revealing conception of life which he believes will enable him to interpret and be at one with the universe. The form his religion takes depends, with but one exception, upon his arrogance or humility before the mystery of the Life Force which without being able to account for he sees in himself and reproducing itself in countless ways in nature. It may well have taken the form of nature worship, animism, in the old days when agriculture itself was a religious art. At various periods, too, primitive man appears to have looked upon life mainly from the standpoint of his own appetite and physical well being as we see still done by the lower order of intelligence. Nevertheless, although gods came and vanished, beliefs changed or became debased, back in man's consciousness there seems to have been ever present the haunting desire to know and be at one with a Supreme Being, the *Primum Mobile*, the Lord of All Life.

If, as seems probable, the continuity of life was the primary animating impulse back of all ancient religions —Life—not only the way life was come by, but life that unfolds, develops through the awakening race, the "son being that which is better"; if this was, in truth, the dream, the aspiration—the desire for perfectioning until at last man is fit to walk with the gods and Life Everlasting is attained, then the motive for existence itself becomes clear.

The moment you bring the race thought to bear the symbolism of the ark, as well as many of the savage customs which Frazer chronicles as taking place at the time a girl reaches puberty, instantly become intelligible. Always keeping carefully in mind, however, that Life to the ancients was not merely physical life and not merely spiritual life but the union of spirit and matter. Even in the oldest religions there is evidence that the ancients reverenced the physical, not as distinct from the spiritual but as the form through which the spiritual manifested itself. That the two forces were looked upon as inextricably interwoven is also shown in ritual, sacrament and symbolism where they blend or counteract each other precisely as in man himself. It is a curious fact that those who would purge the church of these ancient symbols and customs, because founded upon nature worship or sex, end usually by leading nowhere except in the direction of abysmal doubt. One is almost forced to believe, so repeatedly has the effort failed, that the attempt to brush aside these forms as untrue, pagan, profligate is the real profanation which Life itself resents.

To experience the true joy of understanding, of being *en rapport* with Life in all its fullness—one must first, however, divest one's self of one's literal mind and approach these ancient symbols imaginatively—not as theological points to be argued over or explained away, but as something unalterably sweet and true—to be felt as one feels the beauty of nature, to be accepted as a part of our inheritance from the past.

Man, woman, the serpent, of course, and the Sun, giver of all life and light—the moon, earth, air, fire, winds—light and darkness, sun and water—these are the forces symbolised since primeval days, and these are the forces in their relations to religions, to each other and to Life that will be considered in the following pages.

CONTENTS

Contents

FULL PAGE ILLUSTRATIONS

IN–PAGE ILLUSTRATIONS

PAGE

Illustrations

The illustrations on the front and back linings are reproduced from *Signs and Symbols of Primordial Man* with the kind permission of Albert Churchward and his publishers, Geo. Allen and Unwin, Ltd.

Life Symbols as Related to Sex Symbolism

I

THE ELEMENTS

"All knowledge begins and ends with wonder, but the first wonder is the child of ignorance, while the second wonder is parent of adoration."—Coleridge.

"That is true symbolism in which the particular represents the general, not as a dream and a shade, but as a living, momentary revelation of the inscrutable." —Goethe.

I

THE ELEMENTS

THE reverence of the elements and the belief that they were a manifestation of divine power played a large part in Mazdaism, the ancient religion of the Persians.

The four elements were considered eternal by the Hindus. Hence the doctrine that nothing will be annihilated but only changed—souls by transmigration, matter by transmutation.

It was believed by the ancients that the soul also was composed of the four elements—fire, water, air, earth—and that when united these took the form of fire or flame. "The Supreme Spirit was idealised as immaculate fire and symbolised as a pure and elemental flame burning in infinitude. . . . The Egyptians defined spirit as a subtle fire as did the Hindus in whose conception the mystic element spread until it permeated the streams, quivered in the trees and, in fact, pervaded the universe." [1]

The conception of the elements as fire, water, earth, air which was commonly accepted by the Greek and Indian philosophers was not held originally by the Chinese Taoists who resolved the elements into five:—water, fire, wood, metal, earth—and believed that these

[1] Bayley's "Lost Language of Symbolism."

conquered one another according to a definite law. Thus wood conquered earth; earth, water; water, fire; fire, metal and metal, wood.

"No one can do anything against these phenomena, for the power which causes the five elements to counteract each other is according to the natural dispensation of heaven and earth. Large quantities prevail over small quantities, hence water conquers fire. Spirituality prevails over materiality, the non-substance over substance, thus fire conquers metal; hardness conquers softness, hence metal conquers wood; density is superior to incoherence therefore wood conquers earth; solidity conquers insolidity, therefore earth conquers water." [2]

The five elements were also associated with the five planets. Thus Venus represented metal; Jupiter, wood; Mercury, water; Mars, fire; and Saturn, earth.

The Chinese metaphysicians and occultists carried out this inter-relation of the elements with each other and with their planets, designating them as parent, child, enemy, friend. They believed that all misfortunes came about from some disturbance of the five elements, some change in their given position. Thus the Chinese were strongly opposed to any interference with nature, or to doing anything that might perchance alter natural conditions.

Later the Chinese Buddhists adopted the Greek and Indian idea, adding ether, however, to the other elements of fire, water, earth, air. Doing this, no doubt, so that the conception might equal in number the older Taoist form of enumeration.

This Chinese diagram of the elements differs hardly at all from the European. The earth is represented by

[2] From the rule preserved by Liu An, second century B.C., quoted in "Chinese Thought" by Paul Carus.

a square, water by a circle, fire by a triangle, air by a crescent and ether by a gem—*mani,* "the jewel in the lotus" which surmounts the whole. Practically the same diagram or form was employed by the mediæval alchemists of Europe, the only difference being that they considered the two upper symbols as one and called it air.

The *Caitya* or *Stupa,* representing the five elements, is found in the open square of every Buddhist monastery in Japan and Tibet, and all over the interior of Asia wherever the influence of Chinese civilisation extends. There is a well founded reason for the prevalence of

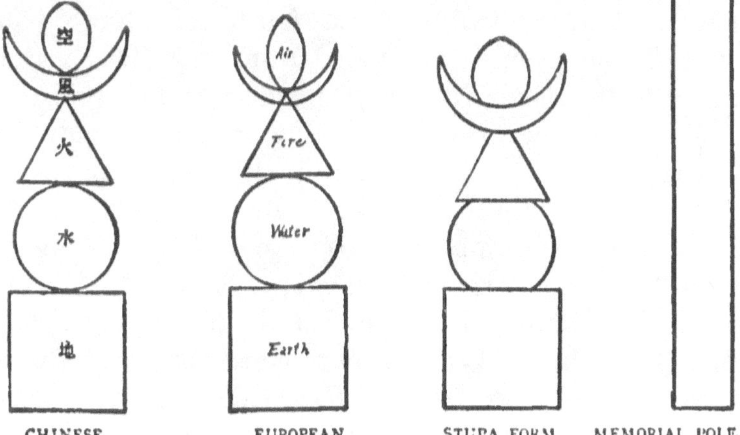

Carus, *Chinese Thought.*

the stupa among the Buddhists. Its purpose is to remind those who are living that the body of the dead has been reduced to its original elements, has been absorbed in the All, has returned to the origin and source of all Life.

In these "elemental" stupas the square becomes a cube, the circle a globe, the triangle a four-sided pyramid and the moon crescent and linga-shaped spike or "gem" are also solid. This symbolism of the five elements is also depicted surmounting the memorial poles which the Chinese place on the tombs of the dead on their All Souls Day.

In considering the various symbols of life, it will be a matter that may induce wonder and later reflection that these five "elemental" symbols march steadily along with man—taking on new meanings, amplifying, while always retaining their original signification.

The position of the elements in the diagrams is also worth noting. It will be seen that the circle (water) stands between the square (earth) and the triangle (fire). And we shall have occasion to refer more than once to the peculiarly important relation that water bears to the earth (matter) and also to fire (spirit). The importance of water in this connection may be likened to fluids in the human body. Nor apparently does this end with the physical. *Le fluide* is a French expression for sympathy, *"Il n'y a du fluide entre nous." "Vous n'avez pas de fluide pour—"* Nor is it wholly a figure of speech that the heart melts, that thought is fluid. We are quite conscious that a hard face indicates inner sterility. Hardening of the arteries means death, as a hard heart causes spiritual death.

II

CREATION MYTHS

"The humid nature being the origin of the universe produced the first three bodies earth, air, fire."—Plutarch.

"In nearly every myth of importance . . . you have to discern these three structural parts—the root and the two branches; the root in physical existence, sun, or sky, or cloud, or sea; then the personal incarnation of that, becoming a trusted, companionable deity, with whom you may walk hand in hand, as a child with its brother or its sister; and lastly, the moral significance of the image, which is in all the great myths eternally and beneficently true."—Ruskin.

"To create a myth . . . to catch a glimpse of a higher truth behind a palpable reality is the most manifest sign of the greatness of the human soul."—Sabatier.

"Every mythological figure is a philosophical concept."—Roeder.

II

CREATION MYTHS

WHETHER the idea of the "sea as the Great Mother of all creation" found its inception in the fact that physical life was supposed to have originated in water, or whether it was used symbolically, water typifying Truth and Wisdom, the two factors Spirit and Water enter into all the ancient stories of creation.

The earliest germ of a creation myth appears to have been based on the idea that night was parent of the day and water of the earth. Out of darkness and death came light and life. Life was also motion. When the primordial waters became troubled life began to be.

The creation myths of Babylonia and Assyria depict "chaotic darkness brooding over a waste of waters. Heaven and earth were not as yet. Nought existed save the primeval ocean Mommu Tiawath (or Tiamat) from whose fertile depths came every living thing."

Tiamat is the chaos demon—the Great Mother. As the origin of good she was believed to have created the gods. She was also the dragon of the sea and therefore the serpent or the leviathan. She is thus seen to have had a dual character. In her beneficent form she survived as the Sumerian goddess Bau who is obviously identical with the Phœnician Baau "mother of the first man." Another name for Bau was Ma. Niritu a "form of the goddess Ma" was depicted as half woman and half serpent with a babe at her breast.

The Egyptian letter M was called ma and also meant country, place, universe. The word "ma" contained for the Egyptians the idea of earth.

In the language of the Mayas, according to Le Plongeon, "ma" likewise meant country, earth.

One of the Babylonian goddesses was called Ama, Mama or Mami or the "Mother of all things." In Chaldea "Mama" signified the "Lady of the Gods."

In this primitive conception the Great Mother deity was believed to be self-created and self-sustaining. The typical Great Mother was a Virgin goddess with a fatherless son. Like the Babylonian Tiamat and the Celtic Danu she was the "mother of the gods from whom mankind was descended." Her characteristics varied in different localities. In one she was associated with the earth, in others with water and in others again with the sky.

In her baleful aspect she was the enemy of mankind. It is she who attempts to destroy all life and to prevent the coming of summer. Her son, on the contrary, is a beneficent being. He is the Spirit of Life, the one who brings summer and who is the lover of all mankind. It is the son with his life giving power who defeats the goddess Mother in her efforts to hold back growth and keep the earth bound in her sterile clasp.

There is a great divergence of ideas in the Egyptian creation myths, although in Egypt as well as in Babylonia there was the early belief that life in the universe had a female origin.

"At the beginning naught save darkness and water. The spirit of night the Great Mother and her

Neith, Libyan Earth Mother
(Metropolitan Museum of Art)

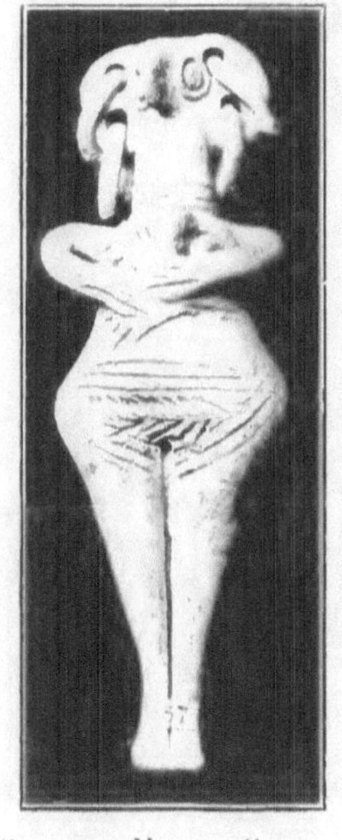

Cypriote, Mother Goddess, Bronze Age 1500–1200 b.c.
(Metropolitan Museum of Art)

Ishtar as the Mother Goddess
(Jastrow, *Civilisation of Babylonia and Assyria*)

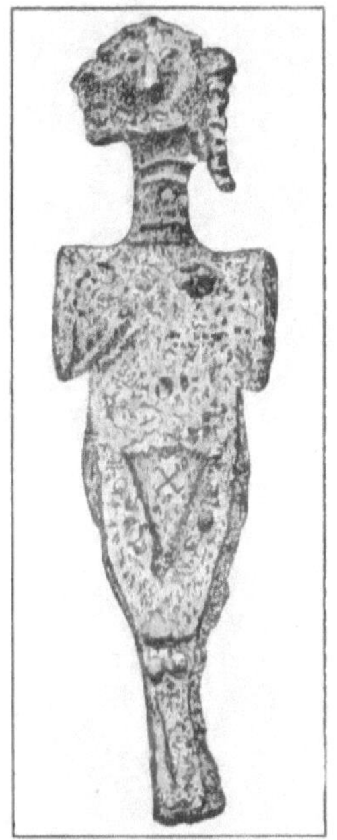

Leaden Idol of Artemis Nana of Chaldea with Swastika Enclosed in a Triangle
Third City
(Schliemann, *Ilios*)

first born the moon child. Life came from death and Light from darkness."

Neith the Libyan Earth Mother was believed to be self-sustaining as she was self-produced. She was the Unknown One, the Hidden One and like other Virgin goddesses she had a fatherless son.

A creation myth of Heliopolis refers to "one god of the primordial deep." It was at Heliopolis, too, that Ra the sun-god was first exalted as the Great Father who created all things. Ra created everything that had being, in the waters and upon the dry land. Men were born from the eye of Ra. Ra the ruler of the gods was the first king on earth.

As related in a creation myth of the Egyptian sun worshippers the world was in the beginning a waste of waters called Nu. Nu gave being to the sun-god who appeared first as a shining egg floating on the waters. The spirits of the deep—the fathers and mothers—were with him there as he was with Nu. Ra, however, was greater than Nu. He was the divine father who created Shu, the wind-god and Tefunt, his consort. Then came Seb, the earth-god and Nut, the sky-goddess whom Shu, the uplifter raised on high so that Nut formed the vault which is arched over Seb, the earth. From the union of Seb and Nut—earth and sky—came forth Osiris and Isis.

Egypt had also the chaos goose who cackled loudly to the chaos gander, when she laid the egg of the sun. Ra became the historic egg and Seb, the earth-god the gander. Later Amen Ra of Thebes who combined many deities represented the chaos goose and gander in one.

The god Kneph whom the Egyptians called "intelligence or efficient cause of the universe" was said to have vomited an egg from which was produced another god named Ptah or Vulcan (the principle of fire or the sun) and that this egg represented the world.

Kneph was depicted as a man dressed in deep blue—the colour of the sky—a sceptre in his hand, a belt—the zodiac—encircling his waist, on his head a cap with feathers and issuing from his mouth the great egg—the world.

Khnemu the 'Moulder' one of the oldest gods of the Egyptian religion also ranked as a 'maker of mankind' and the primeval egg was associated with Khnemu as with the other creator gods.

The cosmic egg the 'germ of the universe' occurs in many mythologies with and without the 'precious goose.'

"Cet œuf mystérieux, resultat d'idées obscurcies par les temps et par les égarements de l'esprit humain, a surnagé au naufrage de toutes les opinions cosmogoniques. Il est resté au milieu des plus nuageuses conceptions comme le type consacré du monde physique." [1]

Bayley in the *Lost Language of Symbolism* suggests that the fairy tale of the goose that laid the golden egg may have been derived from this ancient myth of creation.

P'an Ku, a late but conspicuous figure in the Chinese cosmogony was said to have emerged from the cosmic egg. It was P'an Ku who fashioned the universe out of chaos. He was the offspring of the "original dual powers of nature the *Yin* and the *Yang.*" He is represented as a man of dwarf-like stature dressed in bearskin or leaves, or merely with an apron of leaves. He has two horns on his head, and holds a hammer in his right hand and a chisel in the left, or again he is depicted

[1] *"Histoire et Theorie du Symbolisme Religieux,"* M. l'Abbé Auber.

Nü Kua Shih

(Werner, *Myths and Legends of China*)

with the sun in one hand and the moon in the other. In some pictures he is attended by the four supernatural creatures the phoenix, the unicorn, the dragon and the tortoise. His task of creation took 18,000 years.

The Chinese had several other conceptions of the origin of things that brought in a personal creator. There was Nü Kua who was said to be the creator of human beings when the earth first emerged from chaos. "She or he had the body of a serpent and the head of an ox," or is sometimes represented with a human head as in the illustration.

Sometimes the name is separated and Nü and Kua are brother and sister, the first human pair. "At the creation they were placed at the foot of the K'un-lun mountains. Then they prayed, saying, 'If thou, O God, hast sent us to be man and wife, the smoke of our sacrifice will stay in one place; but if not, it will be scattered.' The smoke remained stationary." [2]

On the whole, however, the Chinese mind seems to have been better content with abstract, philosophical explanations of the cosmos even when too abstruse for the ordinary mind to understand.

According to Charencey the Chinese admitted five primordial agencies *"1° le principe mâle et actif, le dieu inconnu. 2° le chaos ou la matière inerte, représentant le principe femelle; de leur union resultent; 3° le ciel et 4° la terre. Ces deux derniers s'agissant l'un sur l'autre donnent naissance au 5° principe qui est l'homme. Ce principe mâle est appelé Yang et exerce une influence bienfaisante. Au contraire le Yin ou principe feminin a une action néfaste. C'est lui qui cause la mort et la decadence de tous les êtres."* [3]

[2] "Myths and Legends of China," E. T. Chalmers Werner.

[3] *"La Symbolisme des Points de l'Horizon,"* M. H. de Charencey.

The egg is also found in a Hindu theory of creation which relates that the Supreme Spirit laid a golden egg resplendent as the sun and from this was born Brahma the progenitor of the universe.

The ancients in India first worshipped Mother Earth. Ida, the Universal Mother was said to have been formed by Manu, the thinker out of the 'waters which were impregnated with the heavenly seed.' Ida thus represented the purified earth cleansed by sanctifying waters. When she arose from the waters cleansed and purified, the myth relates that Mitra and Varuna the twin deities wished to claim her for their own. Refusing to acknowledge them as parents, however, she remained true to Manu the thinker.

Another Hindu creation myth pictures the Great Originator as infinite, eternal, immaterial, round. "This universe was formerly soul only in the form of Purusha." Purusha having passed an unlimited time in self-contemplation and desiring to manifest himself, he caused himself to fall asunder in two parts. Hence came husband and wife, and these, assuming various animal forms "thus created every living pair whatsoever down to the ants."

Purusha was also called the chaos giant. From him were born the 'Trimurti'—the three gods of the Hindus —Brahma, Vishnu and Siva—Creator, Preserver and Destroyer.

Among the Buddhists, Adi-Buddha the most excellent first Buddha the "saint of the wheel of time" was the beginning deity. "When nothing else was he was." When all was perfect void the mystic syllable Aum became manifest from which at his own will the Adi-Buddha was produced. This mystic syllable Aum signified the three precious Tri-ratna, the Buddhist triad—

Buddha, intelligence, soul, Dharma, matter, the body, and Sangha, the union of the two.

A Creation myth of the Persians divides creation in six *gahans* or *gahan-bars* which represent six periods of time—called by Zoroaster the thousands of God or Light. In the first period God created the heavens, in the second the waters, in the third the earth, in the fourth the trees, in the fifth animals and in the sixth man.

The Etrurians had a similar tradition. The myth of creation in the Zend-Avesta has many points in common with that related in Genesis. There is a first man and a first woman living in a state of celestial innocence. Instead of a serpent, however, the tempter approaches them in the guise of a great lizard, the symbol of Ahrimanes the power of evil. Then the warfare between Ahrimanes, the genius of evil or darkness and Ormuzd (or Ahura-Mazda), the god of life and light, the end of the world in six thousand years, the coming of the lamb or mediator between Light and Darkness, the new world, the life to come, the passage of the soul over the bridge of the abyss to a place of felicity, or despair, the celebration of the mysteries of Mithra, the unleavened bread that is set apart for the initiated—many of these ideas and rites bear a close resemblance to the Hebrew.

"Breathed upon the face of the waters" occurs in many cosmogonies.

One of the oldest of the Hindu myths relates that in the beginning there was one God self-existent who passed through all eternity absorbed in the contemplation of his own reflections. Finally desiring to manifest himself he created matter or substance. The four elements of which the world is composed, lay in a state of mingled confusion till he breathed upon the face of the waters, and they immediately became an immense bubble shaped like an egg. This egg is the vault or globe of the heavens in which the world is enclosed. This god "is the source of motion."

In the Hebrew version of the creation as given in the Book of Genesis "And the spirit of God moved upon the face of the waters" there is the same thought.

Nearly all the creation myths seem to recognise a First Cause, a Great Mover, a Vital Spirit which diffused through all beings animates the vast body of the world. Back of chaos is discerned a *Primum Mobile*, Unknown and Unknowable—then Chaos, then Order. This is the creative process. With rare exceptions, chaos was associated by the ancient myth makers with the feminine principle, and order, organisation with the masculine. The idea of Darkness first, then Light emerging from darkness, or night giving birth to day never varies, nor do the principles themselves ever lessen in importance. Called by many names—fire and water, spirit and matter, positive and negative, active and passive, man and woman—they themselves never change. They pass down through the ages "an inseparable pair"—the same two principles that, although the result is an infinitely varied expression of the creative process, are invariably associated to produce life.

In all the ancient cosmogonies the largest share in the divine government and control of the universe is given to the two powers sun (or fire) and water, as representing the two chief forces of nature upon whose harmonious adjustment rests the prosperity and welfare of mankind.

Troward gives an involved but highly illuminating interpretation of water as related to spirit and matter or fire and earth in ancient symbolism. He describes

Photo. Alinari

Archaic Greek
Statuette of a Woman

Babylonian Goddess. Babylonian
Art 3000 b.c.

(Museo Barracco, Rome)

water as the "universal psychic medium in which the nuclei of the forms hereafter to become consolidated on the plane of the concrete and material, take their inception in obedience to the movement of Spirit or Thought. This is the realm of *potential* forms and is the connecting link between Spirit or pure thought and Matter or concrete form." He adds that the existence of this intermediary between Spirit and Matter must never be lost sight of, and that it may be called the Distributive Medium, in passing through which the hitherto undistributed Energy of Spirit receives differentiation of direction and so ultimately produces differentiations of forms and relations on the outermost or visible plane. "This is the Cosmic Element esoterically called 'Water.' "[4]

Woman or the feminine principle is associated with the earth, matter. The feminine principle is also associated with water. Thus water, the intermediary between spirit and matter, typified "woman the soul, the psychic side of man—the mother of individual life."[5]

The circle symbolised water or the feminine principle in nature, also eternity.

Zigzag lines representing waves or ripples of the sea are also one of the pre-historic symbols of water. The Egyptian hieroglyph for water was a wavy or zigzag line.

Two wavy lines are the zodiacal sign of Aquarius, the Water Carrier.

[4] "Bible Mystery and Bible Meaning," T. Troward.
[5] *Ibid.*

III

THE LOTUS

"The flower that was in the Beginning, the glorious lily of the great Water."

"When Buddha was born a lotus bloomed where he first touched the ground; he stepped seven steps northward and a lotus marked each footfall."

"The entire history of European pre-historic ornament, and therefore of European civilization may receive a new direction from an observation based upon the sepal of a water lily."—Goodyear's "Grammar of the Lotus."

III

THE LOTUS

THE use of the lotus as a symbol of creation or the beginning of life extends back beyond the measurements of time.

A growth of the watery element, without roots in the earth, nourished by the rays of the sun, the lotus was the symbol *par excellence* of the power of nature through the agency of fire and water. As the world was conceived to have come into being by the inter-action of these two elements, the lotus became the dual symbol of spirit and matter or the "spirit moving upon the face of the waters."

LOTUS AND THE MOON GOD.

Assyrian seal.

Goodyear, *Grammar of the Lotus.*

In the Hindu cosmogony the world is likened to a lotus flower floating in the centre of a shallow vessel which rests on the back of an elephant and the elephant on the back of a tortoise.

"Brahma springs from the lotus which in its turn rises from the navel of Vishnu."

Again Brahma is frequently depicted as floating on the waters supported by a lotus leaf.

LOTUS, WORSHIPPER AND WINGED SOLAR DISK.

Assyrian seal.

The myth of Horus as the new born sun rising from a lotus flower expanding its leaves on the breast of the primeval deep, conveys the same idea—the union of fire and water—as does the Hebrew account of creation in the book of Genesis.

LOTUS SUPPORTING WINGED SOLAR DISK.
From a cylinder shown in Lajard, *Culte de Mithra*.

The belief that the lotus is sacred to the sun is one of the most ancient traditions of the Egyptian and Hindu mythologies and has been the most tenaciously held and preserved.

One explanation of the solar significance of the lotus is that "the moment of its opening corresponds to the dawn."

"Je suis un lotus, issu du champ du soleil."[1]

It is used in connection with the sun apparently to suggest the renewal of the sun rather than as a symbol of the sun itself.

"It perhaps symbolised less the sun itself than the solar matrix, that mysterious sanctuary into which the sun retires every evening there to acquire fresh life. This miracle which was believed to be renewed each day was regarded as the origin of whatever exists."[2]

The Egyptians thus believing that the world sprang from the liquid element, made the sun proceed from a lotus which had emerged one day from the primordial waters. From a symbol of solar renascence it became a symbol of human re-birth as well as life in its eternal aspect.

The lotus not only was a symbol of life, immortality, resurrection, fecundity, the feminine principle, re-birth, but it also symbolised nature in her infinite manifes-

[1] *"Livre des Morts,"* Pierret.

[2] "The Migration of Symbols," Count Goblet d'Alviella.

tations, and more particularly the productive power of water.

Goodyear points out that, in considering the Egyptian ideas of resurrection and the future life which played such an important part in their religion, we must never lose sight of the fact that these ideas were practically built up upon a worship of the creative and reproductive powers of nature, which were conceived to be solar in their origin. "It is the supposed passage of the

PHŒNICIAN SEAL.
Lajard, *Culte de Mithra.*

sun at night through a lower world which makes Osiris (the sun at night) the God of the Lower World and of the dead; hence he himself is represented as a mummy. As the God of the Resurrection, his especial and emphatic character, he represents the creative energy of the Sun god. Hence the lotus as an attribute of Osiris is at once a symbol of the sun, of the resurrection, and of creative force and power. . . . This three-fold significance is to be considered in all cases . . . but it is the solar significance which explains the others." [3]

Its association with the mummy and the doctrine of the future life explains the use of the lotus in a mortuary or funerary way. It appears on the sepulchral tab-

[3] Goodyear's "Grammar of the Lotus."

lets of the ancient Greeks and Romans, and was also employed in early Christian art to symbolise the resurrection and immortality of the soul.

LOTUS AND WORSHIPPER.
Ivory plaque from Nimroud.
British Museum.
Perrot and Chipiez.

The lotus—as well as the scarabæus, serpent and palm tree—was an early androgynous symbol of self-creation.

Among the Buddhists the *padma* or lotus is the symbol of self-creation. "The lotus flower, itself a prodigy, coming into existence without being nourished by the earth" became the perfect symbol of the germinating power of water when acted upon by the sun or the active power of the Creator Adi-Buddha.

When all was void Aum became manifest. In Aum Adi-Buddha, the first Buddha "who is present in all things, formless, passionless, who possesses the Tri-ratna—was produced by his own will."

LOTUS PEDESTAL.
Supporting the throne of the Master between two Naga Kings.
D'Alviella, *Migration of Symbols*

As every Buddha and Bodhisattva is self-created and self-existent, the lotus flower as a support typifies his divine birth. Although the lotus pedestal is best known through the statues of Buddha, it is common to all Hindu gods.

The lotus flower support to the solar gods Horus and Vishnu and in the hands of Hathor and Lakshmi the goddesses associated with them, indicates, as does much of the

Eastern symbolism—notably that of the serpent—a shade of thought too subtle to be more than indirectly expressed.

Among the Buddhists the lotus was also the emblem of Nirvana. Its mysterious growth, rising from stagnant water and ooze into perfect flower gloriously white and unsullied, typified the future possibilities of the soul, just as its expanded flower resting upon the surface of the placid waters typified the ultimate repose of the soul after all desire has fled.

Brahma appears on a golden lotus. He is also said to keep watch over the world six months of the year and sleep the remaining six "in a lotus flower of extraordinary beauty."

It is related by the Buddhists that once upon a time Amitabha—god of infinite light, a sun-god who presides over the western paradise—"after giving himself up to earnest meditation caused a white ray of light to issue from his right eye which brought forth Padmapani (Avalokita) into existence. Amitabha blessed him and the Bodhisattva gave utterance to the prayer '*Om, mani, padme, hum.*' 'Oh! the jewel (of creation) is in the lotus.' According to Hodgson the correct translation is 'The mystic triform is in him of the jewel and the lotus.' "[4]

The Mantra *"Om, mani, padme, hum"*—the 'jewel is in the lotus'—is used in the Yoga system to express the union of the Two Parts, the entire system being founded upon the union of the two forces, Spirit and Matter.

Upon the creation of the world Adi-Buddha, the first Buddha was said to have revealed himself on Mount Sumeru in the form of a flame issuing from a lotus flow-

[4] "The Gods of Northern Buddhism," Getty.

er. In Nepal the Buddha is always represented by this symbol (union of fire and water). The flame symbol will also be encountered again and again rising from the centre of a moon crescent. Some of the Nepalese writings thus describe the manifestation of the first Buddha:—

"A lotus flower of precious jewels appeared on the summit of Mount Sumeru which is the centre of the universe and above it arose a moon crescent." [5]

DETAIL OF AN ASSYRIAN SEAL. Goodyear, *Grammar of the Lotus.*

We first see the flame symbol in the moon crescent in the diagram of the elements or in the elemental stupa form. Its shape changes slightly and it is known under various names but its meaning remains unaltered. Whether the flame rests in a moon crescent or in the lotus it is the symbol of the union of the dualistic forces that produce life.

The phallic significance of the lotus as related to the resurrection and the reproductive forces of nature is, of course, obvious. And this is more distinctly implied in the symbolism of the "jewel in the lotus." In its phallic aspect the 'jewel in the lotus' represents the union of the masculine and feminine principles, the jewel indicating the masculine and the lotus the feminine, while the bursting seed pods symbolised fecundity.

The lotus is thus given to Isis in her character of goddess of fecundity.

In the Christian religion the lotus becomes the Lily of the Virgin.

Goodyear in reminding us of the antiquity of the lotus says that the papyrus which is commonly associated with the lotus—the papyrus for the north and

[5] Getty's "The Gods of Northern Buddhism."

the lotus for the south—"sinks out of sight as we go farther back."

The ancients, who did nothing in a meaningless way, creating and developing form not only to shelter and protect life, but to express in all ways, as beautifully as their imagination and skill would permit, their profound belief in and worship of Life, made elaborate use of the leaves, buds and flowers of the lotus as decorative motifs, and this symbol became one of the most important decorative features in the architectural designs of Egypt and India.

Goodyear believed that the egg and dart motif which architects still use was derived from the lotus.

The lotus, the flower of Buddha, was sometimes conventionalised into a wheel design, the petals representing spokes and symbolising the doctrine of perpetual cycles of existence. The wheel symbol was also indicated by the

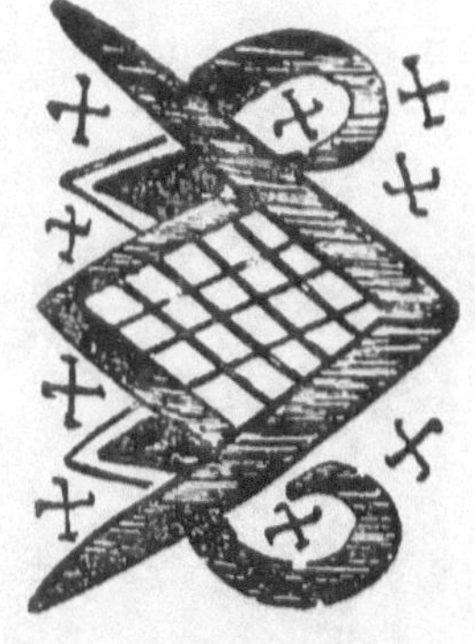

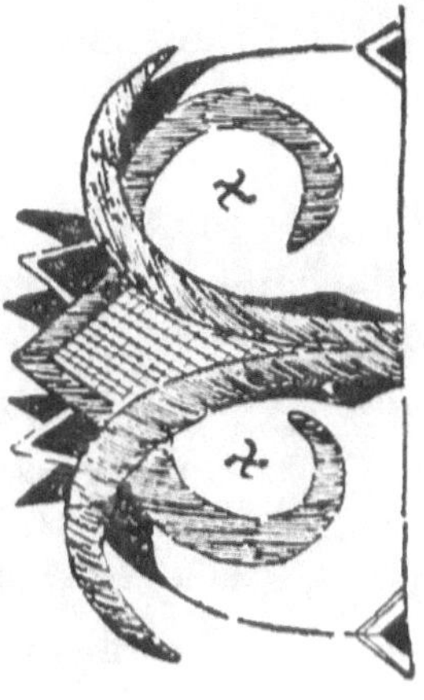

DETAIL OF CYPRIAN VASE SHOWING LOTUSES WITH CURLING SEPALS.
Metropolitan Museum of Art.
Goodyear, *Grammar of the Lotus.*

round top of the seed vessel. An eight leaved lotus flower represented the 'heart of being.'

ASSYRIAN WINGED DEITIES FACING ROSETTE.
Bas-relief from Khorsabad.

The rosettes so frequently found as an architectural ornament were probably derived from the lotus, and thus take on a solar significance.

The Egyptians, according to Breasted, created the column and originated the colonnade. Sometimes these columns represented a palm tree with its capital a crown of foliage, or again "a bundle of papyrus stalks bearing the architrave upon the cluster of buds at the top which form the capital." [6]

On the majority of these columns, however, the capital represented a lotus flower with the upper part cut off, swelling at the base and tapering toward the top, or again the capital is in the form of a calyx whose surface is decorated with convex lobes to indicate the petals of a flower.

Always arriving by way of nature, it is interesting to trace back definitely to the underlying thought of Life. And nowhere is the idea of growth from the soil upward, reaching toward heaven, better expressed than

[6] Breasted's "History of Egypt."

in these Egyptian columns which, resting firmly upon the ground, terminate above in capitals formed like the lotus—symbol of creative energy, life, immortality.

The lotus is called the Flower of Light and Flower of Life, *flower de luce* and *fleur de lys* and "as an emblem of the Trinity is one of the few survivals still retained in the Christian ecclesiology. *Lux lucet in Tenebris.* This light shining in the darkness was like Christ the Light of the World symbolised by the Fleur de Lys." [7]

[7] Bayley's "Lost Language of Symbolism."

IV

THE DUAL PRINCIPLES

"There are in life two elements, one transitory and progressive, the other comparatively if not absolutely non-progressive and eternal."—Gilbert Murray.

"Polarity or the inter-action of Active and Passive is the basis of all evolution."—Troward.

"The very touch of the eternal in the two sexual tastes brings them the more in antagonism; for one stands for a universal vigilance and the other for an almost infinite output."—Chesterton.

"Tranquillity according to His essence, activity according to His nature; perfect stillness, perfect fecundity, this is the two-fold character of the Absolute."—Ruysbroeck.

IV

THE DUAL PRINCIPLES

THE Egyptians built their temples to represent the world as they conceived it to be. "The sun journeying from east to west cut the universe into two worlds, the north and the south. Like the universe the temple was double, and an imaginary line drawn through the axis of the sanctuary divided it into two temples." [1]

This idea of duality was carried throughout into all the ceremonies and rituals. Believing the earth to be a flat, shallow plane, oblong in form, and that Shu lifted up the sky which, stretched over the earth like a vault, was supported by four props or huge pillars, they made their ceilings correspond to the sky, the four corners of the chamber typified the supports, and the temple pavement was the equivalent of the inhabited world. Each part thus was decorated according to its significance. Everything touching the ground was covered with vegetation. The columns represented plants or trees that grew on the banks of the Nile. The base of the walls were decorated with long stems of papyrus or lotus flowers; sometimes cattle were depicted. The temple ceilings resembled the starry heavens, being painted dark blue and sprinkled with golden five pointed stars.

[1] "Manual of Egyptian Archeology," G. Maspero.

"In so far as Egyptian symbolism is concerned it is well to remember that its religious philosophy was a highly refined and intellectual system and that it found expression in pictorial allegories supplied by reptile, beast and bird without detriment to this philosophic quality." (Goodyear.)

The Hindus gave the name of the "pair of opposites" to the dual aspect of nature which manifests itself as sun and moon, light and darkness, heat and cold, fire and water, man and woman, day and night, etc.

From remotest times man, the active principle has been symbolised by fire, by whatever is pointed, direct—a spear, shaft, column, dart, arrow, sword, the "Rod of Jesse." And woman, the feminine or passive principle by water, by everything that is sinuous, concave, curving, receptive—by the earth—the all creative Mother Earth—by mounds, high places, mountains—"as in Germany the famous Hörselberg or Venusberg," by the moon, ark, crescent, pearl—anything, in short, that was hollow, oval, cavernous, circular, a receptacle.

The red of fire typified the masculine principle and the blue of the sea the feminine. The belief in a Saviour God born of a Virgin often named Maria or some word meaning *mare*—sea—was common among many of the ancient races.

The old Chinese religion was based on the idea that Heaven and Earth—themselves the greatest gods—produce all things by the inter-action of the opposites—heat and cold, light and darkness, male and female. Since time immemorial the Chinese have divided nature into two great parts. In this dualistic philosophy *Yang* is the masculine principle denoting light, warmth, life. *Yin* is the principle of darkness, cold, death. *Yang* is the sun, *Yin* the earth. *Yang* is the Celestial Breath and shares supreme sway in nature with the Terrestrial Breath which is *Yin* the passive or feminine principle. Heaven the highest spirit, not only was conceived to be the cause of natural phenomena but the source of the order of nature (the Tao—the way).

"Heaven and earth existing all things got their existence. All (material) things existing, afterwards there came male and female. From the existence of male and female came husband and wife. From husband and wife came father and son. From father and son came ruler and minister. From ruler and minister came high and low. When high and low had existence afterwards came the arrangements of propriety and righteousness."

Moore in his *History of Religions* cites the Chinese imperial sacrifice to heaven as being one of the most grandiose acts of worship ever performed by men. The same definite symbolism is shown in this worship. The sacrifice to heaven is at the winter solstice when the powers of light and warmth begin to prevail against the cold and dark of winter. The sacrifice to earth occurs at the summer solstice for the opposite reason. "For in the dualistic physical philosophy of the Chinese Heaven belongs to the *Yang* the bright, warm male principle, and Earth to the *Yin* the dark, cold female principle. Thus the altar to Heaven is south of the city [Peking] while that of the Earth is north; the former is white and round like Heaven; the latter dark and square and surrounded by water like the earth. Heaven has a round, blue jade stone, Earth a square yellow one."

Among the ancient Chinese jade was the most precious mineral and was always identified in their philosophy with Heaven. Certain things like jade and gold were believed to be imbued with vital energy derived from the great element *yang*. Heaven being the depository of vital energy its symbols must likewise be indestructible, unchangeable. Hence the saying "Heaven is jade, is gold."

Jade and gold were also prominent minerals in alchemy.

The Great Monad, the *ovum mundi* of the Chinese which symbolises the Chinese philosophy of opposites, is a circle divided by two arcs of opposite centres. In this mystic union of the two principles the dark represents *yin* the material or feminine principle and the light *yang* the spiritual or masculine principle.

THE GREAT MONAD.

THE TAI-KIH.

A third arc from above is sometimes depicted uniting them. This represents the "Tai-Kih or Great Ultimate Principle which according to ancient philosophy is the genitor of the so-called Liang-I or Two Regulating Powers or the Superior Breaths *Yang* and *Yin* which create by their co-operation all that takes place in nature. These two Regulators who, mutually extinguishing and giving way to each other, keep at work a ceaseless process of revolution which produces all the phenomena of existence." [2]

The circle is sometimes divided by three lines resembling the Chinese Y, the latter a symbol of vast antiquity used to indicate the Great Unit, the Great Plan, the Great Uniter. The Chinese Y held the same

[2] De Groot's "Religious Systems of China."

FOUNDERS OF THE "THREE RELIGIONS"

Buddha in the centre, Lao-tse on the left (the most honourable place in China) and Confucius on the right.

Henry Doré, S. J., *Researches into Chinese Superstition*

significance as the Egyptian Ankh (the *crux ansata*). The way this symbol was employed to express the Chinese conception of the universe—which is really based on parenthood—will be referred to under another heading.

In attempting to understand the anomaly presented by Chinese thought someone has said that a man in China was born a Taoist, lived a Confucian and died a Buddhist. As a matter of fact the theory of immortality advanced by the Taoists was as little acceptable to the philosophers and thinkers as the Indian conception of Nirvana. Between the two ideas, one of negation or annihilation in the future state and the other of the ultimate union of the two dualistic forces into one thus representing completion stood Confucius with his feet firmly planted on what is, and giving as little thought as possible to life after death "preferring to teach men how to live."

Okakura-Kakuzo relates the Sung allegory of the *Three Vinegar Tasters* as explaining admirably the trend of the three doctrines. "Sakyamuni, Confucius and Lao-tse once stood before a jar of vinegar—the emblem of life—and each dipped in his finger to taste the brew. The matter of fact Confucius found it sour, the Buddha called it bitter and Lao-tse pronounced it sweet." [3]

Yet whether Life was sweet, bitter or sour neither doctrine attempted to disguise the enormous importance of the two principles, which united produce life.

The symbolism of the interaction of the *yang* and *yin* as developed in the famous eight trigrams of the Yi King or Book of Changes forms a fascinating and thought provoking chapter by itself.

[3] "The Book of Tea."

V

THE CHINESE TRIGRAMS

"The reason that can be reasoned not eternal reason,
Name that can be named not eternal name.
The unnamable beginning of heaven and earth,
The namable mother of all things. . . .
These two things spiritual and material, though we call them by different names, in their origin are one and the same. This sameness is a mystery. This mystery the gate of all spirituality."—Trans. of Tao-Teh-King.

'The successive movements of the active and inactive elements make what is called the course of things. Existence and non-existence give rise to each other."

V

THE CHINESE TRIGRAMS

THERE is a legend that a 'dragon horse' emerged from the river Ho bearing on its back an arrangement of marks which gave Fuh-Hi (or Fu-Shi) the idea of the trigrams. These groupings or symbols are supposed by some authorities to go back to B.C. 3322, while others consider that Fuh-Hi lived between 2853—2738 B.C.

These trigrams are contained in the Yi King or Book of Changes. Also the earliest Chinese philosophy is found in notes added to the Yi. This ancient book has been venerated by Chinese scholars and sages of every period, who have looked upon it as a "clue to the mysteries of nature and an unfathomable lake of metaphysical wisdom." [1]

The interpretation of the Yi was raised to a science. Confucius classified and wrote various appendices to it and is reported to have said toward the end of his life that if fifty years more could be given him to devote to the study of the Y he might hope to escape many errors.

According to de Groot the Taoists regarded the Yi King as their Book, *par excellence*. He emphasises this as against the generally accepted opinion that the principal Taoist Bible is the Tao-Teh-King.

[1] De Groot's "Religious Systems of China."

The "I" or "Y" consisted originally of eight trigrams and sixty-four hexagrams made up of a combination of broken and unbroken lines arranged in such a way as not to repeat each other.

These were derived from the two elementary or primary forms called Liang-I. De Groot quotes from the Yi in his *Religious Systems of China.* "Of the system of divination laid down in the Yi King or Book of Changes it says 'There is in the system of the metamorphoses of nature the Great Ultimate Principle and this produces the two Regulating Powers. These Powers produce the four forms which again produce eight trigrams. These trigrams determine good and evil and good and evil cause the great business of human life.' "

The two elementary forms or Regulating Powers are:—

Yang bright, *Yin* dark; *Yang* the principle of heaven, *Yin* the earth which when not acted upon by the heavens is nothing but a cold, dark, lifeless mass. *Yang* is the sun, *Yin* the moon. *Yang* is the active, masculine principle, *Yin* is passive, the feminine principle. *Yang* is positive, *Yin* negative. *Yang* is strong, unbending, *Yin* is weak, submissive, pliant.

Everything produced by *Yang* and *Yin* being the natural result of the Celestial and Terrestrial Breaths, the outcome for good or ill is in exact mathematical proportion to the way these are combined. The struggle between and different admixtures of these two contrasting, elementary forces make all the conditions that prevail.

Yang is symbolised by a whole line ——— indicating strength.

Yin is symbolised by a divided line —— —— indicating weakness.

These lines placed over themselves and each other formed the four Hsiang or Emblematic Symbols.

These same lines placed successively over each other formed the eight Kwa or Trigrams. There are only eight possible combinations of such trigrams, to each of which was assigned a special meaning which formed the basis of divination.

The two fundamental lines added to each of the eight trigrams produce sixteen figures of four lines each. This is carried on to thirty-two figures of five lines each. A similar addition produces the sixty-four hexagrams each of which form the subject of an essay

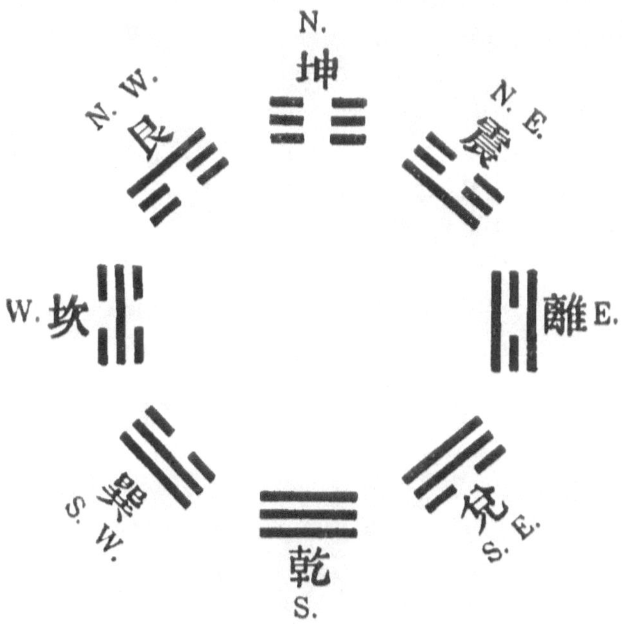

ARRANGEMENT OF TRIGRAMS ACCORDING TO FUH-HI.

in the text of the Yi. The lines increase in an arithmetical progression whose common difference is 1 and the figures in a geometrical progression whose common ratio is 2.

The eight trigrams were called:—

"*Khien*, heaven, sky, celestial sphere.
Tui, watery exhalations, vapours, clouds.
Li, fire, heat, sun, light, lightning.
Chen, thunder.
Sun, wind, wood.
Khan, water, rivers, lakes, seas.
Ken, mountains.
Khwun, earth, terrestrial matter." [2]

Khien represented by three undivided strokes is 'Unalloyed Yang.' Khwun represented by three divided strokes is 'Unalloyed Yin'. In the mixed groups the lower line indicates the place of most importance.

Khien symbolises Heaven which directs the great beginnings of things, and *Khwun* the Earth which gives to them their completion.

Khien and *Khwun* are the gate of the Yi. Movement and rest are the regular and inherent qualities of each.

The six minor trigrams or children are water and fire, thunder and wind, mountains and large bodies of water.

In China the four "heaven spirits" were cloud, rain, wind, thunder, and the worship of mountains and rivers was closely associated with the worship of heaven. Mountains and rivers were believed to control climatic conditions — both physical and spiritual climates. There were four mountains in the four quarters of the empire as well as the four great rivers and the four

[2] De Groot's "Religious Systems of China."

seas which "according to mythical geography bound the earth."

The trigrams contain the three powers, heaven, earth and men. These three are one and the same. When doubled into hexagrams the three powers unite and are one. "But there are the changes and movements of their (several) ways and therefore there are separate places for Yin and Yang and reciprocal uses of the hard and soft." [3]

This system of divination was really an attempt—and an amazingly clever one at that—to explain the

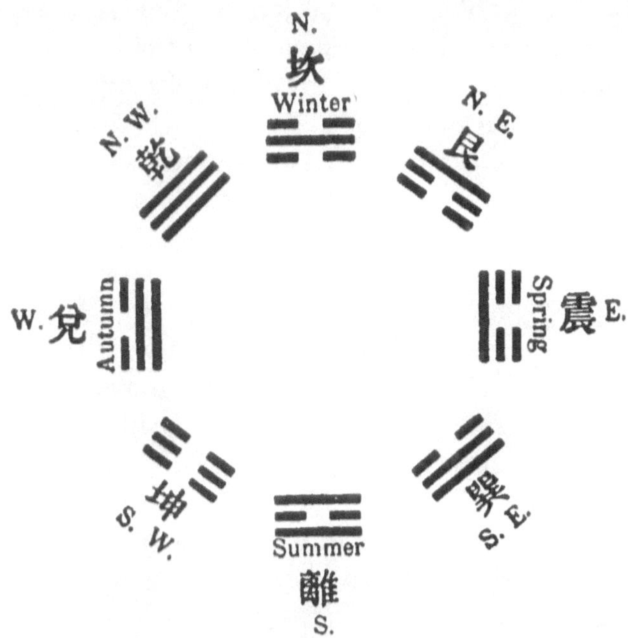

ARRANGEMENT OF TRIGRAMS ACCORDING TO WEN WANG.

origin of nature on mathematical principles. Numbers were conceived of "not as relations predicable of things but as constituting the essence of things." Numbers

[3] Legge's trans. Yi King.

were the rational reality to which appearances as recognised by the senses may be reduced. Troward must have studied the Yi for he speaks of the "three great principles into which all forms of manifestation may be analysed—the Masculine, Positive or Generating Principle; the Feminine, Receptive or Formative Principle; and the Neuter or Mathematical Principle which, by determining the proportional relations between the other two gives rise to the principles of variety and multiplicity." [4]

In the Yi production and re-production are what is called change. The whole system, in fact, is based upon the "contractions and expandings, recedings and approachings of the productive and completing powers of the even and odd numbers."

Yang being represented by an undivided line or one stroke ——— therefore all odd numbers belong to *Yang*.

Yin having a divided line or two strokes —— ——hence all even numbers belong to *Yin*.

Three was assigned to heaven and two to earth.

Heaven was high, earth low. That which is high is noble, honourable. Things low are mean.

Yang was nine, and *Yin* six.

Nine being the triple multiple of the undividable number which represents *Yang* or Heaven, means in Chinese the 'fullness of Yang.'

In Hebrew the number nine was equivalent to Truth. When multiplied the immutable number nine reproduces itself. Thus $2 \times 9 = 18$. $1 + 8 = 9$. $3 \times 9 = 27$. $2 + 7 = 9$ and so on.

The Pythagoreans attached something the same meaning to numbers using the unit and odd numbers

[4] "Bible Mystery and Bible Meaning," T. Troward.

for good and the even for whatever is fluent, crooked, indeterminate, evil.

Plato assigns dexter things and odd numbers to the Olympic gods and the opposite to the dæmons.

Among the Pythagoreans:—

1—is the number of essence.
2—signified otherness, involving difference, diversity.
3—mediation, atonement, completeness—beginning, middle, end.
4—indicated squareness, justice, earth.
5—being the combination of odd and even symbolised marriage.
6—the number of luck or chance.
7—was the number of the entire cosmos, 3 representing the deity and 4 the world. God and the world.
8—solidity.
9—the treble triad. The cube of three being nine, nine was regarded by Pythagoras as the extent to which numbers would go, all others being embraced and revolving within it. Ten but recommences a fresh series capable of infinite expansion.

In the minor trigrams those which contain only one undivided line belong to *Yang*. The *Yang* trigrams represent one ruler and two subjects thus indicating superiority. Those which contain two undivided lines belong to *Yin* and signify two rulers and one subject symbolising inferiority, weakness, dissension.

In the preface to his translation of the Yi King Legge refers a little scornfully to the fact that Chinese scholars are fond of saying that all the truths of electricity, heat, light and other branches of European physics are to be found in the eight trigrams. And if you reflect upon it, as representing an eternal process

The "Pah-Kwa" or eight trigrams with the Great Monad in the centre are also a powerful charm against evil and are often seen above the entrance door of houses or carved on a wooden shield and nailed on the lintel of a door. Henry Doré, S. J., *Researches into Chinese Superstition.*

developed from unity to multiplicity by the inter-relation of the active and negative forces, this may not be untrue.

The most superficial study of the trigrams reveals

a certain authority, that touch of the universal that captivates the imagination. And one finds in them the same undying vitality that pertains to all the ancient symbols of life.

The system or philosophy as developed in the Yi King is strikingly unlike the majority of religious beliefs. There is no sort of a notion conveyed of the ultimate marriage of heaven and earth, nor of a day when the lion and the lamb are going to lie down together. On the contrary, the Chinese, who are intensely practical as well as mystical, seem to have accepted the fact that the lion and the lamb are temperamentally unfitted for any permanent association, and that heaven and earth can only unite for the purpose of production. Indeed, the entire conception of the trigrams is based upon the idea that these forces active and passive, masculine and feminine, heaven and earth not only are directly antagonistic, but that their being so is a part of the scheme of things.

The changeableness of human affairs—union gives way to separation—from separation comes re-union—this is the theme of the Yi King. "The ever changing phenomena of nature and human experience."

"Sun goes, moon comes. Moon goes, sun comes. Cold goes, heat comes. Heat goes, cold comes. That which goes becomes less, that which comes increases. Thus the seasons, year, all life completes itself."

"Notes of the same key respond to one another. Creatures of the same nature seek one another. Water flows toward the place that is low and damp. Fire rises up toward what is dry. Clouds follow the dragon and winds follow the tiger."

It is, perhaps, this very acceptation and development of the idea of displacement and change that gives the Yi King its uncanny fascination. You find yourself repeating "Sun goes, moon comes. Moon goes, sun comes . . . Water flows toward the place that is low and damp. Fire rises up toward what is dry. Clouds follow the dragon and winds follow the tiger." Under its spell you, too, begin to feel that displacement, constant displacement is the secret of continued existence and growth. The weak and the strong alternately give way to each other, just as in the lineal figures of the trigrams strong and weak lines push each other out. And it is this alternation that produces all the changes and transformations.

The weak rule when the *Yang* element is lacking—and civilisations fall. The weak in turn are displaced by the strong and good rises again. Yet each has its purpose in the way of fulfilment.

The Chinese believe, however, that a great man can neither be all heaven nor all earth but must have a blending of both to be truly great.

"A great man is he who is in harmony in his attributes with heaven and earth, in his brightness with sun and moon, in his orderly procedure with the four seasons."

VI

THE CROSS

"The three main forms in which the life force manifests itself are the globe, the star and the cross. . . . Of the third all trees and plants having upright stems and leaves or branches growing at right angles, not forgetting man himself, who, tree-like, with trunk and branches makes with outstretched arms throughout long vistas of human history 'the sign of the cross.'"
—Eva Martin.

VI

THE CROSS

IF you go to the Egyptian rooms of any of the large museums—the Louvre at Paris, the British Museum in London, the Metropolitan Museum of New York or that of Cairo—you will find graven on fragments of temple walls, and on tombs and sarcophagi that existed 4,000 years before Christ, various forms of the cross. You will see it portrayed thus ×—still used as the sign of multiplication—and thus +—used to this day as the plus sign—and again thus T—the "Sacred Tau." You will then notice constantly repeated a figure like this ☥—the tau cross with a circle or ovoid above it. This is known as the *Crux Ansata,* the Egyptian Ankh, the Key of the Nile, the Key of Life or the Cross of Egypt. Although this form of the cross is more closely associated with Egypt, the *crux ansata* was also reverenced as the "hidden wisdom" by the Phœnicians, the Chaldeans, the Mexicans and all other ancient races of whom any records can be found.

Used as a sign by primordial man, found in its different forms as a religious emblem among the most widely scattered races, and in every stage of civilisation, reverenced by the Incas, tattooed on their foreheads by the Patagonians, made a feature of their worship by the Druids, taken over by the Christians as their highest emblem of Life Everlasting, it is significant that the meaning of life attached to the cross has never been lost. Its prevalence, its undying vitality, the tenacity with which it has been preserved and reverenced seems to be an instinct of race consciousness comparable to the instinct for life in the individual, which physicians tell us is the strongest instinct we possess. As a symbol of life it would have been impossible for the Christian religion not to have adopted it.

The cross has been called the cosmic symbol of the four quarters of the earth or universe. Some have believed that it was derived from the two crossed fire sticks. It has been likened to a bird with outstretched wings. It has been traced back to two human figures crossed. Plato saw the divine man stamped upon the universe in the form of a cross. Except that it means life, however, everything else about the cross—its origin and from what source derived is pure conjecture.

The invariable signification of the *crux ansata*—implied also by the simpler cross—is 'Life to Come.'

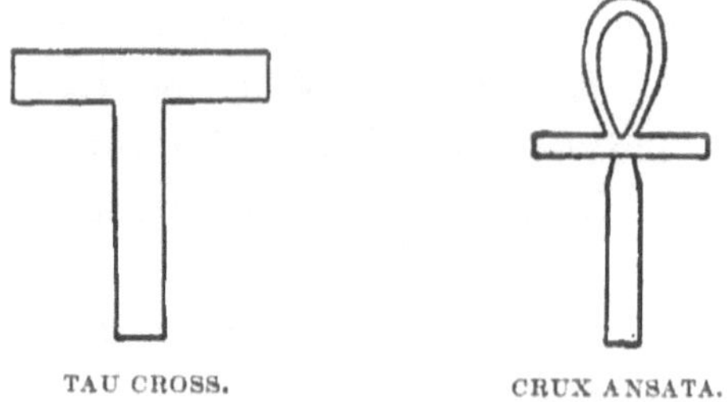

TAU CROSS. CRUX ANSATA.

The *crux ansata* is the inseparable accompaniment of the chief triad of Egyptian deities, nor is its use reserved for superior deities alone. Maat the goddess of Truth is depicted presenting it to the Sun the source of all life, typifying that Life and Truth are eternal.

IBIS-HEADED THOTH PRESENTING THE SYMBOL OF LIFE TO THE FALCON GOD HORUS

Deities are frequently pictured holding it to the lips of a dying man, or sometimes receiving it as a passport to the soul. Placed on tombs and sarcophagi it signified the ever living spirit, the immortality of the soul.

GREEK CROSS. LATIN CROSS. MALTESE CROSS.

The *Tau cross* among the ancient Irish symbolised wisdom.

The tau was considered a divine symbol by the Mexicans, who called it the Tree of Life, Tree of Nutriment, Tree of our Flesh and who later consecrated it to the god of rain.

Thor's hammer was said to be the tau cross. The double hammer of Thor was a symbol of lightning and rain and thus fertility. Thor's hammer has also been called the swastika or fylfot cross. Other authorities, however, consider that the hammer of Thor more properly belongs with the Y—that mystic Y of the Chinese.

THE SWASTIKA.

The tau cross was given to St. Anthony the Hermit, who besides using it as a crutch, was depicted in Greek art with the tau—always blue—on the left shoulder or on the cope.

The candidates for admission into Mithraism are said to have received the mark of the tau on their foreheads at the time of their initiation.

The tau cross as well as other forms of the cross were used as instruments of execution.

As a symbol of life in a perverted sense, a phallic

meaning has been attributed to the tau, and the opinion has been expressed that in the old biblical days of Ezekiel the tau was the mark ordered by the Lord to be placed "upon the foreheads of the men that sigh and that cry for all the abominations." (Ezekiel 9:4.)

The monogram of the Egyptian Tau is formed of three taus ⊢T⊣. This is similar to the Masonic jewel of the Royal Arch. It is interesting to note here that much of the symbolism that enters so largely into Masonic rites goes back through unbroken tradition to the days of primordial man. Churchward finds that the gavel used by the Free Masons was a sacred symbol of the Pygmies. Objects discovered under the obelisk of Cleopatra's Needle reveal that many of the symbols used in the ceremonial rites of modern Free Masonry were employed by building organisations and architects in Egypt in 1900 B.C. The same symbols were also in use among the Mayas, according to Le Plongeon, who, in discussing the origin of Free Masonry, says that, although it has been attributed to Pythagoras and "its esoteric doctrines and symbols can be plainly traced to the doctrine of Pythagoras and from there to the religious mysteries of Egypt"—on the other hand, he goes on to say, although some consider that it was founded by the first Christians, others that it originated in the building of Solomon's Temple and others again that it goes back to the days of Adam, he himself believes that Free Masonry existed before Adam. Bayley notes that the same symbolism was used in Mithraism, preserved by the Gnostics, made a part of their ritual by the Rosicrucians and Templars who "when driven out of Germany reappear in England as Free Masons."

In Egyptian symbolism sometimes four taus are used placed back to back. "These point like the flaming sword that guarded Eden to all four quarters of the universe."

The tau cross is also associated with the sacred axe of the pygmies, when stones took the place of sticks.

The cross with four equal arms, sometimes formed of serpents, has been called the symbol of the four elements.

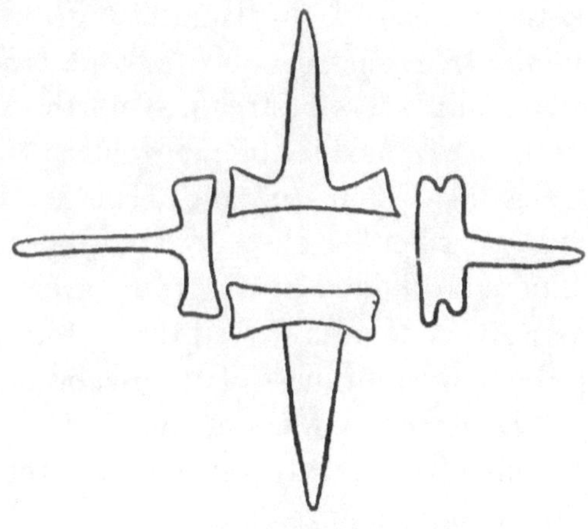

FOUR TAUS PLACED BACK TO BACK.
Bayley, *Lost Language of Symbolism*.

When composed of two or four sceptres with a circle at the point of intersection it indicated "divine potentiality."

The four cardinal points were of great importance in all primitive symbolism. The year with its four recurring seasons and twelve periods of time set off by the appearance of each new moon; the sunrise and sunset, the right and left hand of a man as he faced the east, these all became fixed points of reference. And one may believe that from the latter picture of himself facing the rising sun, man derived the idea of the four cardinal points.

The simple cross enclosed in a circle as a sign of the earth was intended, it may be supposed, to indicate the four quarters—north, south, east, west—or extension in length and breadth.

The tradition of the four rivers of Paradise flowing towards the cardinal points dividing the land cruciformly has been handed down in many mythologies. In the Sinéru of the Buddhist grows the four limbed Damba-tree or tree of life, and from its roots gush forth four sacred streams—north, south, east, west. From the four sides of the golden Mount Meru or the "Celestial Earth" of the Hindus, proceed the four primeval rivers. The "celestial mountain land" of the Chinese is divided by the four streams of immortality. Four rivers of milk flowed through Asgard the Elysium or abode of happiness of the Scandinavians.

The Aztec goddess of rain bore a cross in her hand.

The Greek cross represented the winds from the four cardinal points.

This cross was also used by the ancient Americans to represent the winds which bring rains.

GREEK CROSS REPRESENTING WINDS FROM CARDINAL POINTS.

Dakota Indians

Tenth Annual Report of the Bureau of Ethnology, Fig. 1255.

In the *Swastika* by Thomas Wilson one finds the following legend of the Dakota Indians interpreting the cross which symbolises the winds:

"The four winds issue out of the four caverns in which the souls of men existed before the incarnation of the human body. The top of the cross is the cold, devastating North Wind, the most powerful of all. It is worn on the body nearest the head, the seat of intelligence and conquering devices. The left arm covers the heart, it is the East Wind coming from the seat of life and love. The foot is the melting, burning South Wind indicating as it is worn the seat of fiery passion. The right arm is the gentle West Wind blowing from the spirit land, covering the lungs from which the breath goes out gently, but into the unknown night. The centre of the cross is the earth and man moved by the conflicting influences of Gods and Winds."[1]

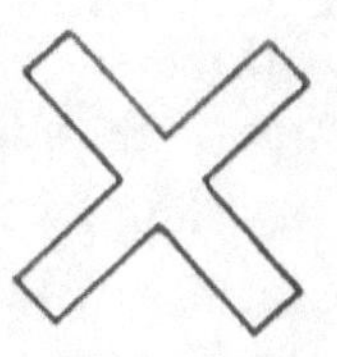
ST. ANDREW'S CROSS.

St. Andrew's cross or Saltire, the *crux décussata* represented perfection. The original meaning of *décusés* was the number ten, the Roman sign for which (X) is made of two Vs (or fives) put point to point.

The crossed fire sticks of the Chinese have been likened to St. Andrew's cross.

The cross with a wheel in the centre called Kiakra, Tschakra or Cakra is regarded as one of the oldest symbols of majesty and power in India. Vishnu the personification of the sun is given the cross to signify his eternal and ever vigilant government and his mighty power of life and light that penetrates heaven and earth and vanquishes darkness and evil.

"The word cross *crux* resolves itself into *ak-ur-os* the Light of the Great Fire. . . . Hammer—anglo-saxon *hamor* means fire or gold of the Immutable Sun." (Bayley.)

Brahma is represented holding a fiery cross.

Fiery Crosses were used in the early days by the Norsemen to summon the nation to a council of war.

The Assyrians represented Anu, god of the sky, by an equilateral cross. The ideogram of the god was formed by four cruciform characters radiating from a centre denoting the sun.

In China a cross inscribed in a square was a symbol of the earth.

[1] "The Swastika," Thomas Wilson, pp. 934-5.

The cross among the Celts and the Germans was the Celestial Two Headed Mallet which symbolised fertility.

The *Mallet* as a religious symbol is also found in Japan where it is called the "Creative Hammer," and typifies the *Yo* and *In* (*Yang* and *Yin*) or the masculine and feminine principles of nature which lead to the creation of all things. On the striking portion was figured a circle the symbol of the *tama* or sacred pearl the "gem of transcendental wisdom, its lambent glow, the emblem of pure essence."

CELTIC CROSS.

The *Celtic crosses* as the name implies are found principally in Ireland and Scotland. They are generally of stone and are usually found distinguishing some spot by the road side.

Numerous forms of the cross are found among the North American Indians as will be seen on page 62.

CELTIC CROSS.

The Maltese Cross was the symbol of the Knights of Malta.

The Cross pattée differs a little having the sides of the limbs slightly curved in. It signified the open wings of a bird and was adopted as their sign by the Knights Hospitaller.

The Latin Cross is the one more closely identified with the Christian religion, although other forms were also used and with the same signification.

Lowrie in the *Monuments of the Early Church*, says "Never has the cross been held in higher estimation than it was in the first centuries of the Church. . . . It was used as a gesture not only in ecclesiastical functions but in private life. Tertullian . . . says 'At every action which we begin, in coming in and in going out, when we clothe ourselves, or put on our shoes, when we bathe, when we seat ourselves at table, at lamp lighting, on going to bed, we trace on our foreheads the sign of the cross."

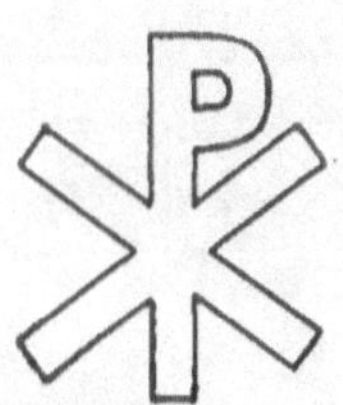

MONOGRAM OF CHRIST. LABARUM OF CONSTANTINE.

Lowrie adds "The Christians saw in these pagan symbols a mystic presage of the Gospel, but the only one of which they make any use during the second and third centuries was the swastica, an ancient oriental symbol which was commonly used in the West for purely decorative purposes."

The old mystical idea of man as the microcosm of which the universe is the macrocosm is a familiar one. Nor is it a new idea that the ancients proportioned their sacred temples from the human figure. The sculpture of the Greeks and Egyptians reveals the fact that they studied the body abstractly in its exterior presentment. The rules for its proportion having been established for sculpture it is not unreasonable to suppose that these same rules and measurements were developed and elaborated upon in architecture. Vitruvius and Alberti both lay stress upon the fact that all sacred buildings should be founded on the proportions of the human body. Troward declares that the "human body forms the basis of the proportions observed in such ecclesiastical architecture as is designed according to canonical rules of which Westminster Abbey and Milan Cathedral are good examples."

One has only to take up the dictionary and glance at the definition of cubit "measure from the elbow to the tip of the middle finger," or watch a woman measure

VARIOUS FORMS OF CROSSES IN USE AMONG NORTH AMERICAN INDIANS, FROM GREEK CROSS TO SWASTIKA.

Second Annual Report of the Bureau of Ethnology, 1880–81, Pl. LIII.

off a yard from the hand with extended arm to the tip of the nose, or an eighth of a yard from the tip of the middle finger to the knuckle, or a man estimating the size of a room by pacing across it heel to toe to realise that man has built up his world on himself—made himself the measure of all things.

It seems plausible, therefore, that the symbol of the cross may have been adapted from man himself standing with outstretched arms, typifying the highest form of life really known to man—his own.

And thus, with the poetic justice that the ancients delighted in, criminals were nailed to the cross, the symbol of themselves, the symbol of life which they had desecrated and profaned. In Greece where the cross also meant future life it was used as a sign of mercy. Criminals who were acquitted had their names marked by a cross—the sign of life. The Romans indicated acquittal in the same way.

To this day a man who cannot write signs his name with a cross.

Interpreted as symbolising man himself, the reason for placing crosses at cross roads where man passes, and in market places where men were apt to congregate is not difficult to understand, nor is the reverence that is attached to the cross in any degree lessened by the thought that throughout his strange and shadowed history, in his painful efforts at self-understanding man has seen in the cross the reflection of his own divine potentiality, that divinity which he recognises dimly at times, overpoweringly at others, as the living part of the inexpressibly complex nature of man.

His religion is thus indissolubly an integral part of himself.

Interpreted as man himself the symbolism of the

cross with the circle above it becomes clear. Universally reverenced as an emblem of life and immortality, the *crux ansata* or tau cross with an ovoid above it has been used from pre-historic days to typify the union of spirit and water, masculine and feminine, the active and passive principles of life. There is something awe inspiring, superb in the continuity of life represented by this one symbol. It goes back to creation itself—"The spirit of God moved upon the face of the waters"—carries us through the human, and on to spiritual life and immortality.

"Toward the spiritual perfection of Humanity the stupendous momentum of the cosmic process has all along been tending."

The swastika, the most ancient of the many forms of the cross will be considered elsewhere.

VII

POLE OR AXIS AND CIRCLE, PILLARS, STONES, ROCKS, ALTARS

"The Universal Pillar which supports all things."

"The Eternal Circle from Goodness through Goodness to Goodness."

"Of the Rock that begat thee thou art unmindful and hast forgotten God that formed thee," Deut. 32:18.

"Jesus saith, wherever there are two they are not without God, and wherever there is one alone, I say, I am with him. Raise the stone and there thou shalt find Me, cleave the wood and there am I."

"Duality . . . the greatest of mysteries . . . for it is the universal mystery of attraction upon which all research even in physical science eventually abuts,"—Troward.

VII

POLE OR AXIS AND CIRCLE: PILLARS, STONES, ROCKS, ALTARS: TWIN BROTHER IDEA, TWIN HORSE-MEN

THE combination of upright and circle—"I the 'Holy One,' the Pole or Axis of the universe" and O—*eau,* water, the Perfect One, the Pearl, the Divine Receptacle, lends itself to an infinite variety of sacred forms and ideas.

In this symbolism the Pole or Axis becomes the stabilising force. It is the Pillar of Heaven, the type of all sacred pillars. Around it revolves the whole universe. "There, too, at the end of the axis are placed those Triune emblems the fleur-de-lys and the trident while the axis becomes the spear, lance, dart of so many classic myths."[1]

PERSIAN SEAL.
D'Alviella, *Migration of Symbols.*

LYCIA.
D'Alviella.

The axis of the universe is also symbolised as a fiery column, or a pillar, staff, spindle, spike, nails, torso, rod, axle-tree, pivot, pole—'under the character of Eros the God of Love or Attraction, the first principle of animation, the father of God and man.' The regulator and disposer of all things was worshipped under the

[1] "The Night of the Gods," by John O'Neill.

name of *Priapus.* He was said to pervade the Universe with the motion of his wings bringing pure light and thence was called the 'Splendid, the Self-illumined, the Ruling Priapus.'

The word pole is a derivative of a Phœnician word which means 'he breaks through' or 'passes into.'

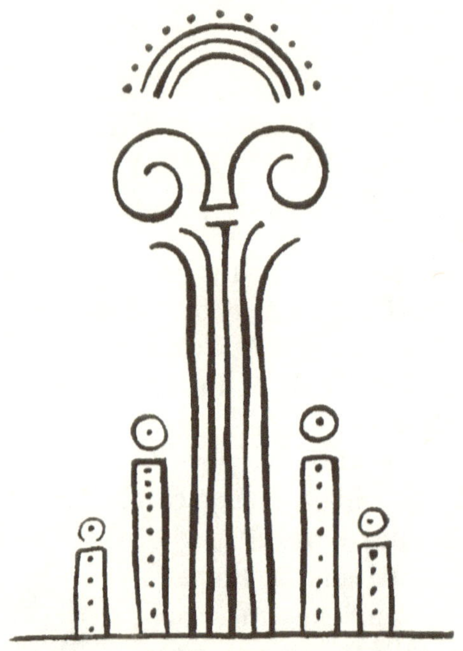

GROUP OF SACRED PILLARS ON MYCENÆAN VASE FROM HALIKI.
Evans, *Mycenæan Trees and Pillar Cult.*

The axis is associated with the great tower of Kronos the mainstay of the universe.

The pillar is constantly referred to in the Bible as a symbol of the Creator.

One of the Egyptian names for the sacred city of the sun signified stone pillar. The traditions of stone worship survived in the Egyptian custom of erecting obelisks similar to Cleopatra's Needle before their temples.

Our church spires are a relic of the same primitive symbolism of creative force and Life Everlasting or belief in the continuity of life.

Pillars, obelisks, columns, monoliths and shafts have an undoubted phallic origin and as symbols of creative energy they were objects of reverential worship among all ancient races.

Photo. Alinari

HERMES (MERCURY)

(Museo Ludovisi Boncompagni, Rome)

The tower is an outgrowth of the pillar, and the Round Towers in Ireland, which are supposed to have been built by Persian refugees probably reflected this same form of worship.

The Sacred Tat Pole of Egypt, the Measurer of the Inundation, is sometimes depicted with a scarabæus and two uræus snakes symmetrically posed on either side. These are all life symbols.

To show their divinity and their association with life, a rayed sun disk is frequently depicted with these pillars or shafts, symbolising the same idea that was conveyed in Egyptian religious art by the two uræus serpents curving up either side of a pole or pillar.

The classic form of the caduceus, a winged rod entwined by two serpents, was originally a rod—believed to be the sacred tau—surmounted by a circle upon which rests a crescent. It was the emblem of life and power and Mercury always bears the caduceus when conducting the souls of the dead.

Serpents twined around a pole were a symbol of Baal Hamman.

The crosier—which was originally in the form of a tau cross and only assumed the bent appearance in the seventeenth century—also the shepherd's crook come under this class of symbols. Osiris in judging the dead is represented as holding in his hands "the crook, the sceptre and the flail, emblems of rule, sovereignty and dominion."

The three pointed wand conventionalised into the *fleur-de-lis* is derived from the same symbolism.

"Pillars supporting a pavilion or tent are found in the older sculptures of Nimroud. They are probably of wood, appear to have been painted and were surmounted by a pine or fir cone, that religious symbol so constantly recurring on Assyrian monuments."[2]

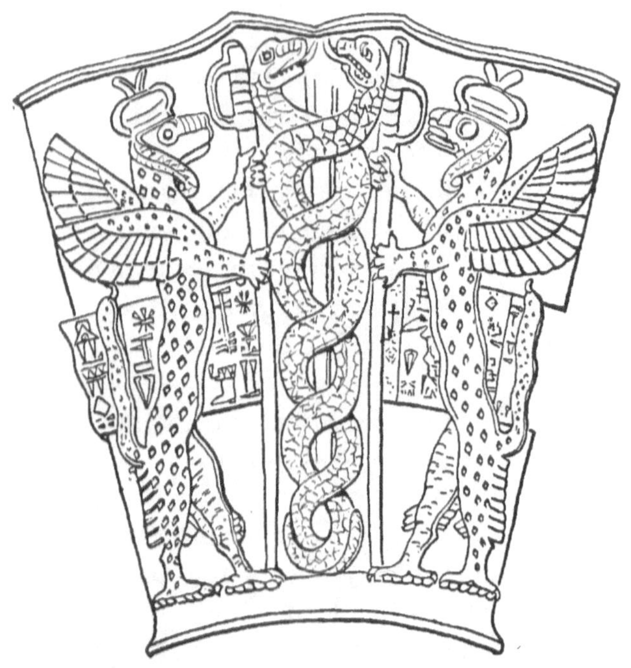

LIBATION VASE OF GREEN STONE.
Jastrow, *Civilisation of Babylonia and Assyria.*

The pine or fir cone had the same meaning as the *crux ansata* of the Egyptians. It has also been interpreted as a symbol of fire, hence life.

Among the Babylonians Ea the Sumerian god of water, as the 'world spine' is symbolised as a column with a ram's head standing on a throne beside which rests a 'goat fish.'

The column symbolising the solar god Marduk (Merodach) terminates in a lance head. Nergal's column bears a lion's head.

[2] Layard's "Nineveh."

In the earliest representations of the pillar in Cyprus and Chaldea it assumes the form of a staff supporting a semicircle.

The Staff of Life depicted in a great variety of forms is found on ancient gems and coins and sculpture.

'The rod of mine anger . . . the staff in their hand' is the battle standard given as a symbol to Ashur, Tammuz and Osiris, who were tree-gods as well as corn and vegetation gods.

The Phrygians depicted lions, bulls or winged sphinxes facing each other, and between them they placed the phallus, or sacred pillar, or an urn.

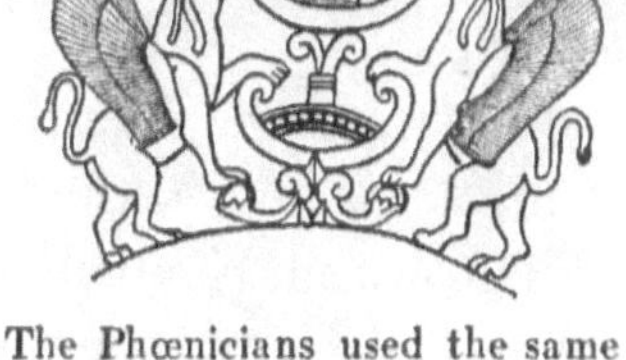

The Phœnicians used the same form. In this case it appears to be the conventionalised lotus.
D'Alviella, *Migration of Symbols.*

In Palestine besides the *stelai* or *hâmmâmin* which symbolised Baal, they also venerated "a *simulacra* of Ashtoreth, representing this goddess of the fruitful and nourishing earth under the form of a tree, or rather a stake begirt with draperies and bandelets. These are the *ashêrîm* which the Hebrews, in spite of the unbraidings of the prophets of Yahvew, did not cease to 'construct' and 'plant.'"[3]

The identification of the *Asherah* or *Ashera*—(singular for ashêrîm)—as an attribute of the goddess Ashtoreth (Astarte) the feminine counterpart of Baal, is disputed by many scholars who consider that the Sacred Pole or Asherah of the Hebrews belongs to the same symbolism of life and reproduction that is expressed in the Old Testament by Aaron's rod which "budded and brought forth buds and bloomed blossoms and yielded almonds." (Num. 17: 8.) And also by

[3] D'Alviella's "The Migration of Symbols."

the Rod or Stem of Jesse, "And there shall come forth a rod out of the stem of Jesse and a Branch shall grow out of his roots." (Isa. 11: 1.)

Representations of the genealogical Tree of Jesse were very popular in mediæval paintings, sculpture and embroideries. And the same account of Christ's descent taken from the Gospel of St. Matthew is elaborated in the Jesse windows which are found in some of the old cathedrals.

The *circle* has always symbolised eternity—that which is without beginning or end. It is also, as we have seen, one of the symbols of water or the feminine principle.

The circle O meaning water enters into the mystery of numbers and in the figure 8 becomes the "twin circles of Love and Knowledge." Christ in "His essential elements His number is eight." Water from remotest times was used as a sacrament of regeneration to wash away sins, its use thus symbolising spiritual re-birth. The baptismal fonts in Christian Churches were made octagonal in form to typify the biblical account of creation, which, having been completed in seven days, thus eight figured regeneration, the beginning anew. The symbolism of the octave also enters in here.

Spirit being the mysterious bond between men this unseen but potent force was indicated by "mystic ties or links." These were frequently formed out of a combination of the S of *spiritus* and the figure 8. Sometimes three circles were used as a symbol of perfection. Again the trefoil is employed, also the cross. "The principle of the Divine Essence" was typified by the trefoil or clover leaf.

The spiral was used in the East to denote thunder from which issues a flash of lightning.

The spiral ornament also appears on Egyptian scarabs, on spectacle stones in Scotland as well as in Crete, France, Denmark, Scandinavia. This spectacle ornament resembled twin wheels or circles and was regarded as a symbol of the Deity.

Among the Egyptians the letter O was the hieroglyph of the sun and was looked upon as a symbol of new birth, new life.

The Trinity which was common to all people of antiquity was sometimes symbolised by three concentric circles.

In the Caves of Ellora three circles arranged in the form of a triangle two below and one above were indicative of a Caitya or Stupa as well as of the Tri-ratna or Three Jewels.

Four circles linked in cruciform shape to a larger central one was used by the mystics as a symbol of Wisdom who is "the mother of fair love and fear, and knowledge and holy hope."

The Egyptians symbolised the "Splendour of Daylight" by five circles. Among the Pythagoreans five typified light as well as marriage. The modern Free Masons have Five Virtues or Points of Fellowship. The Greeks held the number sacred to their solar god Apollo. Five was universally regarded by the ancients as belonging to the God of Light indicating the number of his attributes:—Being, sameness, diversity, motion, rest—or Omnipotence, omnipresence, eternity, omniscience, unity.

The Druids represented the Northern Heavens by a circle and the Southern Heavens by a circle, each circle surrounded by twelve equidistant pillars. These circles were joined together by a smaller circle which also had twelve pillars, the pillars of the latter symbolising the twelve signs of the zodiac. These thirty six divisions were symbolic of the thirty six gates of the "Great House of Him who is on the Hill."

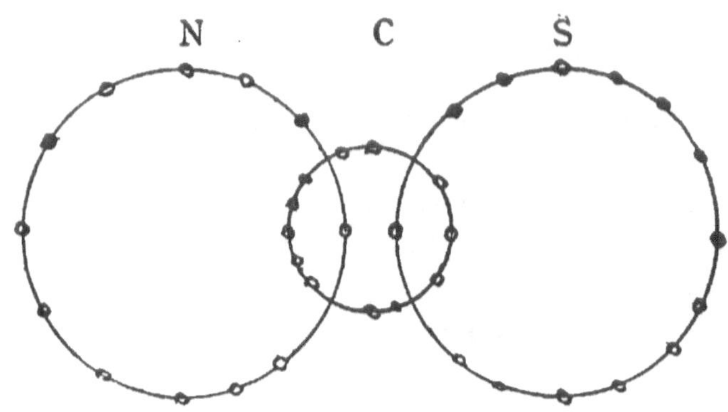

"THE THIRTY SIX GATES."
Churchward, *Signs and Symbols of Primordial Man.*

The Circle also denotes perfection, the Perfect One, the Pearl of Price.

In Japan the circle is associated with the lotus and the *manji* (swastika).

There as well as in China the circle is sometimes divided by three lines resembling the Chinese Y, indicating the Great Unit, the Great Uniter.

The Maoris are said to worship a First Cause under the name of Io.

The decade 10 is a combination of upright and circle and was interpreted by Pythagoras as forming, as it were, a monad with which re-commences a fresh series capable of infinite expansion.

In Bayley's *Lost Language of Symbolism* there is an illustration of a spear or dart typifying "the primal, energising force of Light or Rod of Jesse," transfixing a wavy line which terminates in a circle. Bayley interprets this as "being the M of *mare,* sea or a com-

Photo. Alinari

Demeter (Ceres)

(Museo Nazionale delle Terme, Rome)

bination of I the Holy One and *o—cau*—a variant of the symbolism known to underlie the Maypole and its ring."

Nowhere is the nature of this symbolism more clearly shown than in our modern Maypole and its ring, which is simply a survival of some ancient springtime festival in which the pole, the symbol of the reproductive powers of nature, is laden with garlands of flowers and all the conventional attributes of life and productivity, and ceremoniously planted in the warm, receptive earth, while those who celebrate the return of spring sing and dance about it.

In this symbolism of pole and circle, the dominant, forceful upright was looked upon as Creator, and the circle was the "regulator or bridle of time and motion." One sees here also the esoteric connection between the circle and the tides of the sea.

The ancient metaphysicians were not always complimentary to the passive principle. True, as Chesterton says, "In all legends men have thought of women as sublime separately but horrible in the herd."

Nevertheless, in spite of her legendary beginning in which she is depicted as a malignant force, a monster like the Scottish Hag—in spite of Eve, the very tempting first woman of the Hebrews, the mystics of all ages have delighted in portraying woman as enclosing, guarding, protecting—as the "house or wall of man without whose bounding and redeeming influence he would inevitably be dissipated and lost in the abyss."

The supreme importance of these forces Life itself proves. And the rise and fall of civilisations and the happiness and misery of individuals can be largely interpreted by their juxtaposition. The trouble with the circle, of course, is that it cannot go forward without returning to itself—without coming back to the beginning, and with the pole or dart or arrow, that it loses itself, goes on and on until spent unless bounded and restrained by the circle.

To this ancient conception of the active and passive principles of life as angular and curved, has been attributed many of the intricate and elaborate designs used from time immemorial in architecture—such as the egg and dart motif, the bead and reel, and many others that one still sees pictured on friezes, and carved on capitals and mouldings. Whether, as Goodyear believes, the egg and dart is derived from the lotus, or whether the inception comes from some earlier form, one may assume without fear of contradiction that it represented this tenaciously held conception of the dualistic principles.

This feeling for life was carried into mediæval church architecture where one tower—the feminine—was always a little lower. Nor is it altogether fanciful that it was this thought of Life—used reverently and with full knowledge of its meaning—that creates the difference between ancient and modern art.

The statement that all architecture had a phallic origin is one of those fragmentary truths that mankind is so fond of uttering—a shallow and surface way of expressing a tremendous, vital, underlying truth. Looking around upon the work of his hands and brains, if man finds nothing but imitation and ugliness if he is honest, he will say "This is myself." When he resorts to imitation, however, or merely expresses the ugly and meretricious his best is perverted, he is no longer an honest workman. It is one of the unbreakable laws, apparently, that when an architect or artist does not express in his art from the very depths of his inner consciousness this union of spirit and matter he is actually saying nothing to us. His buildings, pictures, statues are meaningless forms.

And this leads one to modern church architecture. In the old days towers, columns, church spires symbolised the creative impulse reaching up toward the sky, toward the spiritual—to the divine union of heaven and earth, spirit and matter. In building our modern church without spires—the old phallic emblem—it may be the shame of knowledge that overtook Adam or Eve, or possibly a reflex of puritanical training that instead of sublimating the natural instincts we should deny their existence, but is it not more truly an unconscious betrayal of how little we ourselves enter in—does the absence of the church spire symbolise only too truthfully that the church has lost its aspiration to lift the whole of man up?

Whatever we do is so apt to indicate more than we dream.

Among all ancient races *rocks* and *stones* were worshipped as symbols of the Creator.

A theory has been advanced that in simpler times when man lived closer to nature he was responsive to all her subtle influences, so that even the spirit of the stone, which we are now too dulled and atrophied to recognise, carried a message to him. Hence arose the belief in the magical and medicinal qualities, in the luck or ill luck, that have been since time immemorial, attributed to certain precious stones.

The Egyptians perpetuated the worship of trees and wells, stones and mounds. A great block of stone was believed to be inhabited by one of the spirits of the sun-god.

The early Cretan religion seems to have consisted largely in the worship of natural objects such as trees and stones, or artificial, such as the sacred pillar, cones, the 'horns of consecration' and the double axe.

In the worship of the Druids the stone pillar or menhir was associated with their sacred trees. In the primitive religions of India there was the same custom of setting up sacred stones underneath holy trees.

Rocks, stones, altars and pillars are constantly referred to in the Old Testament as symbols of the Creator. Jacob sets up a pillar where he had talked with God, "even a pillar of stone." And again he takes the stone which he had used for a pillow and sets it up for a pillar and pours oil upon the top of it, "And he called the name of that place Beth-el." Evans identifies Beth-el with bætylic or the heaven sent meteoric stones.

The Israelites at the command of the Lord take twelve stones from the bed of the river Jordan and Joshua later sets them up at Gilgal.

When the psalmist says, "The Lord is my *rock* and my fortress and my deliverer; my God, my strength in whom I will trust; my *buckler* and the *horn* of my salvation and my high *tower*," (Ps. 18:2.) he is not originating these images out of his own mind; he is simply making use of old symbols of life that had been known and believed in since time began.

A. J. Evans in his *Mycenæan Trees and Pillar Cult* says of the cavern shrines of the Diktæan Cave that "it is clear that the natural columns of this cave were regarded as the bætylic forms of the divinity just as the cave itself is here his temple. Some of the shorter stalagmitic formations of this 'Holy of Holies' are perfect representations of the omphalos type and may supply the true explanation of the origin of this form of sacred stone."

The ancient Greeks appear to have had the idea that men were derived from trees and rocks.

"Mithra was said to have been born of a rock, to have wedded a rock and to have been the parent of a rock."

MITHRA BORN FROM THE ROCK.

His head is adorned with a Phrygian cap. He has a dagger in one hand and a lighted torch in the other.

Bas-relief found in the Crypt of St. Clements at Rome. Cumont, *Mysteries of Mithra.*

Bayley finds justification for thinking that the word rock is associated with Great Fire. Hence Stonehenge, seat or stronghold of Resplendent Fire. Stone circles were symbolic of the Immutable Sun.

"The reference in Jeremiah 'Saying to a stock Thou art my father and to a stone—Thou hast brought me forth' means, no doubt, the sacred stock (ashera) and the sacred stone (masseba) of the sanctuary which the Israelites regarded as their father and mother. The sacred stock seems to have been a tree stripped of its branches. The sacred stone was usually shaped like a pillar, cone or obelisk."[4]

In their worship of the sacred stone or pillar known as Masseba, pouring oil on the stone was a part of the ritual.

In the cult of Asherah it might be either a living tree or an artificially constructed pole or post before which the Canaanites placed their altars.

Stone pillars and shafts and monuments to mark graves were originally placed there not only as a symbol of the Creator—of the animating force of life here

[4] Frazer's "The Golden Bough."

and hereafter, but also as a place of indwelling for the ghost of the departed. Stones and trees were thought to be the depositories of the divine life, and were therefore worshipped, not as things, but for the divinity they were supposed to contain.

In the old Jewish burial ground in Prague—one of the oldest in existence and long since disused, one sees a curious exemplification of this ancient reverence for stones, in the quantities of small stones which still lie piled up upon the graves and tombstones where they were placed, according to Jewish custom, as a token of esteem by relatives and friends of the deceased.

Altars and *rocks* were modified forms of pillars; the rock a simplification of the pillar, and the altar a place of offering. In the early religions of Northern India the first sacrifice was to Mother Earth which was the feminine manifestation of creative energy. The altar, a heaped up mound of earth, was a symbol of the sacred mother. This altar not only was the earth itself but the earth as woman. The original altars among the Jews were also of earth.

In time these altars became slabs for votive offerings and were placed over the "pillar shrines which were of a slightly conical shape." The corner posts which were only added for security gave rise to a table form and "when the aniconic image had been superseded, to a Cretan form of altar and certain types of tripod." [5]

In the most primitive form of stone and pillar worship, the offerings were simply placed on the holy stone. Again a basket or some receptacle will hold the offering. The symbolism of fruitfulness and plenty is obviously indicated in a Græco-Roman relief where the "shovel shaped basket of Bacchus laden with grapes and fruit"

[5] A. J. Evans's "Mycenæan Trees and Pillar Cult."

is depicted surmounting a divine pillar. The same type of basket plays an important part in the religious ceremonies of the Hittites and Babylonians. There, too, it is sometimes placed on the summit of what "must certainly be recognised as a bætylic cone." [6]

A close relationship appears to have existed between moon and stone worship. The moon spirit was believed to inhabit the lunar stone. Moon worship also links itself with earth worship and both with water worship, or in other words, with the feminine cult, all three being looked upon as manifestations of the feminine principle.

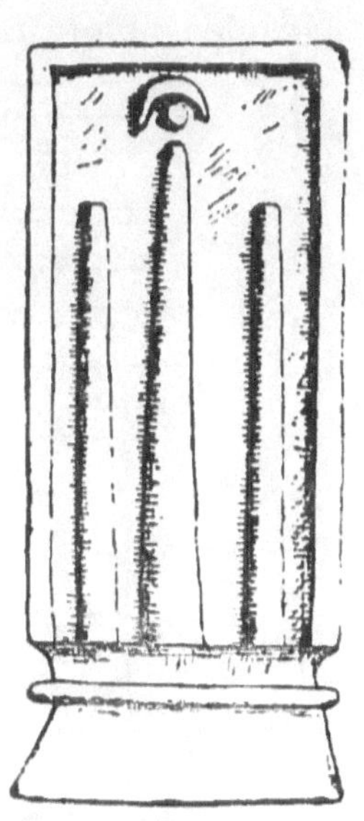

CARTHAGINIAN PILLAR SHRINE ON STELE, NORA, SARDINIA.

The moon-spirit was believed to inhabit the lunar stone.

Evans, *Mycenæn Trees and Pillar Cult.*

The Urim and Thummim (lights and perfections) were, according to Josephus, twelve precious stones of extraordinary beauty and purity worn on the breast plates of the Jewish high priests. These were the sacred symbols worn 'upon his heart' by the high priest and by which God gave oracular responses to His people for their guidance and safe conduct in all matters temporal. Josephus also speaks of two additional stones worn on the shoulders. These were supposed to be two sardonyx buttons, which were said to emit luminous rays when the response was favourable. Although all definite knowledge of what the symbols were seems to have been lost in obscurity since the days of Solomon, some authorities incline to the belief that

[6] *Ibid.*

the Urim and Thummim were contrasting symbols representing light and darkness or *yang* and *yin*, and while probably unlike the Chinese, they typified the same forces and were used for the same purpose of divination. On the other hand, modern Egyptologists seem to find the clue in Egypt where the Egyptian high priests who were also magistrates wore around the neck a jewelled image representing Truth on one side and

ENTRANCE TO TATTU IN AMENTA.

Showing the two Tat Pillars, and Ra the God in Spirit, and Osiris who is God in the Body or Mummy-form.

Churchward, *Signs and Symbols of Primordial Man.*

Justice or Light on the other. When the accused was acquitted the judge held out the image for him to kiss. Osiris as judge of the dead wears around his neck the precious stones representing "Light and Truth."

The custom of wearing charms is a relic of stone worship.

The two opposite forces were also represented as two pillars, twin horsemen, the "primeval twins."

In the Indian Rig-veda there were the twin deities Mitra and Varuna who were the regulators of the sun, moon, stars, winds, tides, waters, seasons; the bestowers of all heavenly gifts and who measured out the length of human life. Varuna represents the concavity of the sky (as does the Greek Ouranus) and carries the noose associated with death.

In the Vedic mythology Yama the god of the dead and his sister Yami were the first human pair.

Yama's messengers were the owl and the pigeon. Yama also had two dogs each with four eyes. These two brown, four-eyed dogs of Yama who guard the way to the abode of death bear a strong resemblance to the four-eyed dog or white dog with yellow ears of the Parsi who was supposed to drive away Death, as well as to the three-headed Cerberus that watches at the gateway that leads to hell.

There were also the Persian Celestial Twins, Yima and Yimah, who are likened to Mitra and Varuna.

The "Celestial Twins" were sometimes symbolised by two children, two eyes, two circles as well as by two pillars which become II the zodiacal sign of Gemini.

The Açwins, the twin horsemen in Indian mythology resemble the Greek Dioscuri—Castor and Pollux. They were called *Vitrahana* because they "ushered in the Sunlight and destroyed Vritra the Darkness." They are pictured as beautiful youths, children of Dyaus (heaven) and brothers of Ushas (the dawn) and are next in importance to Indra, Agni and Soma in the Rig-veda. "In early India the twin horsemen seem to have represented father and mother and afterwards day and night." [7]

The Açwins were the special gods of horsemen

[7] "The Early History of Northern India," J. S. Hewitt.

and charioteers and were symbolised by two interlacing Vs.

In Egypt the Dioscuri were symbolised by two lions who in their solar phases represented Day and Night.

The "Twin Brother Idea"—one of whom envies and slays the other, or deprives him of his birthright, as in the story of Jacob and Esau—plays a most important part in all ancient mythologies. It appears under various names such as Cain and Abel, Baldur and Loki,

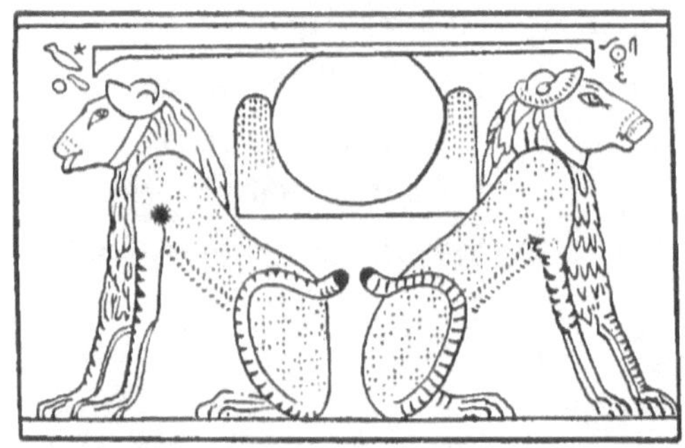

EGYPTIAN LION GODS "YESTERDAY AND TO-DAY" SUPPORTING SOLAR DISK.

Osiris and Set. It is a theme that is still used in modern romances. Guy de Maupassant employs it in "*Pierre et Jean.*" The Twin Brother Idea is merely a dramatic version of the old struggle between Light and Darkness, good and evil, growth and destruction or the positive and negative forces which represent Life.

It was an ancient Babylonian belief that the sun-god re-enters the inhabited world each morning between two pillars. Thus it was customary to place two pillars in the Semitic temples. And long after the meaning was lost, even in the temples of Jerusalem the two brazen pillars were never missing. The Phœnician sailors believed that the two rocks of Gibraltar were the two pillars of Melkarth through which the sun-god passed on his descent to the lower world of darkness.

The Two Pillars were called in Egypt the North Pole or Light and the South Pole or Darkness and typified the Door of Heaven, the Gateway of Life, the Portals of Eternity, the Double Gate of the Horizon.

This symbolism was reversed, as we have seen, by the ancient Chinese. With them the North indicated cold, darkness, the feminine principle, and the South light, warmth, the masculine principle, Heaven.

The psalmist, however, agrees with the Egyptians and pictures Zion on the North. "Beautiful for situation, the joy of the whole earth is Mount Zion, on the sides of the North, the city of the great King." (Ps. 48:2.)

One of the most important features of Solomon's Temple are the two pillars which guard the entrance.

The building of Solomon's Temple 'without sound of hammer nor axe nor saw' has been interpreted as a mystical way of describing the universe which is "created silently and by natural development."

The Temple of Solomon has also been likened to the "New Jerusalem, the City of the Sun, the spiritual city which lay four square and whose length was as large as its breadth." [8]

In the description of the Temple given by the Hebrew chroniclers one notes how lavishly and with what profusion the Oriental symbols of life, reproduction and fecundity are employed either as supports or decoration. There were palm trees, lily work, pomegranates, wheels, axle-trees. There were "nets of checker work, and wreaths of chain work which were upon the top of the pillars; seven for the one chapiter, and seven for

[8] Bayley's "Lost Language of Symbolism."

the other chapiter. . . . And round about upon the one network . . . were pomegranates. . . . And the chapiters which were upon the top of the pillars were of lily work." Twelve oxen support a molten sea "and the brim thereof was wrought like the brim of a cup, with flowers of lilies. . . . And on the borders that were between the ledges were lions, oxen and cherubim."

The cherubim in the Temple of Jerusalem and in Solomon's Palace are identical with the winged bull of Assyria.

The priests bring in the ark of the covenant. The ark, a most precious symbol in all ancient religions, is invariably associated with the feminine principle. They bring the ark "into the most holy place even under the wings of the cherubim; for the cherubim spread forth their wings over the place of the ark and the cherubim covered the ark and the staves thereof above." (II Chron. 5:7-8.)

"The sacred symbols apply, not only to man, but also to his environment. The Tabernacle of Moses and the Temple of Solomon not only represent the Microcosm but also the Macrocosm. And this leads us to the threshold of a very deep mystery, the effect of the spiritual condition of the human race upon Nature as a whole. . . . The Building of the Temple is thus a three-fold process, commencing with the individual man, spreading from the individual to the race, and from the race to the whole environment in which we live. This is the return to Eden where there is nothing hurtful or destructive." [9]

The symbolism of the Two Pillars was so well known that they must have been used advisedly as symbols of

[9] "Bible Mystery and Bible Meaning," T. Troward.

high import, as was, indeed, the case with all the other decorations that were used in the building of this gorgeous temple.

"And he reared up the pillars before the temple, one on the right hand and the other on the left; and called the name of that one on the right hand Jachin ('The Stablisher') and the name of that on the left Boaz ('In it is strength')." (II. Chron. 3: 17.)

Troward in identifying the English J with the Oriental Y interprets Jachin as being an intensified form of the word *Yak* or One, thus denoting first the "principle of unity as the foundation of all things and then the mathematical element . . . since all numbers are evolved from the one." This, he affirms, is the element of measurement, proportion. The pillar Jachin is therefore balanced by the pillar Boaz which may be interpreted as Voice or Spirit, the vital element of Feeling, Volition. "And the only way of entering 'The Temple' whether of the Cosmos or the individual is by passing between these two pillars."

Back we are again to the two potent forces which whether represented by the *crux ansata* of the Egyptians, by the broken and unbroken lines of the Chinese trigrams, by the 'jewel in the lotus' of the Hindus, or by stones, rocks, columns, poles, pillars—back we come to the active and passive, positive and negative, masculine and feminine principles—those two extraordinarily complex and interesting forces that guard the portals of Life.

One may add here that much that has been found confusing and contradictory will be avoided, if we keep constantly in mind that the ancients were not specialists and that their religious symbols are almost as manifold in their meanings as life itself.

Inman and many other writers of a former generation and a similar turn of mind, found but one meaning and that an obscene one in the phallic symbols of fecundity.

Others of more tolerant disposition dismissed them a little superciliously as representing the "infancy of man's mentality" when, unable to comprehend the forces and wonders of the world about him, "he clothed them with the imagery of his untutored mind."

Later and more chastened investigators, however, in the light cast upon ancient civilisations by excavations going on in Egypt, Babylonia, Crete and elsewhere, are less positive that they are arriving at the "infancy of man's mentality." Moore in his *History of Religions*, commenting upon the high order of civilisations shown by these remains, emphasises the fact that the cult of phallicism was a phase rather than a religion.

In other words the symbols of life and fecundity did not originate in phallic worship, nor, apparently, does phallic worship end in that remote and mythical past.

It seems nearer true that whenever phallicism came to be worshipped *per se,* instead of as a symbolical representation of a high and holy mystery, degeneracy had already set in. Logically enough, therefore, when civilisations became decadent and Life itself profaned and debased, the symbols that typified Life were correspondingly debased and profaned. Decadence invariably exaggerates the process instead of the manifestation, concerns itself with the means of life and ways of prolonging it, rather than with the renewal of life—forgetting that it is this stream of continuity that comes into and flows out of us that is all that makes life significant. Phallicism represented clearly and unmistakably this attitude. And in these periods of phallic worship the life symbols reflected accurately the measure of men's thoughts. Instead of creative power, they merely typified the instincts and passions of various races at various times as strength oozed out of them and the spirit fled.

Seemingly, one may assume, therefore, without going far wrong, that in their origin these symbols were used reverently and with high intent. Thus the intricate maze of ideas and poetic fancies—ideas sacred and profligate, reverential and obscene, imaginative and literal that have clustered about these ancient symbols of life resolve themselves simply enough to Life itself—to the interplay of those primal, transcendent forces known since time began as Fire and Water, Light and Darkness, Man and Woman.

It is *tout simplement* the world man and world woman, not in relation to their trappings, their individual caprices, their present day revealings, wants, desires—but their relation to the earth, air, heavens, sun, moon, stars, heat and cold, wind and storm, and above all their relationship to each other that is forever being typified by the life symbols.

Thus the meaning of pillars, columns, poles and circles is the same as that commonly ascribed to the tau cross with circle above it, which is seen so frequently on ancient tombs and temple walls as an emblem of life and immortality.

None can gainsay that the union of spirit and matter forms the paradox of existence, for man is sternly bent on accomplishing it, and equally bent on disregarding it. How can we doubt that the ancients knew this? The ancient man did not need Freud to tell him that he was a complex. His symbolism proves that his knowledge of this point in his make up was precise and far reaching, displaying an understanding of life so comprehensively true and subtle, that it still keeps scholars gasping. In truth, it is a little staggering to our *amour propre* when it first dawns upon us how much the ancients really did know about this very interesting thing called Life.

The real difficulty in adjusting the different meanings attached to any one of these symbols of life, seems to arise from our inability or unwillingness to grasp the fact that each symbol typified, not spirit alone to the ancient religionists—as the cross is now used by the Christians—nor matter alone as many have interpreted the phallic emblems, but the divine union of spirit and matter, fire and water, positive and negative, masculine and feminine—in other words, Creation, Life. Different forms were used to represent the Creative Life Principle, but there is the same idea of essential and derived life, of unity passing into multiplicity, the same creative idea carried up from the physical to the metaphysical, from its material aspect to the spiritual until it is one again with the "universal life which is over all and through all and in all."

VIII

THE TREE OF LIFE

"Wisdom is a tree of life to them that lay hold of her."

"Cet arbre mysterieux, symbol d'immortalité, toujours vert, oderiférant, chargé de fruits."—Gaillard.

"The old standing feud between those who heard the pipes of Pan and those who would deny them into ridicule and silence."—Bayley.

PAN-ESQUE

If, walking in the forest gnarled and old,
Some wind-sweet, magic day,
Behind the shelter of a moss-hung tree
The laughing face of Pan peers out at me,
I shall not run away—
But rather, with surprise and joy grown bold,
"Oh, tarry here, Wood God!" my prayer will be—
"One little hour, and play
Upon your pipe of reeds those notes that make
The timid nymphs hide listening in the brake,
Though greatly longing, they,
To yield them to your lilting melody!
Play me the message of the whispering trees—
The mystery of the pine,
The sorrow of the oak that sighs and grieves,
Tune my dull ears to hear the singing leaves—"
And Pan, whose heart, like mine,
Loves the deep woods, will pipe me songs like these!

—Mazie V. Caruthers.

VIII

THE TREE OF LIFE

THE pillar or dolmen is found constantly associated with sacred trees. There is the same religious idea that the thing worshipped, whether pillar or tree is possessed by divinity. It is perfectly easy to see how the two objects would merge into each other. The pillar being formed of the wood of the living tree retained the sacred character of the other —became its reflex, a part of the same expression of life.

Nor is it difficult to understand why trees were objects of worship. Nothing in all nature was a more perfect symbol of the miracle of reproduction and man's belief in immortality than the tree with its leaves and blossoms and fruit. It became again the symbol of 'dying to live' which is the framework of all ancient religions.

The cypress, fir, pine and palm—continually green —were symbols of the ever living spirit, green symbolising the everlasting.

On the other hand, the trees that shed their leaves in the autumn only to put forth again into quickening life in the spring, conveyed the message of re-newal, of dying only to live again in greater beauty and glory— a message that man was quick to apply to himself.

The Sumerians believed that the spiritual—the *Zi* was that which manifested life. The test of life was movement. "All things that moved possessed self-power."

Bergson elaborately re-affirms the same idea:—

"In reality life is a movement, materiality is the inverse movement, and each of these two movements is simple, the matter which forms a world being an undivided flux, also the life that runs through it cutting out in it living beings all along the track . . . . In order to advance with the moving reality you must replace yourself within it. Install yourself within change."[1]

Believing this, the ancients saw life in everything that moved. Rivers were living things, the sun and moon were vessels in which the divine spirit sailed across the sky. A beneficent spirit spoke in the life giving winds on a sultry day. The god of destruction made himself heard in the howling storm winds and tornadoes. Trees groaned and sighed from the buffettings of these furious blasts, yet the voice of divinity forever murmured in their rustling leaves.

The life principle in trees was believed to have been derived from the "Creative tears of the gods." And the living tree as the receptacle of divine life was doubtless placed near pillars in the cult of pillar and stone worship with the thought primarily in mind of assisting or bearing witness to the divine life in stock and stone.

Aiding the gods has ever been the desire of man. He not only apes them but ceremoniously assists them. In the first stages of all his religious conceptions, however, he is always true, simple, sincere. Unfortunately his very nature obliges him to elaborate, to graft on

[1] Bergson's "Creative Evolution."

more and more, to lose himself in subtleties and neglect the substance, to pay greater and greater attention to form or its visible aspect and forget the invisible spirit which makes form a living thing.

SACRED TREE TERMINATING IN LOTUS BUDS OR PINE CONES.
Layard, *Nineveh.*

The Sacred Tree which, worshipped in the beginning for its divine essence formed a part of all ancient religious systems and was universally reverenced and adored as a symbol of highest import, became later merely an intricate and indispensable artistic form.

Both the Aryan and the Semitic races had a Tree of Life, a Tree of Knowledge and a Tree of Heaven. The fruit of the latter related to the "igneous or luminous bodies of space, the Tree of Life produced a liquid conferring eternal youth and the Tree of Knowledge had the power of foretelling the future or of divination." [2]

The Haoma whose sap gave immortality was the traditional Tree of Life of the Persians, and was preserved in almost the same form as found on the Assyrian monuments until the overthrow of the Persian empire by the Arab invasion. This is the Cosmic Tree which produces ambrosia and dispenses salvation.

Fruits of the vine and the tree yielded by fermentation a liquid which is still called *eau de vie.*

There were two trees that stood out above all others in the Garden of Eden. "And out of the ground made the Lord God to grow every tree that is pleasant to the sight and good for food; the tree of life, also in the

[2] D'Alviella's "Migration of Symbols."

midst of the garden, and the tree of knowledge of good and evil."

After Adam and Eve, tempted by the serpent, partake of the tree of knowledge of good and evil, they are driven forth and the Lord places "at the east of the garden of Eden cherubim and a flaming sword which turned every way, to keep the way of the tree of life."

It is the Tree of Life that is so jealously guarded.

The Chinese Tree of Life was one of seven marvellous trees that grew on the slopes of the Kuen-Luën Mountains—the terrestrial paradise presided over by Si Wang Mu. This tree, which was 10,000 cubits high and 1,800 feet in circumference, was all of jade and chrysoprase, and bore fruit but once in three thousand years. Si Wang Mu the goddess of the Tree of Life, the "Royal Mother of the West" is the queen of immortal beings. Originally a sun-goddess, the Jesuits associate her with the Queen of Sheba, and others liken her to Juno—or the daughter of heaven and earth. The fruit of this tree over which she presides was supposed to be the sacred peach which enters so largely into the mystical fancies of the Taoists, who used the peach tree as a symbol of marriage, longevity and immortality. The Chinese goddess is depicted bestowing the fruit on her votaries, one of whom was the Emperor Wu. Anyone to whom she gave the fruit became immortal. In Chinese art Si Wang Mu is symbolised by a peach and the phoenix.

The Buddhists have a legend of an enormous tree with four boughs from which great rivers are continually flowing. Each river bears golden pips which it carries down to the sea. This tree the Buddhists call the Tree of Wisdom. The legend bears a strong resemblance, however, to the Hebrew Tree of Life and the four rivers of paradise.

The *Bhagavad-Gita* speaks of the Ashwattha, the eternal sacred tree which grows with the roots above and the branches below. The Ashwattha tree "is the Primeval Spirit from which floweth the never ending stream of conditioned existence."

In Teutonic myths the Polar star around which the heavens are supposed to revolve was called the 'world spike' while the earth was said to be sustained by the 'world tree.'

The American Indians had a "World Tree."

In *Certain Iroquois Tree Myths and Symbols,* Arthur C. Parker relates the Seneca's myth of a Celestial Tree on whose branches hung flowers and fruit the year around. Its branches pierced the sky and its roots extended to the waters of the underworld. The Big Chief ordering it to be pulled up, a great pit was seen where its roots had been. Into this pit fell the Sky Mother on the wings of a waterfall who placed her on a turtle's back.

In another myth after the "birth of the twins Light One and Toad-like (or dark) One the Light One noticing that there was no light created the Tree of Light."

The Delawares, who also had a Central World Tree believed that all things came from a tortoise. "It had brought forth the world and in the middle of its back had sprung a tree from whose branches men had grown."

This resembles the Hindu myth of the Tortoise who supports the world.

The Five Nations always expressed peace under the metaphor of a tree. "We now plant a Tree whose tops will reach the sun and its Branches spread far abroad

. . . and we shall shelter ourselves under it and live in Peace."[3]

Crosses, used by the ancient Indians and Mexicans to represent the winds which bring rain, were often given a tree-like form or that of a stem with two branches. A bird is frequently depicted standing upon

MEXICAN SACRED TREE.
D'Alviella, *Migration of Symbols.*

the fork. Sometimes the tree is flanked on either side by two persons with wreaths of feathers on their heads facing each other.

A bird standing on the fork of the Sacred Tree or resting near it is also a feature of the Persian representations of the Tree of Immortality.

FROM A SASSANIAN BOWL.

SICILIAN BAS-RELIEF.

D'Alviella, *Migration of Symbols.*

In this symbolism of life as typified by the world tree, the bird and the serpent are constantly employed. The spirit is depicted in the form of a bird which descends to give life to tree or stock or stone. In the pillar

[3] "Certain Iroquois Tree Myths and Symbols," Arthur C. Parker.

cult twin pillars frequently bear the symbolic eagles of the god to express this wide-spread belief that life is in the soul.

The serpent in all countries and among all nations is also associated with the Sacred Tree or Tree of Life. Sometimes it is coiled about the tree and again it appears in the background.

SERPENT IN BACKGROUND.
Chaldean cylinder. British Museum.
Perrot and Chipiez.

The Chaldeans "saw in the universe a tree whose summit was the sky and whose foot or trunk the earth."

The tree in its earliest form in Chaldea and also in Cyprus was a staff supporting a semi-circle.

The Assyrian Tree of Life is one of the oldest as well as the most famous of all sacred trees, and still gives definite form to various ornamental designs. Starting in Assyria where Layard believes it to have been connected with the worship of Venus (or Ishtar) it was introduced into Arabia on the one side, and Central Asia, Asia Minor and Persia on the other.

It first appears on Chaldean cylinders as a pillar or 'world spine' surmounted by a crescent. Sometimes this pillar is thrice crossed by branches resembling bulls horns each tipped by ring symbols. The highest pair of horns have a larger ring between them which shows but a part of itself as if it were a crescent. These rings are frequently replaced by flowers and fruit.

About the beginning of the tenth century B.C. the tree becomes more complex. It has been conventionalised into elaborate and graceful forms and is one of the most conspicuous objects found on the sculpture and monuments of Khorsabad and Nimroud. From the "mystic flower of the Assyrians" which Goodyear identifies with the lotus, innumerable branches spring from an intricate scroll work or interlacing design. The

SACRED TREE SHOWING DIVIDED PILLAR.
Layard, *Monuments of Nineveh.*

pillar or trunk of the tree is sometimes divided, suggesting the same idea of duality or union of spirit and matter that was conveyed by the bird and serpent. The divided pillar is surmounted by a conventionalised form of the mystic flower or lotus. Sometimes the branches terminate in the same form of the lotus, or they will bear a fruit resembling the pomegranate. Frequently the fruit is shaped like a fir or pine cone. Again it is suggestive of a lotus bud. In each case, however, the fruit of the tree is one of the well known symbols of life and fecundity.

Sometimes the wild goat or sacred bull with expanded wings is represented kneeling before the mystic tree. A bird or human figure frequently takes the place of the bull or goat. On some of the older cylinders the tree is represented between two animals which may be

Two Kings Kneeling Beneath the Emblem of the Deity

Winged Females Standing Before the Sacred Tree
(Nimroud)

unicorns, winged bulls, or eagles with the bodies of men. It is often shown between two Kings facing each other in an attitude of worship. Sometimes the kings are flanked by two priests who carry in the one hand the sacred cone—which among the Babylonians and Assyrians was a symbol of life, fire, the masculine principle, and in the other a metal, shovel-shaped basket which is also when filled with fruit and flowers one of the attributes of Bacchus. Its use here has puzzled many students. The suggestion that it contained holy water and the fact that the "ritual watering of sacred trees from a natural or artificial source was a regular feature of this form of worship" lends credence to the idea that we are once more confronting one of the simplest yet most profound and persistent associations in ancient symbolism—the union of fire and water to produce life.

Two priests clad in fish robes as attendants of Ea or the goddess Ishtar are seen on either side of the Sacred Tree. Again it is represented between two winged females who are depicted with one hand extended toward the tree in a gesture of adoration, while in the other they hold the ring or circle, symbol of eternity, water, the feminine principle.

To indicate the high significance of the tree as a religious symbol the winged circle of the deity is frequently shown above it.

Jastrow calls the various animals or winged figures "guardians of the sacred tree with which the same idea was associated by the Assyrians and Babylonians as was with the tree of life in the famous chapter of Genesis as well as with other trees of life found among other ancient races. The cones which the winged figures beside the tree hold indicate the fruit of the tree plucked for the benefit of the worshippers by these guardians who alone may do so. A trace of this view appears in the injunction to Adam to eat of all trees except one which being of the tree of knowledge was not for mortal man to pluck—as little as of the fruit of the 'tree of life.' "[4]

The tree of life and wisdom was a theme which "lent itself both to the refinements of ornamentation and to the fancies of the symbolical imagination." Yet, although conventionalised into all sorts of fantastic forms until its tree-like appearance is nearly lost, the symbolic idea conveyed is precisely the same. Strangely enough, too, although other features are inserted and the tree itself is sometimes replaced by other symbolic objects, the grouping remains essentially the same.

CAPITAL OF THE TEMPLE OF ATHENE AT PRIENE.

PERSIAN CYLINDER.

Sometimes an altar or pyre takes the place of the tree.

In China the tree becomes the Sacred Pearl between two dragons.

In India the two figures become Nagās or Snake Kings, their heads entwined with cobras.

The Tree of Life is sometimes represented between two peacocks. The peacock, besides being an emblem of immortality was believed to kill serpents.

[4] "Religious Belief in Babylonia and Assyria," Jastrow.

In adapting this idea to the temptation and fall of man, the only change necessary was "to give a different sex to the two acolytes."

An interesting illustration is shown by Count Goblet d'Alviella in his *Migration of Symbols.* It is a Phœnician bowl discovered by Cesnola on the Island of Cyprus. The Tree stands between two figures who are plucking the lotus blossom with one hand and hold the

PHŒNICIAN BOWL.

crux ansata in the other. Thus showing that the tree, the lotus and the Key of Life are but variations of the same religious thought—the quest of Life. D'Alviella points out that the Assyrian priests and gods hold the pine cone precisely as the gods of Egypt sometimes handle the *crux ansata.*

Sometimes the myth varies, and the two monsters, griffins, unicorns or other fabulous beasts are shown

BAS-RELIEF OF THE BAPTISTERY OF CIVIDALE.

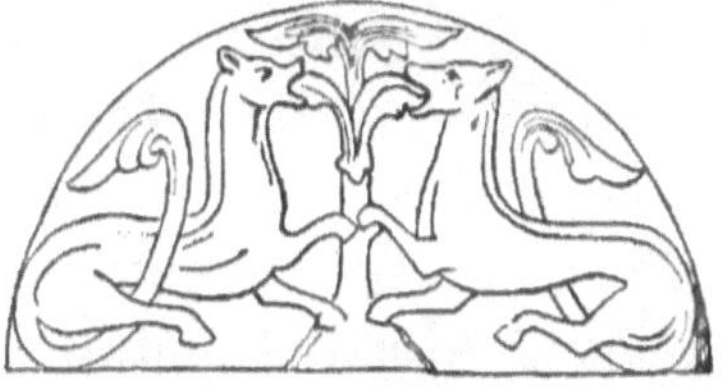

FROM THE CHURCH AT MARIGNY.

approaching the tree as if to pluck the fruit or flower. In general, however, the tree is usually portrayed as being jealously guarded by mythical beasts or birds who protect it from demons or rivals who are seeking to gain possession of it.

The Christians in making use of this symbolic form sometimes depicted the two figures as lambs or again doves or peacocks. The cross of Christianity was be-

FROM ATHENS CATHEDRAL.

SYRIA.

lieved at one time to be like a tree. This symbolism is typified in the Holy Rood or Rod.

Lowrie in the *Monuments of the Early Church* says that "of all the various notions which attached themselves to the Christian cross none were so common nor so fundamental as that which regarded it as the tree of life. . . . In a fresco in S. Callistus the cross still dissimulated is represented under the figure of a green tree with two horizontal branches under which stand two doves." He also notes that the symbolic significance of the early chalice, the classical cantharus which appears upon the altar in two mosaics of Ravenna and which is almost invariably associated with the Eucharist is plainly indicated by the "vine which springs out of it, the two harts which approach it on either side panting to quench their thirst with the water of life, and by the peacocks which symbolise its potency for immortality." He believes that it was rarely if ever used in administering the wine to the people, that it was a "conventional decorative motive which the Church borrowed from ancient art and to which it attached its own meaning." The design, which was originally the Sacred Tree of Life of the Assyrians with its animal guardians, is altered by the Christians, who make the vase in which the tree grew the chief motive, substitute the symbolic vine, and instead of panthers or griffins place the gentler animals as guardians.

The Sacred Tree of the Mayas was often depicted with two branches springing out horizontally from the top of a pillar or trunk in the form of a tau cross.

The Sacred Tree, the one that was the supreme object of worship, varied in different localities. Apparently each race and country adopted as its highest religious emblem the one that was considered the most valuable.

In Europe *the oak* was venerated because of its strength and vitality. It was associated with the gods of fertility and lightning including Thor and Jupiter.

The Greeks had a Tree of Heaven. This was the oak which gave shelter to the Dioscuri—the twin brothers of Light and Darkness.

The leaves of the oak, eight-lobed and flaming in autumn, suggested re-generation and fire. Then, too, the acorn in its cup was one of nature's most perfect and manifest symbols of the lingam and yoni or the 'jewel in the lotus' or the "combination of I the Holy One and O the generating cup or crater."

The oak was the sacred tree of the Druids. In consecrating their holy oak trees they made them cruciform or shaped like the fylfot cross, either by cutting off or by inserting branches. They chose oak-woods for their sacred groves, and no rites were performed without oak leaves. The cutting of the mistletoe (the druidical name meaning All Heal) from an oak of thirty years growth was a matter of great ceremony. The Druids were said by Pliny to worship the mistletoe because they believed it to have fallen from heaven, and to be a token that the tree upon which it grew had been chosen by the god himself. The mistletoe was rarely met with but when found, provided the tree was an oak, it was gathered with impressive ceremony on the sixth day of the moon when the moon was believed to have its greatest vigour. A white robed priest climbed the tree and with a golden sickle cut the mistletoe which was not permitted to touch the earth but fell into a white cloth held by votaries below. Then followed the sacrifice of two white bulls whose horns had never been bound before, and prayers that God might make his gift prosper with those upon whom he had bestowed it.

A tree struck by lightning was naturally thought to be "charged with a double or triple portion of fire." Fire kindled by lightning was looked upon with superstitious awe. God himself spoke in the thunder and lightning.

The reverence paid to the oak by the ancient peoples of Europe may be due, therefore, to the "greater frequency with which the oak appears to be struck by lightning than any other tree of our European forests." A peculiarity which recent scientific investigations seem to have confirmed. For this reason the ancients believed that the great sky god "loved the oak above all the trees of the world and often descended into it from the murky clouds in a flash of lightning, leaving a token of his presence or his passage in the riven and blackened trunk and the blazed foliage. Such trees would thenceforth be encircled by a nimbus of glory as the visible seats of the thundering sky god. . . . Both Greeks and Romans identified their great god of the sky and of the oak with the lightning flash which struck the ground and they regularly enclosed such a stricken place and held it sacred." [5]

In this connection Frazer hazards the conjecture that the real reason why the Druids worshipped above all others a mistletoe-bearing oak was the belief that the mistletoe had dropped on the oak in a flash of lightning and that the oak thus bore among its branches a "visible emanation of celestial fire."

Thus, too, the "rich golden yellow which a bough of mistletoe assumes when it has been cut and kept for some months" indentifies it with the celestial fire of the sun. "The bright tint is not confined to the leaves but spreads to the stalks as well, so that the whole branch appears to be indeed a Golden Bough." One may suppose, therefore, Frazer ingeniously concludes, that "in the old Aryan creed the mistletoe descended from the sun on Midsummer Day in a flash of lightning."

It was a rule strictly adhered to by the ancient Germans, Celts and Slavs that the Sacred Fire should be ignited annually by the friction of two pieces of oakwood. "In some places the new fire for the village was made on Midsummer Day by causing a wheel to revolve round an axle of oak till the oak took fire. This curious custom may have had its origin from the idea that the oak tree symbolised the Cove, Pole or Axis of Immaculate Fire." [6]

"It may be" or "It may have been"—quite unlike Tennyson's doleful "It might have been"—are the most enchanting phrases of archæology. One may believe that the original man—if there ever was a first man—in

[5] Frazer's "The Golden Bough."

[6] Bayley's "Lost Language of Symbolism."

pondering upon various inscrutable things, that alas! still remain inscrutable, said to himself: "It may be that *le bon Dieu* intends." Or, perhaps, when life was simpler he went to the Great Source for an explanation. It may be—some believe this—*it may be* that the original man knew.

His descendants, however, soon fell victim to mankind's insatiable love of embroidering with picturesque phrase and florid explanation some ancient, elemental, outstanding truth. Later generations take the past seriously and say: "It may have been that he thought thus," when the ancient may simply have been amusing himself by letting his imagination go, as we are letting ours go when we try to interpret him.

The game of supposing is a very old and delightful pastime. History and science as well as fairy stories and myths are built upon it. And we are indebted to it for many of the most enthralling fancies, especially those that have been entwined about the oak and the mistletoe. This was doubtless a very simple form of worship originally. The same that the ancients extended to whatever in nature grew without roots in the earth—whatever remained ever green and living while other things fell into decay. Thus the mistletoe growing on the oak and remaining green while the oak was barren and leafless was another of those mystical emblems that gave man such reassurance of the potency of the divine union of spirit and matter, and renewed his belief and faith in the glorious continuity of life.

The Senal Indians of California "profess to believe that the whole world was once a globe of fire whence that element passed up into the trees and now comes out when two pieces of wood are rubbed together."

Agni the fire-god of India was spoken of as "born in wood, as the embryo of plants or to strive after them."

The *Sien* trees of the Chinese are those that confer life, strength, health, immortality, such as the jejube, plum, pear, peach—any trees, in short, that produce fruit or aromatic or edible matter.

From time immemorial it has been the custom in China to plant trees on graves in order to impart strength to the soul of the deceased and thereby preserve his body from corruption. The cypress and pine, because they were evergreen, were thought to be fuller of vitality and were therefore preferred for this purpose above all other trees.

The *fir and pine tree* were also worshipped for their straightness, their uprightness. The fir tree was a symbol of elevation and was related to the God of Israel.

It has been suggested that the pyramidal form of certain trees was one of the factors that contributed to their worship.

The *"pyramidal Yache"* was the sacred tree of the Mexicans.

A flame-like tree is likened to the Fire of Life or rod or stem of Jesse.

The *poplar tree* once sacred to Hercules was an obvious symbol of the Holy Rood, pole, spike, spire or rod.

The *laurel* was sacred to Apollo.

The All Father was identified with the mighty *ash*. This tree was also an object of reverence because of its clusters of red berries.

Ezekiel compares the Assyrian to a "Cedar in Lebanon with fair branches."

The *pine tree* was sacred to Attis, Dionysos and other spring time gods. The sanctity of the pine tree is thought by some scholars to have originated possibly from its resemblance to a spiral of flame, and that the cone from its inflammable nature as well as its shape was originally a symbol of fire. Here the analogy and the later use of the pine cone as a phallic emblem becomes perfectly clear for fire was invariably regarded as one of the most powerful attributes of the direct, pointed, creative masculine principle.

Tree terminating in the Sacred Cone protected by birds and lions.

From the Cathedral of Torcello. D'Alviella.

The *sacred cone* was used to typify an existence united yet distinct. As has been said before in another connection it had the same meaning among the Semites as the *crux ansata* of the Egyptians, and was also looked upon as a talisman of high import exclusive of its phallic meaning.

It is found on sepulchral urns and tombs of the Etruscans or sometimes on top of a pillar.

"In Græco-Roman paganism the fruit of the pine discharged prophylactic, sepulchral and phallic functions." [7]

The pine cone enlarged and conventionalised is still seen on gateways in Italy as a talisman of fecundity, abundance, good luck.

The traditional sanctity of *doorways* and *portals* or *gateways*—anything that gives entrance to something beyond, or something secluded, hidden—has come down from the most ancient times and portals and gateways with their two pillars are frequently depicted in connection with the sacred tree.

After the 'aniconic idol' had been superseded by

[7] "The Migration of Symbols," D'Alviella.

representations of the gods in human form, the original meaning seems to have been lost. The Sacred Cone on burial urns was supposed to be the attribute of some hero, whereas it was simply one of the symbolic expressions used to "represent life in its dual aspect—the dual type of the Creator, of the God himself."

The *banyan tree* in India symbolises "eternal life, productive powers, perfect happiness, supreme knowledge." These are the gifts of the tree which represents the universe.

The Buddhists depict the Sacred Tree between two elephants facing each other. This is the sacred *Bo Tree* or *Bodhi Tree* under whose shade Sakya-Muni sat for seven years before he received enlightenment and became the Buddha. The elephants are an allusion to the legend that when Sakya-Muni left the Tushita heavens to be born again on earth as Gautama Buddha, he descended in the form of a white elephant.

One notes that the Sacred Tree among the Buddhists also dwindles into the mystic flower of the lotus flanked by the same two elephants. Again the connection between the two is obvious, the *fleur de lis* or lotus, the sacred plant is called the Tree of Life of Mazdaism.

In the symbolism of the Buddhist Triad or Tri-ratna Buddha (intelligence, soul) is given the trisula placed upon a pillar surrounded by flames. Dharma—(matter, the body)—a wheel, and Sangha who represents the union of Buddha and Dharma, or soul and body—is given a tree.

Each Buddha had a special Bo-Tree or Bodhi-Tree, the Tree of Wisdom or Enlightenment under which he is supposed to have been born, to do penance, preach and die.

Although some have pictured it as the Banyan Tree

—dear to the hearts of the Hindus—whose branches lean down only to take root again when touching the ground, the fig tree—*ficus religiosa*—is the one under which Gautama Buddha is usually represented as receiving *bodhi* or knowledge.

The *Sacred Fig Tree—ficus religiosa*—was held in especial veneration as an emblem of life—combining both masculine and feminine attributes. Its tri-lobed leaf, suggesting the masculine triad, became the symbolical covering in sculptured representations of nude figures, while the fruit—the eating of which was supposed to aid fecundity—was identified in shape with the yoni. In all the countries bordering on the southern shores of the Mediterranean the fig tree was an object of worship. And although the cypress, plane and pine as well as the fig tree were held sacred in Crete, the traditional sanctity of the fig tree, Evans finds, was well marked in the later cult of Greece as well, being, because of its fruitfulness and the belief in its prophylactic power against lightning, an object of special sacredness in the primitive Ægean cult. Besides being a sacred tree of the Mycenæan world it was also worshipped in Rome. He notes that "near the original seat of ***Ficus Ruminalis*** was the cave of Pan connected with the old Arcadian cult, and that the fabled suckling of twins beneath the tree by the she wolf reproduces a legend of typically Arcadian form." [8]

In the primal principle this recognised duality was believed to have been androgynous or bi-sexual. Thus the palm tree as well as the lotus, the serpent and the scarabæus were believed to be self-created and were all androgynous symbols.

The ***Palm Tree*** was especially reverenced because it

[8] "Mycenæan Trees and Pillar Cult," A. F. Evans.

Photo. Alinari

Pan and Olympus

(Museo Nazionale, Naples)

was the only tree known to the ancients that never changed its leaves. It was believed, therefore, to be self-renewed. Hence the miracle of reproduction represented by the symbolical Tree of Life found its highest expression in Chaldea, Assyria and Babylonia in conventional representations of the date palm.

It is "quite conceivable that the inflorescence of the date palm may have performed a symbolical function . . . . as a pre-eminent emblem of fertilising force."

Thus the palm that the Christians used as a symbol of martyrdom, although I believe it has a deeper meaning—the triumph of life over death—was an ancient symbol *par excellence* of creative force, the universal matrix, the generating power of nature, the flame of fire. Baal Tamar a Phœnician deity is called 'Lord of the Palm.' A palm tree encircled by a serpent is depicted on Phœnician coins.

The Sacred Tree in Japan is the *Sa-ka-ki* tree. In the various ceremonies in the temples branches of the Sa-ka-ki tree to which are attached a mirror, a sword and a jewel are among the offerings. These ceremonies are followed by two dances one by men and the other by a dozen girls twelve or thirteen years old who carry in their hands branches of the Sa-ka-ki tree.

The "divine Lady of Eden or Edin" was called in Northern Babylonia the "goddess of the Tree of Life."

The Sacred Tree embodying as it did a conception of the renewal of life, frequently typified the feminine principle in nature under the name of Astarte, Ishtar, Mylitta and other nature goddesses. A *cypress* is sometimes depicted on the coins of Heliopolis in place of the conical stone which commonly symbolised Astarte. The name of Cypress was given to Venus of Lebanon. "Upon an altar of the Palmyrene is depicted on one side a solar god, and on the other a cypress with a child carrying a ram on its shoulder showing in its foliage. The pine in which Cybele imprisons the body of Atys till springtime belongs to the same class of images. The tree becomes the symbol of the matrix." [9]

In the legend of Osiris the body of Osiris is concealed in "the branches of a bush of Tamarisk which in a short time had shot up into a tall and beautiful tree" which grew around the sea-drifted chest in which his body was hidden.

The Phrygian Atys (or Attis) was said to have met his death by self-mutilation under a sacred tree. Adonis sprang from a tree. Diamid hid in a tree when pursued by Finn. Tammuz died with the dying vegetation.

The Tree of Life of the Egyptians was a 'high *sycamore* tree upon which the gods sit.' The sycamore with its thick foliage which gave grateful shade was thought to be the resting or the abiding place of the beneficent tree spirit who gave sustenance to the parts of the dead. Hence the deep veneration accorded to the sycamore particularly in the vicinity of Memphis. The sycamore was always associated with a goddess. In the south it was called the "living body of Hathor."

The *Ivy* which the Greeks consecrated to Bacchus was called by the Egyptians 'Osiris's Tree.'

Nowhere is the reverence for trees more clearly shown than in the Old Testament. The Old Testament is filled with references that indicate how deeply imbedded was this ancient association of divinity with trees. Divine revelations take place under trees. Sometimes it is a palm tree, sometimes a cypress and again an oak, terebinth or tamarisk. Deborah the prophetess of the Children of Israel sat under a palm tree. The

[9] D'Alviella's "The Migration of Symbols."

Photo. Alinari

Attis

(Louvre, Paris)

angel of the Lord who sent Gideon to deliver the Israelites "sat under an oak which was in Ophrah." Jehovah declared himself to Moses "in a flame of fire out of a bush . . . . and behold the bush burned with fire and the bush was not consumed." (Ex. 3:2.) The pomegranate, fir, apple, cedar, palm, vines, grapes and berries which are alluded to in a figurative sense in the Songs of Solomon are all ancient symbols of life.

JESSE WINDOW, DORCHESTER CATHEDRAL.

The Tree of Life becomes the genealogical tree, the family tree, the tree of Jesse. The latter, representing the genealogy of Christ as related in the gospel of St. Matthew was a favourite subject for ecclesiastical paintings and embroideries in the Middle Ages as we have already seen. In these representations the roots of the tree encircle the body of Jesse who is reclining upon the ground. On the branches which stretch out from either side of the tree are the different personages who composed the links in the chain of descent, while at the very top standing in an aureole of glory are Christ and the Virgin Mother. Candlesticks formed like a tree with branches were called Jesses. The Jesse windows in mediæval churches show the same subject treated in stained glass.

Bayley points out that the word *leaf* is identical with love and life and further adds that it is a scientific fact that a tree lives by its leaves.

Troward places together the Bible, the Great Pyramid and the Pack of Cards, the three showing a unity of principle and each throwing light upon the other. "The three stand out pre-eminent all bearing witness to the same one truth." [10]

Besides the enormous diversity of combination, and the mathematical fascination of cards, it is an odd fact that the four designs are all symbols of life. The spade is derived from the leaf, the heart is the source of life, the diamond or lozenge is a symbol of the yoni or the feminine principle and the club (*tréfle* in French) is the trefoil, one of the most ancient symbols of the Trinity or the three-fold aspect of life.

Early serpent worship was associated with groves, and tree worship undoubtedly had a dark side and degenerated into a form of phallicism just as darkness alternates with light. From earliest times, however, the Tree of Life has been one of the most cherished symbols of man's estate, and Ruskin believed, and I am glad to believe with him, that in itself tree worship was always healthy and becomes instead of symbolic, real. "Flowers and trees are beloved with a half-worshipping delight which is always noble and healthful." [11]

In this connection the thought occurs, if some reformer—a purist of a prohibitory turn of mind—were to blot out from the Bible all reference to trees, stones, altars, rocks, hills, pillars, pomegranates, vines, grapes, wine, sun, moon, stars, rivers, seas—because at some periods these manifestations of the power of Yahveh

[10] Troward's "Edinburgh Lectures on Mental Science."
[11] Ruskin's "Queen of the Air."

were worshipped or made symbolic use of to express excess of life in its lowest form—degeneracy—how much of the Bible, one wonders, would there be left!

Having done this, having stripped it of all poetry and imagery, the next step logically, of course, would be to demolish Nature itself. And that *is* a bit difficult even for a reformer of an aridly righteous and unimaginative mind.

ASSYRIAN CYLINDER.

IX

SACRED BIRDS

"The bird in which the breath and spirit is more full than in any other creature and the earth power least." —Ruskin.

"There are no myths . . . by which the moral state and fineness of intelligence of different races can be so deeply tried and measured as by those of the serpent and the bird."—Ruskin.

". . . . The Bird that halting in her flight
Awhile on boughs too light,
Feels them give way beneath her yet sings,
Knowing that she has wings."—Victor Hugo.

IX

SACRED BIRDS

THE bird symbolises the spirit of the air, the spirit of life.

The wing of a bird symbolised the wind.

A circle or globe with bird's wings issuing from it on either side, was an Egyptian and Assyrian symbol of the deity.

DETAIL OF ASSYRIAN RELIEF, LAYARD.

In one of the early Egyptian triads of gods Nut is heaven, Seb the earth and Shu the air or space which separates them. The hieroglyph of Shu is an ostrich feather "the most imponderable object for its bulk that could be selected," hence the symbol of space.

Maat the Egyptian goddess of truth carried a feather.

ANUBIS, THE JACKAL-HEADED GOD OF THE DEAD, ADJUSTS THE SCALES ON WHICH THE HEART OF THE DECEASED (WHO IS ON THE EXTREME LEFT) IS BEING WEIGHED AGAINST RIGHT AND TRUTH, SYMBOLIZED BY THE FEATHER. THOTH, THE IBIS-HEADED GOD OF LEARNING, STANDS READY WITH A SCRIBE'S PALETTE AND BRUSH TO WRITE DOWN THE VERDICT OF THE BALANCE.

FROM A COLORED VIGNETTE IN THE PAPYRUS OF ANI, WHICH IS NOW IN THE BRITISH MUSEUM. DYN. XVIII (ABOUT 1500 B.C.)

BALANCE USED TO WEIGH THE HEART IN THE JUDGMENT OF THE DEAD

It was thought that after a man died he was brought before Osiris the judge of the dead and "his conscience, symbolised by the heart, was weighed in the balance before him." In the Egyptian representations of the Last Judgment the heart of the deceased is weighed before an assemblage of the gods over against a feather the symbol of truth, to test the truth of his plea. The lightness of the feather, the ease with which it ascends symbolised the eternal quality of truth which, when "crushed to earth rises again." We still say "Heart as light as a feather" to indicate freedom from care, happiness, a good conscience.

The *panache* is a part of this same symbolism, as well as the three feathers of the Druids—"three rods of light"—light meaning power, divinity, Light of the

Anubis
(Owned by Mrs. Myron C. Taylor, New York City)

World, and which later were adopted by King Edward and other Princes of Wales as a badge.

The bird power was humanised by the Greeks in their flying angels of victory. It is also associated with the Hebrew cherubim which guard the Tree of Life.

The soul, which was commonly believed to be exhaled from the mouths of the dying in the last breath was frequently pictured as a bird. It was a part of the funeral rites of a Roman Emperor to burn his waxen image on a pyre. As the flames were seen ascending an eagle was let loose from the burning pyre to carry the soul to heaven.

In Egypt the soul is often portrayed as a human-headed bird hovering about the mummy. Or again it will be depicted perched in a tree near by regarding curiously its own funeral.

The sun-god Ra is pictured as a falcon winging his swift course across the sky.

The *hawk* is connected with all solar gods and was particularly venerated in Egypt. Horus is the falcon god. The hawk of Horus typified the spirit of the sun.

HAWK ON LOTUS ANTHEMION.
Greek pottery fragment.
Goodyear, *Grammar of the Lotus.*

Layard quotes from a fragment of the Zoroastrian oracles preserved by Eusebius, "God is he that has the head of a hawk. He is the first, indestructible, eternal, unbegotten, indivisible, dissimilar; the dispenser of all good, incorruptible; the best of the good, the wisest of the wise; he is the father of equity and justice; self-taught, physical and perfect and wise and the only inventor of the sacred philosophy."

Sometimes the head of the hawk is given to the body of a lion, the latter is also associated with the might and power of the sun.

The hawk or falcon, vulture and phoenix in Egypt, and the eagle in India and Babylonia are birds of the sun, fire, wind, storms, immortality.

Among the Egyptians where decomposition set in so rapidly, the *vulture* was regarded as an emblem of purification, of compassion, as a worker of all good. The vulture also symbolised maternity. Nekhebet the vulture goddess is identified by the Greeks with Eileithyia the goddess of birth. She is generally represented as a vulture hovering above the king. Mut another Egyptian goddess whose name signified mother, 'queen of the gods,' 'lady of the sky,' was supposed to represent nature the mother of all things and like Nut, Neith and Isis and other great mother goddesses was symbolised by the vulture. Hathor, who was the female power in nature, wears a head-dress in the shape of a vulture and above it a disk and horns. Hathor is called 'lady of the sycamores' and 'mistress of the gods.'

THE BIRD OF FIRE.

Bayley. *Lost Language of Symbolism.*

The *phoenix* a fabulous bird of the sun, one of the four supernatural creatures of the Chinese, has symbolised life and immortality from remotest antiquity. According to the legend this "bird of wonder" combines both feminine and masculine attributes. "It lives five hundred years or a little more, when it will become young again and leave its old age."

When its time to put off old age arrives, it makes for itself in some secret place somewhere in Arabia a nest of rarest spices. These, becoming ignited by the heat of the sun and the fanning of the bird's own wings, burst into flames consuming the phoenix, which arises from its own ashes, buoyantly young, to pursue "the same never ending life and re-birth."

In the Egyptian religion the phoenix is the embodiment of Ra the sun-god. The Egyptians believed that this mystic bird came out of Arabia every five hundred years and burned itself on the high altar in the Temple of the Sun of Heliopolis, rising again from its own ashes young and beautiful.

Among the Romans, where cremation was practiced, the symbolic use of the phoenix signified resurrection and immortality. This emblem of life was taken over by the Christians as a symbol of immortality and was also used by the alchemists.

The *eagle* among the Greeks was the symbol of supreme spiritual energy. It is a solar bird like the hawk and shares with the latter the power of being able to out-stare the sun.

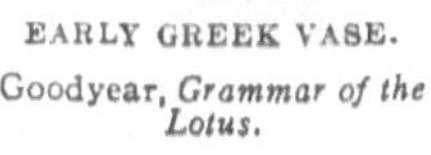

EARLY GREEK VASE.
Goodyear, *Grammar of the Lotus.*

The eagle is the symbol of royalty, power, authority, victory. Zeus is attended by an eagle. On ancient Greek medals and coins the eagle of Zeus is often portrayed carrying the thunderbolt.

The Babylonian shepherd Etana (or legendary King) is borne aloft by an eagle to the Celestial Mountains where grows the plant of life.

The Etana eagle figured as a symbol of royalty in Rome.

The eagle is associated with Ashur, the solar god of the Assyrians, and occupies a prominent place in the mythologies of Sumeria and Assyria as a symbol of fertility, of storm and lightning, the bringer of children and the deity who carries souls to Hades.

The eagle was looked upon as the inveterate enemy of serpents. The contest between the sky or sun and the clouds was symbolised as a fight between serpents and eagles.

In its cruel aspect the eagle is identified with the *Zu bird,* a storm demon, a worker of disaster, a prolific source of evil. The Zu bird symbolised also a phase of the sun, also fertility and slays serpents.

Garuda the solar vehicle of the Indian god Vishnu, half eagle, half giant—was also a destroyer of serpents and, like the Babylonian Etana eagle when it was born it "issued from its egg like a flame of fire, its eyes flashed the lightning and its voice was the thunder."

In a hymn which Mackenzie quotes in the *Myths of India* the Garuda is lauded as the "bird of life, the presiding spirit of the animate and inanimate universe, destroyer of all, creator of all. It burns all as the sun in his anger burneth all creatures." The same hymn identifies the sacred bird with Agni, the god of fire, with Brahma, the creator, with Indra, god of fertility and thunder and with Yama, god of the dead who carries off souls to Hades. The Garuda is also called the "steed-necked incarnation of Vishnu."

The double-headed eagle—a form of the Garuda bird—was worshipped by the Hittites as a symbol of omniscience. It was the emblem of the King of Heaven and as such was given to kings and emperors who were his Divine representatives on earth. The Hittite Bird of the Sun is also identified by some with the magic

Photo, Alinari

GRIFFINS AS TABLE SUPPORTERS

(Vatican, Rome)

Roc, mortal enemy of serpents, the bird that bore Sindbad aloft.

"The cherubim guarding the Tree of Life are modelled on the Double-Headed Eagle."

The double-headed eagle of the Hittites figured until recent days on the royal arms of Austro-Hungary and Russia.

In Layard's *Nineveh* he notes that eagle-headed or vulture-headed human figures were constantly represented in colossal proportions on walls or guarding the portals of chambers. Often they were depicted contending with other mythic animals such as a human-headed lion or bull. In these contests the eagle-headed figure was always victorious, which he believes may denote the superiority of the intellect over mere physical strength.

Assyrian eagle-headed genii are depicted advancing towards the Sacred Tree holding the symbolic cone.

In Christian art St. John the Divine is given the eagle, or sometimes he is depicted as an eagle, when as one of the four evangelists they are represented by the four creatures of Ezekiel—a man, an ox, a lion, an eagle.

EAGLE HEADED FIGURES HOLDING SYMBOLIC CONE.
Lajard, *Culte de Mithra.*

The lion with the wings of an eagle typified strength and power—the union of spirit and matter.

Doves played a prominent part in the worship of Astarte the great goddess of nature of the Phœnicians. The dove was a symbol of Bacchus, the First Begotten of Love!

Doves were also an attribute of Ishtar.

Doves bring ambrosia to Zeus.

Doves and snakes were associated with the mother goddess of Crete, typifying her connection with air and earth.

It was believed that Semiramis, the mythical founder of Nineveh, took flight to heaven in the form of a dove.

Doves were sacrificed to Adonis.

The dove, swallow, sparrow, wry-neck and swan were sacred to Aphrodite.

Doves and pigeons were sacred birds in Egypt.

In Vedic literature Yama is the god of the dead and his messengers are the owl and the pigeon.

A dove with an olive branch was used as a symbol of Athene or re-newed life.

In the Hebrew story of the Great Flood Noah sends forth first a raven and then a dove. But the dove found no rest for the sole of her foot, and returned to the ark. In seven days Noah sent her forth again. "And the dove came into him in the evening; and lo, in her mouth was an olive leaf pluckt off." Noah "stayed yet other seven days; and sent forth the dove; which returned not again to him any more."

In the Babylonian flood myth Pre-napish-tim the Babylonian Noah sends forth a dove on the seventh day. The dove finding no resting place returns. Next he sends a swallow which likewise returns. "Then Pre-napish-tim sent forth a raven and the raven flew away."

Sacred doves are usually associated with the sepulchral cult. Evans gives an illustration of one of the "dove shrines" of Mycenæa. These shrines were also connected with sacred trees and pillars.

In Christian art the dove is the symbol of the Holy Ghost. It is used pre-eminently as the emblem of the soul and in this sense is seen issuing from the lips of dying martyrs. The dove as the Holy Spirit hovers about the Virgin. It is also given to certain saints who were believed to be divinely inspired.

The 'primeval goose' that laid the golden egg of the world comes down through the ages as an object of endearing worship. It is safe to say that no woman ever really resented being called a "silly goose."

While the ancients looked upon blood as the primary vehicle of life, believed that the blood of a god flowed in the sacred waters, that inspiration and renewed life came from drinking blood—hence the Eucharist—they also saw that life was in the breath, that air was life, without air man could not breathe. Thus they reverenced the atmospheric gods—the gods of the moving winds. Hera is the "Queen of the Air." Anu is the sky and atmosphere god of the Babylonians. Zeus and Jupiter are gods of the winds and storms as well as of "heaven, earth, fire, water, day and night." As the gods grew more highly complex—and thus indicating the growing tendency towards monotheism—the solar gods eventually took over all the powers that had formerly been given to other gods. But whether centralised or scattered the forces that lie back of all vegetation and growth—sun, storm, wind, earth, water, fire, air—were none the less worshipped as divine manifestations of life.

From earliest days, perhaps because of its sibilant hiss, the goose became associated with the sound of the rushing wind.

The Hindus depict Brahma the Creator, the Breath of Life riding on a goose. The goose or 'breath bird' was sacred to Juno the Queen of Heaven (the Greek Hera). In Egypt the goose was the attribute of Seb the earth god who in the creation myth was the 'chaos gander.'

The goose was associated with the sun in Egypt, India, Greece and Britain. Thus as a solar bird it was given to Osiris, Horus, Isis. It was also sacred to Apollo, Dionysos, Hermes, the Roman Mars and Eros. Eros the god of love is depicted riding on a goose. The

GEESE AND THE LOTUS, SWASTIKA AND DIAGRAMS.
Detail of Rhodian vase in Metropolitan Museum.
Goodyear, *Grammar of the Lotus.*

'beautiful goose' is sacrificed to Venus in Cyprus where it was an emblem of love. It was sacred to Priapus in Italy. Among the Hindus it was the symbol of eloquence. The Greeks gave the goose to Peitho the "goddess of winning speech." In Germany and France the goose was believed to be endowed with the power of forecasting events as well as being a good weather prophet.

"The goose represented love and watchfulness, the 'watchfulness of a good housewife.' " It was called the "blessed fowl." The mystics likened themselves to "unslumbering geese." A goose with flames issuing from its mouth typified the Holy Spirit and symbolised the way of life or regeneration.

The oath taken by Socrates and his disciples was "by the goose."

The goose or Bird of Heaven was held sacred in China where it was regarded as peculiarly a bird of *yang* or the principle of light and masculinity.

The word for goose has a common origin in Latin, Greek, Sanscrit and German.

The *Crane* in China and Japan is a sacred bird said to live to a fabulous age. It symbolises longevity and happiness; "longevity" coinciding with our idea of immortality. It is often represented standing on the back of a tortoise. The crane also transported to heaven those who had attained immortality.

The *Stork* was one of the symbols of *hsiao,* "filial piety," which occupies such a high place in Chinese ethics. Confucius whose ideals lay in the past, or in modelling conduct upon the best that had gone before, defined filial piety as "carrying on the aims of our forefathers." Hence the "nursery lore of the stork bringing babies—doing as our fathers have done."

"There is a tradition of the Great Wisdom whose emblem is the serpent surrounding a pair of storks." [1]

The *Mandarin Duck* is a Chinese symbol of connubial affection and fidelity.

Crows in pairs were the symbol of conjugal fidelity in Egypt where the same quality has been given them that attaches itself to the pigeon in other countries—that if either dies the other never consoles itself—never re-mates.

Birds not only symbolised the soul, sun, wind, storms, fecundity, growth, immortality but they were 'fates.' Certain birds had the gift of presage. The *screech owl* was a bird of ill omen. The hooting of an owl even now brings a sense of coming disaster. Instinctively we still experience the inherited shudder.

In Japan the *crow* is looked upon as a bird of ill omen. If the crow cries when anyone is ill, death is near. The same idea of misfortune attaches itself in

[1] Bayley's "Lost Language of Symbolism."

Duran, *Historia de las Indias de Nueva España.*

Italy and France. In the fable of "*Les Deux Pigeons*" La Fontaine makes the pigeon who is urging the other not to leave him say:—

> "*Qui vous presse? Un corbeau*
> *Tout à l'heure annonçait malheur à quelque oiseau.*"

In the stories of wanderings, which are a part of every myth and saga, the spirits that aid or accompany the heroic figure or dragon slayer are birds or wild beasts. The bird Mimi delivers over the secret to Siegfried. "A little bird whispered it in my ear," is still a common saying, relic of an ancient belief.

St. Francis of Assisi preaching to the birds has come down the centuries as a touching evidence of the purity of his soul.

X

THE SERPENT

"It is fate itself, swift as disaster, deliberate as retribution, incomprehensible as destiny."

"Swift, powerful, graceful, without feet or paws, yet it can glide, coil, stand erect, leap, dart and likewise swim."—Waring.

"The serpent in which the breath or spirit is less than in any other creature and the earth power greatest. . . . It is the strength of the base element that is so dreadful in the serpent. It is the very omnipotence of the earth. It moves like a wave but without wind, a current but with no fall . . . all with the same calm will and equal way . . . one soundless, causeless march of sequent rings and spectral processions of spotted dust, with dissolution in its fangs, dislocation in its coils. Startle it, the winding stream will become a twisted arrow, the wave of poisoned life will lash through the grass like a cast lance."—Ruskin.

X

THE SERPENT

THE *Serpent* is a notoriously complicated symbol. Its meaning is subtle and contradictory. It has figured as a life symbol from remotest times, sometimes in a positive and again in a negative sense. No symbol has a more confused variety of meanings—good, evil, life reproduction, wisdom, power, eternity—everything also that is base, dark, evil, low. It is one of the universal attributes of the creative principle and is found in every portion of the globe as a symbol of life. It is common to both elements earth and water, is closely associated with groves and tree worship, and from earliest times has been inseparably connected with sun worship.

The earth in early days was thought to be surrounded by a celestial river whose circumambient course was likened to a serpent biting its tail.

The serpent with tail in its mouth forming a circle was an Egyptian symbol of eternity and immortality.

The fact that the serpent was believed to be androgynous—self-creating—added to its reverence. Its annual sloughing of its skin made it a symbol of renewal, of being born anew.

It was the emblem of destruction and death. "As the worm of corruption it is the mightiest of all adversaries of the gods."

Typifying darkness in this connection, it is the especial enemy of the gods of light and creative power. Apollo the god of day kills the python of darkness as soon as he is born. Ra, the sun-god of Egypt spends his nights in mortal combat with Apep the great serpent of mist, darkness, discord, destruction. In India Indra, the martial god of heaven kills the serpent Vritra, and liberates the waters which the serpent had kept imprisoned in mountains or clouds. Among the sun worshippers the serpent was believed to be the incarnation of evil and darkness.

The serpent was also used as a symbol of solar rays, lightning, clouds and rivers.

The undulating movement of the serpent was thought to typify the motion of the waves of the sea. This and its association with earth as well as water made it a symbol *par excellence* of the feminine principle. All the more so because, although used to denote evil, disaster, darkness, it was also employed with equal potency to signify life, understanding, wisdom, power, re-generation, re-production, eternity.

In the very early days in India there is found traces of an ancient religion which consisted of the worship of Mother Earth and the Great Snake Father.

In the Indian flood myth Manu is warned by the fish-god of the coming destruction, and counselled to build a large ark in which Manu and the seven Rishis are saved. The tradition of a Great Flood is found among all ancient peoples. The flood myth is thought by some to be a variant of the Indra myth which shows how Indra destroyed the snake worshippers. This in turn may have found its origin in Babylonia, where Ea the fish-god and water snake ordered the building of the ark and the destruction of the wicked snake wor-

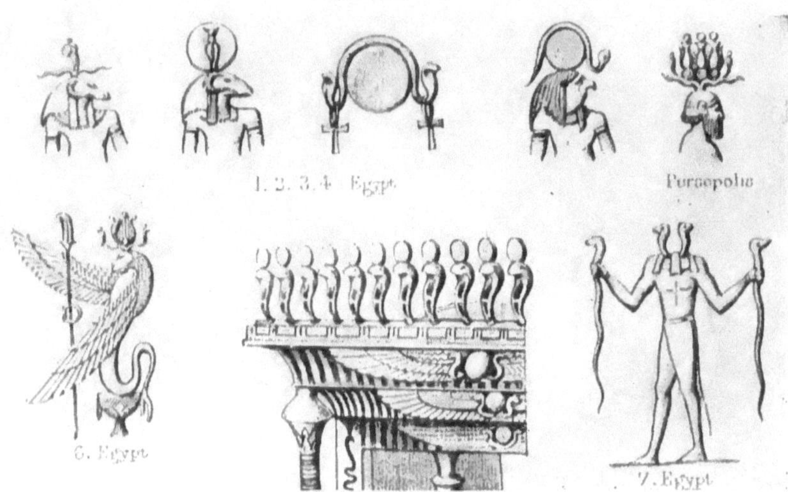

SERPENT SYMBOLS IN EGYPT

Fig. 6, "Kneph or Phanes, the most powerful deity, lion-headed, serpent bodied, winged and bearing on head the usual emblems of wisdom and fecundity, contemplating the sacred staff of his divine office and resting upon the sacred Nile jar."

In place of head fig. 7 is given the serpents of divine wisdom and "holds wisdom in each hand as a sign of power."

Waring, *Ceramic Art in Remote Ages*

shipping race. In the Egyptian flood myth it is Ra who becomes angry with the rebellious acts of men and consults with Nu, the god of primeval waters who orders the wholesale destruction of mankind. The Mexican deluge is caused by the 'water sun' which suddenly discharged the moisture it had been drawing from the earth in the form of vapour. That fire and water unite to destroy a race inimical to both, is evident in all the

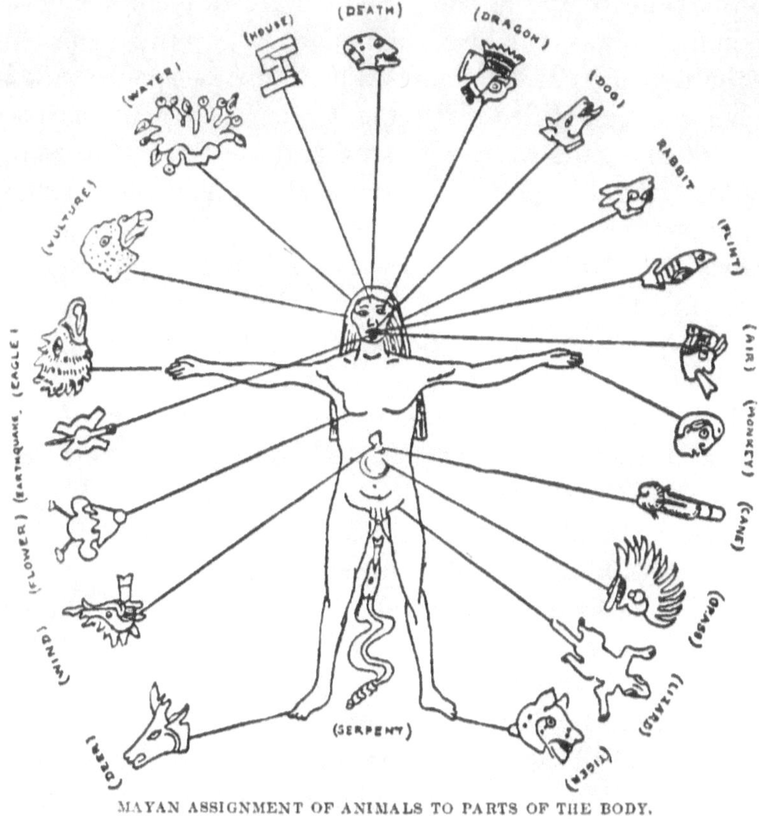

MAYAN ASSIGNMENT OF ANIMALS TO PARTS OF THE BODY.
Carus, *Chinese Thought*.

flood legends. These may have been snake worshippers or races far gone in the iniquities symbolised by the serpent.

The Maoris have a legend that in the beginning heaven and earth were united. The union was later destroyed by a serpent. This resembles the serpent in the Garden of Eden.

The Indian Nāgas are said to be "snakelike beings resembling clouds." They are said also to occupy eighth rank in the system of the world. Other enumerations put them next to the Devas. The Nāga world was beneath the ocean. There were heavenly Nāgas, divine Nāgas, earthly Nāgas and Nāgas who guarded the treasures of the deep. The Indian serpent-shaped Nāga is identified with the Chinese dragon because both are gods of rivers, seas and the givers of rain. The Nāgas were "Lords of the earth more than anyone else and send, when having been insulted, drought, bad crops, diseases and pestilence among mankind."

The Nāgas are represented in three ways in the Indian Buddhist art, first as human beings having on the head a uræus-like snake which curves out of the neck, often with several heads. Second, they are depicted in their snake-like form, and third they are shown with the trunk of a man, the lower part of the body and the head being that of a serpent.

In one of the legends of Gautama, when the Buddha sat under the tree where he received enlightenment, his brilliant light shone into the Nāga's palace under the sea, just as the light had spread from his three predecessors who had sat in the same spot. The Nāga rejoicing in the new Buddha, arose from the water and surrounding the Buddha with "seven coils covered him with his seven heads." For seven days and seven nights the Buddha sat motionless protected from storm and tempest by the royal snake. Thus, the legend concludes,

"These fearful serpents by the influence of Buddha's Law became blessers of mankind."

The Nāgas or serpent-gods were believed to be superior to men. Gautama Buddha was said to have put the Sacred Book under the protection of the Nāgas "until such time as man should have acquired sufficient wisdom to understand it."

NĀGA KINGS SUPPORTING THE LOTUS PEDESTAL.

D'Alviella, *Migration of Symbols.*

The Nāga kings Nanda and Upananda are depicted as entirely human with five serpents over their heads. They were said to have created the lotus, and are frequently shown in a kneeling attitude at the base of Buddha's pedestal supporting the lotus.

The Nāga god has practically disappeared from India except in the south where it is still reverenced.

The Nāgas were worshipped in China from earliest times. It is related that two heaven-sent serpents presided over the first washing of Confucius. The snake symbol is much less common in China, however, where its place is taken by the dragon.

From pre-historic times the serpent has been an object of worship in Japan, and Nāga shrines may still be found there. Benten, one of the seven gods of good luck, is usually represented riding on a snake or a dragon.

The mighty and powerful Nāgas were only helpless before their deadly enemies the Garudas, the fabulous, golden winged birds of the sun, of whom they stood in constant terror.

The snake inspired awe, fear and worship among all primitive races. Many of these customs and traditional observances still survive among the American Indians.

The Egyptian goddess Neheb-kan was represented as a serpent. The beneficent mother goddess Nazit of Buto was also a serpent and the goddesses Isis and Nephthys had serpent forms. The serpent was a symbol of fertility and as a mother was a protector. All the great nature goddesses of fertility are given the serpent.

The serpent is found in greatest profusion on Egyptian tombs and temple walls. The kings and gods of Egypt wear the uræus serpent crest in their crowns. Ra the Egyptian sun-god who had the sun's disk for an emblem was frequently represented with the head of a hawk crowned by the disk of the sun upon which rests the curving uræus snake.

Ruskin speaks of this, "The serpent crest on the king's crown, or of the gods on the pillars of Egypt is a mystery, but the serpent itself gliding past the pillar's foot, is it less a mystery?"

In hymns to Amen-Ra—who is a later form of Ra and took over many of the attributes of Ra and other gods as well—Amen-Ra is called "Lord of rays, creator of light . . . he that placest the uræus upon the head of its lord. . . . Lord of the uræus crown; exalted of plumes, beautiful of tiara, exalted of the white crown; the serpent 'mehen' and the two uræi are the ornaments of his face . . . the two uræi fly by his forehead. . . . The flame makes his enemies fall, his eye overthrows the rebels, it thrusts its copper lance into the sky and makes the serpent Nak [Apep] vomit what it has swallowed."

"He that placest the uræus upon the head of its lord" seems to deliver the secret. As the solar gods were always engaged during the night in fighting the serpent of darkness, mist, storm, evil, it may be that the uræus serpents worn on the crowns of the sun-gods

Photo. Alinari

Athene (Minerva)

(Museo Nazionale, Naples)

and the Pharaohs of Egypt were placed there to convey the same symbolic idea that is typified by the lion's skin which Herakles wears, in other words, they were worn as trophies of victory.

Serpents were worshipped as defenders of households, and images of them hung up for luck or protection as horse shoes were hung up as lucky omens in the peaceful, mid-victorian days before the horse was superseded by the automobile.

Snake charms, snake rings and snake bracelets were worn as fertility and protective charms.

The serpent in Rome was connected with the worship of Lares the household gods of the Romans, and among both Greeks and Romans it was regarded as a guardian spirit of places. A serpent kept in a cage in the temple of Athene at Athens was called the "guardian spirit of the temple." A snake is one of the symbols of Athene the goddess of wisdom. The Romans regarded the serpent as an object of divination.

Vishnu the preserver of the Hindu Trimurti sleeps on the World Serpent's body.

It was believed that Mercury the herald of the gods, with the caduceus—a rod with wings entwined by two serpents—in his hand "could give sleep to whomsoever he chose."

Æsculapius god of medicine and son of Apollo carries a staff encircled by a serpent, symbolising healing, the re-newing power of life.

Hippocrates is also given the same symbol.

Hygeia the goddess of health is depicted bearing a serpent in her hand.

There is an interesting communication that throws

a great deal of light on serpent symbolism, in the *American Journal of Archeology* for Jan.–Mar., 1922, from Prof. A. L. Frothingham of Princeton University, regarding a former contention of his, which identified the so-called Medusa in the temple at Corfu as Artemis. An inscription found after the publication of his theory proves that the temple was, in fact, a temple of Artemis and his theory of the identification of Medusa with both the goddess and the sun has been accepted by Dr. Dörpfeld. Prof. Frothingham goes on to say:—

"There are two phases in the creation and development of the Gorgon Medusa. Originally she is pre-Olympian. She is a child of Mother Earth and belongs to the primitive stage of proto-Hellenic religion, the matriarchal stage when the mother goddess was supreme and when the great snake, the emblem of life, was also the emblem of the great productive forces of mother earth. Medusa was the embodiment of this material, productive force. The second stage in the Gorgon evolution coincided with the substitution of the male for the female deity as leader of the Pantheon, when in the duality of productive forces the father sun heat took the upper hand of the other element in the production of life, the mother-earth-moisture element. In this second phase the darting snakes of the solar heat around the Gorgon's nimbus were symbolic of one side of the Gorgon's function, in the same way as the great snakes at her girdle were symbolic of the earth moisture forces of the great mother. . . . The two children of Medusa represent the two elements of heat and moisture. Chrysäor is Apollo in his character as sun god. In historical times the epithet of Apollo as a solar god was Chrysaor and his darting arrows are described as snakes. Pegasus, the horse is of course the well known symbol of Poseidon, the god of waters, and therefore in primitive Medusa symbolism represented the other element moisture. At Corfu, therefore, Medusa is the great producing force of the universe through a combination of heat and moisture. She is the presiding genius over the creative evolution out of which world order is produced."

The Serpent coiled about the Egg of the World symbolises the same idea of production by generative heat.

The cross entwined by a serpent was the emblem of spiritual re-birth.

Frazer finds the serpent associated with life-giving plants, and that there is a close connection between the fertility of the soil and the marriage of woman to the serpent; also that there seems to have been a Greek notion that women may conceive by a Serpent God.[1]

According to the legends Jupiter Ammon, appearing to Olympias as a serpent, became the father of Alexander the Great. Similar legends were told of Jupiter Capitolinus as the father of Scipio Africanus.

Jastrow considers that "In the Biblical narrative the sexual instinct and the beginning of culture as symbolised by the tree of knowledge are closely associated. According to rabbinical traditions the serpent is the symbol of the sexual passion."[2]

Conceived of in this way the whole analogy of serpent symbolism becomes stupendously clear and enters into the very essence of our being.

Another authority says "The serpent among the

[1] "Adonis, Attis and Osiris."

[2] Jastrow's "Religion of Babylonia and Assyria."

Eastern nations had the subtle significance of representing an emotion, the animating spirit of procreation, the sexual instinct, the Divine Passion. While this instinct as a factor in the work of the Creator was the source of all good, when it represented the sexual nature in its sensual and lustful aspect the serpent became the symbol of sin." [3]

As the manifestation of the Life Principle in obedience to law it becomes the symbol of wisdom, power, goodness. In the negative or evil sense it becomes the deadly reptile with no higher aspirations than materialism and sensuality. It was the serpent in this latter aspect that brought about the expulsion of Adam and Eve from the Garden of Eden, or Garden of the Soul.

With this interpretation in mind it is not difficult to understand how the snake came to be thought of by the literal minded and the ignorant, for whom the original meaning had been lost, not as a symbol of the means of creation but as the Creator himself—the Great Snake Father. Or again by others as an object whose presence gave potency to the life impulse. Even the sinister chapter that relates to serpent worship no longer puzzles, although it is a bad chapter in the history of humanity. It is the dark side made manifest. An amazing phase that defeats itself.

Troward sums it up very clearly:—"The serpent a favourite emblem in all ancient esoteric literature and symbolism, is sometimes used in a positive and sometimes in a negative sense. In either case it means life—not the Originating Life Principle but the ultimate outcome of the Life Principle in its most external form of manifestation. Recognized in full realization that it comes from God, it is the *completion* of the Divine

[3] "Sex Symbolism," Clifford Howard.

work by outward manifestation. In this sense it becomes the serpent which Moses lifted up in the wilderness. Without the recognition of it as the ultimate mode of the Divine Spirit, it becomes the deadly reptile not lifted up but crawling flat upon the ground; it is that ignorant conception of things which cannot see the spiritual element in them and therefore attributes all their energy of action and re-action to themselves, not perceiving that they are the creations of a higher power. Ignorant of the Divine Law of Creation the Serpent symbolizes thus that conception of Life which sees nothing beyond secondary causation." [4]

Nothing beyond Sex, in other words. Thus the Freudian theories of "Sex urge," the Œpidus complex, as well as other abnormal complexes that have seized upon modernism, especially the modern novel, are comparable to the phallicism of an earlier age. The only difference is that the modern uses words to symbolise precisely the same thought on life that was expressed in the degenerate stages of phallicism.

And whenever, as we have seen, phallicism is worshipped *per se* either by 'graven images' or by the written word, it is clear to the observing that the relation of the sexes is about to describe another circle.

D. W. Lawrence who is a sex expert—not with the definition in mind that "an expert knows nothing else," for I find him extremely well versed in symbolism—seems to foreshadow the male revolt against the sexual supremacy of the modern woman in the closing chapter of *Aaron's Rod.*

One character asks the old, old question that the ages have asked tirelessly, "But can't there be a balancing of wills?"

[4] "Bible Mystery and Bible Meaning," T. Troward.

The other says "My dear boy, the balance lies in that, that when one goes up the other goes down. One acts, the other takes. It is the only way in love. And the woman is nowadays the active party. Oh, yes, not a shadow of doubt about it. They take the initiative and the man plays up. That's how it is. The man just plays up. Nice manly proceeding, what?"

Lawrence goes on about the "power urge" which will have to issue forth again in man. He would not be modern, of course, if he did not put it that way. To keep to the old terms, however, this sounds like the recrudescence of the masculine. And when the masculine principle, as typified by heaven, light, fire, strength, the spiritual comes uppermost, hybridism goes out and the brazen serpent is once more lifted high.

XI

THE FOUR SUPERNATURAL CREATURES OF THE CHINESE

THE DRAGON, UNICORN, PHOENIX, TORTOISE

In unravelling the meaning of the lotus, dragon, tama, nimbus, or wheel of the law they become living records of the thoughts and beliefs of ancient peoples." —Maude Rex Allen.

"The simplest truths in philosophy are hidden in the Hindu allegory that the world rests on an elephant and the elephant on a tortoise."—Lloyd P. Smith.

"The dragon is the spirit of change, therefore, of life itself . . . taking new forms according to its surroundings yet never seen in a final shape. It is the great mystery itself. Hidden in the caverns of inaccessible mountains or coiled in the unfathomed depth of the sea he awaits the time when he slowly arouses himself into activity. He enfolds himself in the storm clouds, he washes his mane in the darkness of the seething whirlpools. His claws are in the fork of the lightning . . . His voice is heard in the hurricane . . . The dragon reveals himself only to vanish. He is a glorious symbolic image of that elasticity which shakes off the inert mass of exhausted matter."—Okakuro-Kakuzo.

"Cloud follows the dragon, Wind follows the tiger."

XI

THE FOUR SUPERNATURAL CREATURES OF THE CHINESE

THE DRAGON, UNICORN, PHOENIX, TORTOISE

IT has been suggested that the *dragon* may have been the traditional form of some huge saurian or prehistoric monster, or perhaps a conventionalised form of the alligator found in the river Yangtse. Whatever its origin, from the remotest times the dragon has figured in the folk tales and mythologies of nearly every ancient race as the personification of the malign forces of evil and chaos. "The combination of every bad feature in nature—the sum of every creature's worst."

In Babylonia Tiamat, the chaos dragon or Great Mother is the serpent or leviathan of the sea. In Egypt it is associated with the great serpent or night demon Apep with whom Ra the sun-god battles. In China he is a sun and moon swallowing monster during an eclipse. In India the dragon is the serpent Vritra who keeps the waters imprisoned in the clouds. Hydra the water serpent slain by Hercules belongs to the same class of images. There were dragons, too, of the wells. In all these representations the dragon is merely the idealised serpent.

In Egypt the dragon is also associated with the crocodile.

The dragon symbolised water, clouds, rain, floods, sin, evil.

It is the sea monster of the Hebrews. "In that day the Lord with his sore and great and strong sword shall punish leviathan the piercing serpent, even leviathan that crooked serpent; and he shall slay the dragon that is in the sea." (Isa. 27:1.) St. John describes the dragon "A great red dragon having seven heads and ten horns and seven crowns upon his heads. And his tail drew the third part of the stars of heaven and did cast them to the earth." (Rev. 12:3–4.) And again he sees an angel who came down from heaven and "laid hold on the dragon that old serpent which is the Devil and Satan and bound him a thousand years." (Rev. 20:2.)

The scriptural phrase 'the jaws of hell' was rendered literally in early Christian art by depicting a dragon with jaws open from which are seen issuing flames. St. Michael is the victorious angel over the "great dragon that deceived the world," and in devotional pictures he is frequently represented in full armour, carrying a sword, standing with one foot on the half-human, half-dragon form of Lucifer. St. George was another dragon slayer as were nearly all the heroes of myth and saga.

The Chinese, however,—and also the Japanese who borrowed most of their religious ideas from China—give a much wider meaning to the dragon. Water which is associated with the dragon is a source of greatest good as well as evil, and in China the dragon becomes the most potent symbol of the blessing, the rain-giving, the wonder working gods of water.

It is almost impossible for the Western mind to grasp the mystical subtleties that are embodied in their dragon symbolism nor the profound hold it has. The dragon and all that it implies enters into the very warp and woof of Chinese thought and imagery.

It is the symbol of power, royalty, sovereignty. It is the symbol of floods, clouds, rain. It is one of the four supernatural creatures who preside over the fate of China. But above all else—that thought so dear to the Chinese mind—to the Chinese who believe that their civilisation is eternal—"the dragon is the spirit of change."

Lao-tse defines the Tao, "I do not know its name and so call it the Path. With reluctance I call it the Infinite, Infinity is the Fleeting, the Fleeting is the Vanishing, the Vanishing is the Reverting."

Commenting upon this in *The Book of Tea* Okakuro-Kakuzo says, "The Tao is in the Passage rather than in the Path. It is the spirit of Cosmic Change—the eternal growth which returns upon itself to produce new forms. It recoils upon itself like the dragon, the beloved symbol of the Taoists. It folds and unfolds as do the clouds. The Tao might be spoken of as the Great Transition. Subjectively it is the Mood of the Universe. Its Absolute is the Relative."

In the Yi King; the Book of Changes, the dragon is the symbol of *Chén* (or Kan) one of the *yang* trigrams meaning thunder.

There is a legend that a 'dragon horse' emerged from the river Ho bearing on its back an arrangement of marks which gave Fuh-Hi the idea of the trigrams. The 'dragon horse' with wings at its sides that could walk on the water without sinking symbolised the vital spirit of heaven and earth.

According to the Yi King the symbol *chén*, corresponding to the third of the four primary developments of the creative influence, is synonymous with *lung* the dragon and in conformity with this dictum the powers and functions of nature which are governed by the forces thus indicated, such as east, spring, etc., are ranked under the symbol of the azure dragon. This also designates the Eastern quadrant of the Uranosphere, as the White Tiger is given to the Western Quadrant.

The four cardinal points and the four seasons were thus represented:

East,	Spring,	Blue,	Dragon.
South,	Summer,	Red,	Bird.
West,	Autumn,	White,	Tiger.
North,	Winter,	Black,	Tortoise.

De Groot places the azure dragon as highest in rank among all the dragons in China because blue is the colour of the East. This idea may have been derived from India where Indra the rain and sky god is the patron of the East and Indra-colour is blue or blue-black, the colour of rain clouds.

According to other authorities, however, the yellow dragon is the most honoured.

The blue dragon symbolises the vital spirit of water.

The yellow dragon is the essence of divine, manifesting power.

"The dragon can be bigger than big, smaller than small, higher than high, lower than low."

The dragon wields the power of transformation and invisibility. He conceals himself or becomes brilliant.

When the dragon breathes his breath changes to a cloud upon which he rides to heaven. He mounts to the sky at the time of the spring equinox. When he flies too high and cannot return the "thirsty earth must

Dragon

(Musée Chinois, Fontainebleau)

wait for his blessings and sorrow prevails." At the time of the autumnal equinox he plunges down into the depths. He sleeps in the pools in winter and arouses himself in the spring. He is the god of thunder and appears in the rice fields as rain, or as dark clouds in the sky.

The symbol of imperial sovereignty is an ascending dragon which belches forth a ball. The ball in this case is the thunder and not the sun pursued by the dragon. Sometimes the object depicted between two dragons is shaped like a spiral, the spiral denoting the rolling of thunder from which issues a flash of lightning.

The dragon devours the moon during an eclipse, and the ball between the two dragons has been identified as the moon which the dragons are attempting to swallow. The conjunction of moon and water is obviously a magical one and was a symbolism used for the purpose of drawing down the fertilising rains.

More frequently, according to Chinese belief, the ball is a 'precious pearl,' a form of the *tama* or sacred gem which typified the spirit or divine essence of the gods and also denoted the force which controls the ebb and flow of tides. The pearl was believed to be the "concrete essence of the moon distilled through the secret workings of the secondary principle of nature within the mussel of the shell which produces it. Hence it acts as a charm against *fire,* the active or primary principle."[1]

The intense desire of the dragons to regain possession of this jewel, which has been wrested away from them by the covetousness of man, is a favourite subject in myth and legend and is constantly being de-

[1] Mayer's "Chinese Reader's Manual."

picted in Oriental art, where the dragons are shown either guarding or battling for it.

In *The Dragon in China and Japan* M. W. de Visser describes a great ball of glass covered with gold which is said to hang from the centre of the roof of the great hall of the Buddhist Temple Fa(h)-yū-sze, "Temple of the Rain of Law." Eight dragons are carved on the surrounding "hanging pillars" eagerly stretching out their claws towards the ball in the centre—the "pearl of perfection." This is again explained as the "divine pearl." He divides the dragon into five sorts: 1. Serpent dragons, 2. Lizard dragons, 3. Fish dragons, 4. Elephant dragons, 5. Toad dragons.

The usual number in China, however, used in the ethical or abstract sense are four. These are the dragons of the four seas. They are four brothers named Yao who govern the North, South, East, West seas. They are called:—

JAPAN.

Nāga Kings with two dragons on shoulders upholding the lotus pedestal of the god.

D'Alviella, *Migration of Symbols.*

1. The Celestial dragon who upholds the heavens, guarding and supporting the mansions of the gods so that they do not fall.

2. The Spiritual or Divine dragon who benefits mankind by causing the wind to blow and the rain to fall.

3. The Earth dragon who marks out the courses of rivers and streams.

4. The Dragon of Hidden Treasure who watches over the wealth concealed from mortals.

The connection of the dragons with pearls is here obvious. The masters of the sea would jealously guard its treasures.

As far back as 2700 B.C. Yao the dragon was one of the six symbolic figures painted on the upper garment of the emperor.

Imperial coffins used to be painted with a sun, a moon, a bird, a tortoise, a dragon and a tiger.

Coffins of grandees displayed the blue dragon, symbol of the Eastern quarter on the left side, and a white tiger representing the West on the right. The sun and moon are on the top. The burial garments for women had dragons embroidered on them surrounded by clouds, bats, phoenixes, stags, tortoises and cranes—emblems of fertilising rains, longevity, bliss, immortality, prosperity, happiness.

De Visser quotes from the philosopher Kwan who writing on the nature of dragons says, "Those who, hidden in the dark can live or die are *shi* (a plant the stalks of which are used in divination), tortoises and dragons. The tortoise is born in the water; she is caused to disclose (what she knows) in the fire and then becomes the first of all creatures, the regulator of calamity and felicity. A dragon in the water covers himself with five colours, therefore he is a god (*shen*). If he desires to become small he assumes a shape resembling that of the silk worm and if he desires to become big he lies hidden in the world. If he desires to ascend he strives towards the clouds, and if he desires to descend he enters a deep well. He whose transformations are not limited by days and whose ascendings and descendings are not limited by time is called a god (*shen*)."

Japan has three kinds of dragons coming from India, China and Japan. These may all be classed, however, as thunder, storm arousing, rain bestowing gods.

The dragon in Japan is the symbol of the Mikado, whose garments are the robes of the dragon, whose face is called the dragon face and who is seated on a dragon throne.

The dragon is depicted with flame-like wings or appendages curving out from shoulders and hips. Its feet are given either three, four or five claws. The Japanese dragon has three claws. The imperial dragon of China is always given five. This may be in allusion to the fact that Japan has but three kinds, whereas China has five, or it may symbolise the Chinese myth that the dragon in water covers himself with five colours.

"The people paint the dragon's shape with a horse's head, and a snake's tail. He is given five fingers, three joints and 'nine resemblances'—the horns of a stag, head of a camel, eyes of a demon, neck of a snake, belly of a clam, scales of a carp, claws of an eagle, soles of a tiger, ears of a cow. Upon his head is a big lump—*ch'ih-muh*. If a dragon has no *ch'ih-muh* he cannot ascend to the skies." [2]

The symbolism of the dragon and the tiger preceded the *yang* and *yin*. The dragon typified spring, heaven, the sky and the tiger autumn, the earth. They are often depicted together symbolising power.

The dragon, being the fullest of *yang* is chief among the four supernatural, divinely constituted beasts called *Ling*. These are the unicorn, the phoenix, the tortoise and the dragon. "They are called the *Ling*."

Ling has been translated by Couvrez as *"animaux qui donnent des présages."* Dr. de Visser believes that it has a stronger meaning and translates it as spiritual

[2] "The Dragon in China and Japan," M. W. de Visser.

The Lady with the Unicorn

(One of six tapestries in the Musée Cluny, Paris)

beings, adding that the "effective operation of the *Tsing* or vital spirit of these four creatures is, indeed, enormously strong and therefore they may be justly called 'the four spiritual animals, par excellence.' "

Their appearance was considered to be an omen but this was due to their symbolic spiritual powers. The dragon being full of *yang* symbolises those of mankind who are fullest of light and its appearance is the presage of their coming. The Emperor, the greatest of all men, being the fullest of the heaven power *yang*, was symbolised by the dragon.

The dragon diffused light, "A black dragon vomits light and makes Darkness (*yin*) turn into Light (*yang*)."

Of the others of the four supernatural creatures the *unicorn*, called *K'i-lin* in Chinese and *Ki-rin* in Japanese (*K'i* male and *lin* or *rin* female) like the phoenix was believed to combine both the masculine and the feminine principles. The unicorn appears in the earliest examples of Chinese art, where it closely resembles the dragon-horse. It is depicted in ancient Egyptian hieroglyphics. It is spoken of in the psalms, "But my horn shalt thou exalt like the horn of an unicorn," (Ps. 92:10.) as well as being mentioned in other books of the Old Testament.

The horse has invariably symbolised wisdom, intelligence, the intellectual side. The white horse typified innocent and pure intellect or reason. The white horse when given one horn becomes the unicorn which has figured in all countries from pre-historic days as a symbol of purity, strength of body and virtue of mind. It was regarded as the "noblest form of animal creation, the emblem of perfect good." Among the Chinese it was considered to be the incarnate essence of the five primordial elements, and was believed to live one thousand years. It ranks first among the four sacred animals which preside over the destinies of

BULL UNICORN AND SACRED TREE OF LOTUS BUDS.
Assyrian relief.
Layard, *first series 46.*

China and only makes its appearance when some great event is about to occur.

The unicorn, adopted by the Christian religion as a symbol of female chastity in allusion to the fable that it "could never be captured except by a virgin stainless in mind and life," was given only to the Virgin Mary and St. Justina. In the art of the Renaissance the unicorn figures frequently with the lion.

Fêng (phoenix) a fabulous bird of a mystic nature, second among the supernatural creatures is associated with the sacred Ho-o or Ho-ho—which was represented in the earliest art in China as a huge eagle bearing off large animals in its claws. The ho-o had the same characteristics and functions as the sacred garuda of the Hindus, the Persion rukh and the Greek gryphon. Later it is depicted as a compound of the peacock and the pheasant. The female was called *hwang* or *luan* and this name combined with *féng* the male becomes *féng-hwang* or *féng-luan* the name by which this wondrous bird is usually designated. The phoenix like the *k'i-lin* or unicorn is supposed to unite in itself both

CHINESE LONGEVITY SYMBOLS.
Carus, *Chinese Thought*.

masculine and feminine principles. "In poetry many covert allusions to sexual pairings are intimated by references to the inseparable fellowship of the *féng* and *hwang*." [3]

[3] Mayer's "Chinese Readers Manual."

The plumage of the phoenix was of five colours typifying the five cardinal virtues. Its appearance was the forecast of wise and beneficent rulers. This supernatural bird was looked upon as the essence of fire, and Chinese mystics believed that it symbolised the entire world. "Its head is heaven, its eyes the sun, its back the crescent moon, its wings the wind, its feet the earth, its tail the trees and plants." [4]

The phoenix as a royal emblem was given to the Empress, as the dragon was given to the Emperor.

Kwei—astrologically this is the *divine tortoise* which was thought to be embodied in Ursa Major. Another account says that the first dragon sprang from the great *Yuan*—a form of tortoise and dragon which accompanies the god of waters—and from this came the divine tortoise. It was the divine tortoise who presented to the sage Lü a scroll of writing on its back composed of the numbers 1 to 9. Lü made this the basis of his philosophy or "nine divisions of the Great Plan."

The tortoise was a symbol of longevity, the faculty of transformation and was believed to conceive by thought alone. It was believed also, that the tortoise could create by its breath a cloud, a fog or an enchanted palace.

As has been said before 'longevity' among the Chinese means life everlasting, immortality, as well as long life on earth. The five blessings which are so constantly symbolised are, longevity, riches, peacefulness, serenity, the love and attainment of virtue. The five eternal ideals are humaneness, propriety, insight, uprightness and faithfulness.

[4] "Japanese Art Motives," Maude Rex Allen.

"The characters which stand for the five blessings and also the five eternal ideals are the most popular symbols all over China. . . . Among them the characters 'longevity' and 'blessing' are most used of all. . . . Blessing is called *fu* in Chinese which is an exact homophone of *fu* meaning 'bat' and so the five blessings *wu fu* are frequently represented by five bats. The word 'longevity' is commonly transcribed by *sheu* 'long life.' "[5]

The life of the tortoise was supposed to be one thousand years, although it is sometimes represented in art with a long bushy tail which it is said to attain in its ten thousandth year.

The Chinese had two chief modes of divination, one was by the stalks of the yarrow and the other by the tortoise shell. The latter was regarded as the nobler method. It consisted in applying a thick black pigment to one side of the tortoise shell and fire to the other side until cracks appeared in the coating, which the diviner interpreted according to the rules of his art. Thus the tortoise was believed to hold the secrets of life and death.

The tortoise is also a symbol of fecundity and it was thus used by the Egyptians. The Greeks give the tortoise to Venus as well as the dove, dolphin, ram, hare and swan. In Greek art Venus is sometimes represented standing on a tortoise.

As one studies into its symbolism one finds that the tortoise had no mean function to perform in the estimation of the ancients, for besides everything else—the power of divination, of transformation, of fecundity, of longevity, it was said to carry the world on its back. The belief that it does this is almost universal.

[5] "Chinese Thought," Paul Carus.

Sometimes it upholds the treasure mountain of the mystic jewel the '*tama.*' In Japan it upholds the mountain abode of the gods. In the Hindu legend the tortoise sustains an elephant upon whose back rests the world. The Delaware Indians believed that the Cen-

Three worlds supported by elephants resting on a tortoise the whole encircled by a serpent with tail in its mouth.

Waring, *Ceramic Art in Remote Ages.*

tral World Tree grew out of the middle of the back of a tortoise. Among the Senecas the sky mother fell into a great pit on the wings of a waterfall who placed her on a turtle's back. In an ancient Arab myth a whale performs the 'all sustaining office' of the tortoise. Earthquakes were caused by the awakening of the earth tortoise, the tortoise yawned and all nature was convulsed.

The use of the tortoise as a support in various representations in bronze, or sculptured in stone is no doubt derived from this widespread legend. The symbolism of the four supernatural creatures has been fascinatingly expressed in ancient Chinese art.

In the *Bhagavad-Gita* a man who is confirmed in spiritual knowledge is likened to the tortoise who "can draw in all his senses and restrain them from their wonted purposes."

XII

THE SUN

"Set (Darkness) and Horus (Light) are the first two elemental powers."—Churchward.

"Whoso venerates the Sun that is immortal, brilliant, swift-horsed . . . he venerates Ormazd, he venerates the Archangels, he venerates his own soul."—From the Nyaishes or Zoroastrian Litanies of the Sun.

"If, for us also, as for the Greek, the sunrise means daily restoration to the sense of passionate gladness and of perfect life—if it means the thrilling of new strength through every nerve,—the shedding over us of a better peace than the peace of night, in the power of the dawn,—and the purging of evil vision and fear by the *baptism of its dew;—if the sun itself is an influence, to us also of spiritual good—and becomes thus in reality, not in imagination, to us also a spiritual power,—we may then soon over-pass the narrow limit of conception which kept that power impersonal, and rise with the Greek to the thought of an angel who rejoiced as a strong man to run his course, whose voice calling to life and to labor rang round the earth, and whose going forth was to the ends of heaven."*—Ruskin.

"In the commencement was Brahman without beginning or end, unborn, luminous, free from decay, immutable, eternal, unfathomable, not to be fully known."—Mahabharata.

"To the Brahmans the sun is the most glorious and active emblem of God."—Goodyear.

XII

THE SUN

MOST of the ancient religious rites, while accumulating in the long processes of time all sorts of rubbish which now seems puerile and childish—all sorts of dogmas, priestly terrors, magical rituals and practices—appear, one can scarcely doubt, to have been based upon that profoundest of all instincts reverence for the most holy, the great and insolvable mystery of life.

In this quest of life it was inevitable that almost from primeval days the *sun* should be exalted above all the other gods of nature as the Supreme Creator, the source of all Life, Light, Power.

The Egyptian religion has been called a solar drama. Their gods, typifying the forces of nature, presented a dramatic and moving picture of the universe. The cult of one god superseded another, the attributes and symbols were frequently transferred, one god might be confused with another, but the fundamentals of the Egyptian religion—based upon the enduring and unchangeable powers of nature remained always the same.

Back of the ancient worship of the various gods of nature there seems to have been even at a very early time, especially in Egypt, a belief in the existence of one God—self-existent, almighty, eternal—one great God who created all the other gods of sky, storms, sun, moon, earth, stars. These were worshipped, not as the divine, self-created power—but as glorious manifestations of that mysterious First Cause, the *Primum Mobile*.

It is probable that the sun worshippers placed this power in the sun, figured that it resided in the sun, as later cults have said God is in the heavens. As no attempt apparently was made to symbolise this mysterious Life Force or to realise it in visible, objective form, the sun, as the highest manifestation of this Unknown Power of creative energy and life, came to typify that power and was addressed as that power.

"The material symbol of God was the sun, who was personified under the form of Rā, or later Amen-Rā; and although Osiris who was probably an indigenous god, is far older than Rā in Egypt, Rā was declared to have been the father of Osiris, and Osiris was his only son. Osiris was of divine origin, and he reigned wisely and well on earth, but at length he was slain and mutilated by Set, the personification of the powers of darkness. But he rose from the dead, and became the god of the underworld and of the beings who were therein. Because he suffered, died and rose from the dead, he became the type of the RESURRECTION to the Egyptians who based all their hopes of everlasting life upon the belief that Osiris was immortal and eternal." (Budge.)

The solar gods changed in Egypt as elsewhere, one god displacing another, but the force symbolised remained ever the same.

Tum, the primeval sun-god of the Egyptians, is lost sight of and Horus and Set typify the elemental

Photo. Alinari

THE GOD BES, SERAPEUM

(Louvre, Paris)

powers of light and darkness. Horus, the falcon-god was also originally the sky—the "sun is the eye of Horus."

Horus prepares the way for Ra the great sun-god—the "Horus of the Two Horizons."

Later Horus reappears as the morning sun—the son of Osiris and Isis.

"Ra at the beginning rose from the primeval deep in the form of the sun-egg or lotus flower.

He that openeth and he that closeth the door;
He who said 'I am but one.'
Ra who was produced by himself;
Whose various names make up the group of gods;
He who is Yesterday (Osiris) and the Morrow (Ra)."[1]

Men were born from the eye of Ra. Ra the ruler of the gods was the first king on earth.

The Egyptian hieroglyph of the sun-god Ra was a point within a circle. The life of Indian and Egyptian gods was in the egg. The 'dot within the circle,' a symbol that goes back to remotest times, may have typified the seed within the egg. This is the 'Orphic egg,' symbol of the universe whose yolk in the middle of a liquid surrounded by an encompassing vault, represented the globe of the sun floating in ether and surrounded by the vault of heaven.

A point within a circle is still used as the astronomical sign of the sun, as a circle divided by a cross is the astronomical sign of the earth. In Egypt the circle also symbolised the course of the sun about the universe.

Worship of the sun-god Ra became first prominent

[1] "Egyptian Myth and Legend," Mackenzie.

at Heliopolis where it received its fullest development. The priests of Heliopolis were the first religious thinkers of Egypt of whom any records are extant. Their theology gained wider and wider acceptance, until with the Fifth Dynasty (2700 B.C.) the solar religion of Heliopolis became the religion of the state.

Ra was exalted as the Great Father who created gods and men. Hymns proclaimed him as self-begotten, king of the gods, lord of heaven and lord of earth, creator of those who dwell in the heights and of those who dwell in the depths. "Thou art the ONE god who came into being in the beginning of time. . . . Worshipped be thou whom the goddess Maat [goddess of truth] embraceth at morn and at eve. . . . Thou stridest across the sky with heart expanded with joy. . . . Hail thou Disk, lord of beams of light, thou risest and thou makest all mankind to live. Grant thou that I may behold thee at dawn each day."

The sun was frequently represented as a falcon, and from this idea of the sun as a hawk or falcon taking his lofty flight across the sky, may have originated the Egyptian symbol of the deity, a sun disk with the outspread wings of a hawk. This solar emblem of life, omnipotence, power was also widely venerated in Asia Minor. Horus the falcon-god is symbolised by the solar disk. The emblem of Ra was a sun disk. In papyri and on bas-reliefs he is depicted with the head of a hawk, wearing the disk over which curves the uræus serpent. Ra is also identified with the ass, cat, bull, ram and crocodile.

Amen-Ra, a later form of Ra, who was extensively worshipped at Thebes, is given the ram's head, the ram symbolising the masculine principle or solar creative energy.

Under Amen-hetep IV (Ikhnaton or Khu-en-Aten), the 'Heretic King' who preceded Tut-ankh-amen, Amen-Ra was temporarily dethroned. The sun-god was clearly distinguished from the material sun. To the old name Ra was added Aton or Aten, 'Heat which is the sun'—the solar disk, which was looked upon as the source of all things. The king was thus deifying the vital heat which is found accompanying life. The god was everywhere active by his rays and his symbol was a disk in the heavens darting down towards the earth diverging rays which terminated in hands, each holding the symbol of life. "In so far as it rejected all other gods the Aten religion was monotheistic." Upon the death of the king, Amen-Ra was restored and the old gods found favour again.

"The sun was the great Proteus, the universal metamorphist."

The three steps of the sun indicated "His Going Down, His Period of Darkness and His Rising Again."

The heat and glow of the noonday sun represented Ra. The sun going down typified the death of Osiris. In the morning sun Osiris lives again as the incarnate Horus.

Dawn, noon, sunset, represented "three in one of the sacred substance of the sun as three divine persons existed perpetually in the substance of Uncreated Light."

In this thrilling drama, the sense of contest, suspense, struggle between the power of light and the power of darkness is never lost. What the sun does during the long hours of the night is a mystery, appealing to all the emotions of curiosity, fear, hope, apprehension, mystification. When the orb of day re-appears in the morning after a night of mortal combat with his old enemy Set—now in the guise of Apep or Nak, the huge serpent of mist and darkness—there is rejoicing, the tension goes, the play ends well. Good has triumphed over evil. The meaning of life is fulfilled. Yet the drama begins again with each night. There is always the constant, never ending struggle, if light is to win over darkness. The legend of Isis and Osiris becomes more personal. The human forces enter in—the eternal feminine and the eternal masculine. Osiris, who is dismembered by Set, is avenged by his son Horus and his mutilated remains found and restored by Isis. It is as fascinatingly complex yet simple as life itself. From the days of Plutarch down every generation has sought to explain to its own satisfaction the solar myth of Osiris and Isis.

To one who would understand the race thought and its marvellous persistence, nothing is more deeply satisfying than to trace back these old religious beliefs and myths to their perfect simplicity—to the 'first narrow thought' and then, as Ruskin puts it, to see, as the intelligence and passion of the race develops, how leaf by leaf their beloved and sacred legends expand, until "the real meaning of any myth is that which it has at the noblest age of the nation among which it is current."

It is questionable whether the present day city dweller is able to realise or comprehend the loving intimacy of the ancients with nature, and the number of sacred ideas that owe their inspiration to the revolution of the universe, to the orderly movement of the heavenly bodies, and to man's supreme reverence for the Unknown Power that lies behind that all containing motion. Even among the most primitive and savage races there is found the desire to understand the forces and wonders of the universe, the causes of phenomena, —the winds, the seas, the tides, the transmission of life from one generation to another, the fecundity of nature, growth—the secret of that omnipotent, creative power that causes a plant to spring from a tiny seed. All this man, savage and scientist, has brooded over, seeking the solution since time began.

So close and so normal is man's association with nature, it represents such a large part of his religious life, constantly reminding him of eternal processes, of the wondrous works that are beyond the power of the human mind, however avid for the knowledge, to grasp, that, apparently throughout the ages, whenever he forsakes nature and shuts himself up in the artificial life of cities, he loses God. As cities and commerce grow, his religion develops into an ethical sense which ultimately loses force as it loses its direct, yet mythical and awe inspiring association with the hidden powers of nature.

The same great drama that is represented by the Egyptian religion, the drama of Life and Death, Light and Darkness and the magical, miraculous return to Light, Life, Immortality is played out by all the other great religions.

Sun worship was of great antiquity in Babylonia. The Babylonians had many gods, but the most important place, as we have seen, was given to the gods of fire and water as representing the two chief forces of nature that control and preserve the health, prosperity and happiness of mankind.

Anu, one of the earliest Babylonian gods, is originally a sun-god and Enlil is a storm-god like the Hebrew Yahveh and is described as a mighty ox or bull. The bull is associated with the gods of humidity.

To this ancient duality is added Ea, god of water, whose symbol is a goat-fish. In this triad Anu becomes god of heaven and Enlil god of earth. Ea, the god of water is pictured as always beneficent, constantly on the side of humanity, the embodiment and source of wisdom.

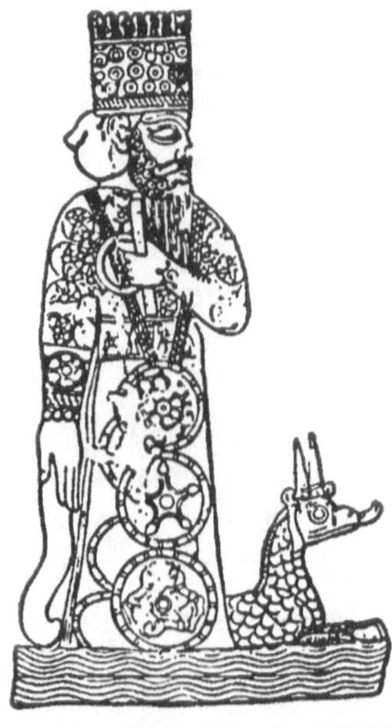

MARDUK THE CHIEF BABYLONIAN DEITY
From Jastrow.

These transfer their powers to Marduk (Merodach) a solar god who in his complexity resembles the Egyptian god Osiris.

Marduk is called the son of Ea. He is pictured as the victor over Tiamat the primeval chaos monster. Marduk died to give origin to human life. He commanded that his head should be cut off and that the first pair should be formed by mixing his blood with the earth. "He was lord of many existences . . . the mysterious one, he who is unknown to mankind. It was impossible for the human mind a greater than itself to know."

It is Marduk who directs and controls the forces of the chief triad. To him are given the attributes and supremacy that was formerly attached to all the other great gods, to Sin, the moon-god, to Ninib, Shamash and Nergal the three great sun-gods, to Ea and Nebo, gods of the deep; he also absorbs the powers of Adad,

Marduk Killing Tiamat the Chaos Monster. He Holds the Double Trident or Thunderbolt in Each Hand
(Jastrow, *Bildermappe zur Religion Babyloniens und Assyriens*)

the storm-god; he is the wind-god who brings the air of life; he is the god of thunder and the sky.

Marduk "starting out at Babylon by the absorption of the character of Ea, combining in his person the two powers water and sun which comprise so large a share in the divine government and the control of the universe, he ends by taking over all the duties of Enlil of Nippur. . . . He becomes, like Enlil Lord of many lands. It is he who seizes the tablets of fate from the Zu bird—the personification of some solar deity—and henceforth holds the destiny of mankind in his hands. . . . Addressed in terms that emphasise the fact that he is the one and only god we find all the tendencies toward true monotheism centering on Marduk the solar deity of Babylon." [2]

ADAD THE GOD OF STORMS.
From Jastrow's *Civilisation of Babylonia and Assyria.*

The *lion* was given to Marduk also the *goat*.

Nergal typified the destructive power of the sun and heads the pantheon of the lower world where dwell the dead.

Shamash the other great solar deity of the Babylonians is constantly associated with Adad or Rammon—the Rimmon of the Bible—a storm-god, a hammer-god, god of wind and thunder, a rain bringer, a corn-god, a god of battle resembling Jupiter, Indra, Thor and other gods of storm and sky. Adad is represented with the symbol of the *thunderbolt* or *forked lightning* which he holds in his hand.

[2] Jastrow's "Religious Belief in Babylonia and Assyria."

Shamash is given no other powers save those beneficent ones which reside in or emanate from the sun. He is Lord of the living, a mighty judge who loves righteousness and abhors darkness and sin. His light shines over all. Without him all mankind would die. He illumines the world, his rays penetrate into every corner revealing all things. "He dominates by his majesty and power. He sees all things. Nothing can be hidden from Shamash."

In the Babylonian flood legend it is the sun-god Shamash who decides the time when the heavens shall rain down destruction.

The symbol of Shamash was the solar disk from which flow streams of water. The union is again significant, showing the pertinacity of this ancient conception of the powers which produce life. These rays were apparently 'fertilising tears' like the rays of the Egyptian sun-god Ra.

Ashur is the sun-god of the Assyrians. All the other gods are of Babylonian origin, but Ashur is the god of his people and reflects their aspirations and experiences. He is the national hero, but he also reflects the origin of the greatness of Assyria, as well as exemplifying in himself its power and might.

Ashur also absorbs the attributes of the other and older gods. He bears a close resemblance to Marduk, has traits in common with Tammuz, the god of vegetation, takes of the functions of Ninib, Nergal and Shamash, as well as those of the older triad of gods Anu, Bel Enlil and Ea. He is a god of fertility, a corn-god, a water-god, and thus the rippling water rays appear on his solar disk. He becomes the dominating figure, overshadowing all others. "He is the Great God, God of Gods, the embodiment of the genius of Assyria."

Photo, Alinari

Winged Bull with Human Face from Sargon's Palace, Khorsabad

(Louvre, Paris)

Having absorbed so much, Ashur becomes, like Osiris and Marduk an exceedingly complex and mystical deity. "Like the Indian Brahma he may have been in his highest form an impersonation or symbol of the 'self-power' or 'world soul' of developed naturalism, the creator, preserver and destroyer in one, a god of water, earth, air and sky, of sun, moon and stars, fire and lightning, a god of the grove whose essence was in the fig and fir cone as it was in all animals." [3]

The Assyrian *winged bulls* and *lions* typified the power of the sun.

Ashur was not the goat but the bull of heaven. He was also given the lion and the eagle. As the bull he was the ruling animal of heaven.

The symbol *par excellence* of Ashur is a sun disk with wavy lines extending to the circumference of the disk. He is also symbolised by a winged disk with horns enclosing four circles radiating around a middle circle, with rippling rays streaming down from either side of the disk; Also by a circle or wheel with wings, and inside the circle a warrior drawing his bow to discharge an arrow. And again by the same circle, the warrior having his bow in the left hand, however, and the right hand uplifted as if to bless his worshippers. It has been conjectured that the Assyrians drew the circle to denote eternity, the wings omnipotence and the human figure supreme wisdom. Jastrow considers that the warrior was added

[3] "Myths and Legends of Babylonia and Assyria," Mackenzie.

to the old solar symbol of the winged globe, and that its presence evinces a de-spiritualisation which "reflects the martial spirit of the Assyrian empire."

Other authorities contend, however, that the sun symbol on the sunboat of Ra enclosed a similar figure which was seemingly conceived to represent the soul of the sun—"the life of the god was in the 'sun egg.'"

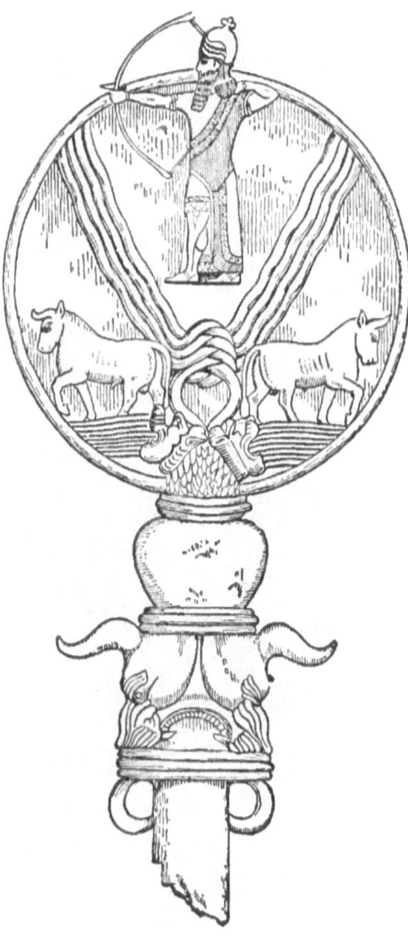

ASSYRIAN STANDARD.

The *arrow* is associated with the sun, moon and gods of the atmosphere. It is a symbol of fertility, rain, lightning, as well as war, famine, disease, death.

Apollo gave Hercules a solar arrow.

It seems credible, therefore, that the archer was as truly solar as his rays, and that the warrior in the sun-disk represents Ashur as god of his people.

An Assyrian standard shows the disk mounted on a bull's head with horns. The warrior's head, part of his bow and the point of his arrow protrude from the upper part of the circle. The rippling water rays, which are V shaped, stream out from either side, and two bulls are depicted in the divisions thus formed. Two heads, that of a lion and a man, each with gaping mouths are also shown symbolising possibly the scorching, destructive power of the sun.

In the Sabæan system, which is one of the most ancient religions of which there is any record, preceding even that of the Egyptians, the heavenly bodies were worshipped as visible evidences of the power and majesty of the supreme deity of which the sun was the highest divine manifestation. Emblems of the sun, moon, etc., were often depicted with seven disks which may represent the seven great heavenly bodies—'that mysterious number so prevalent in the Sabæan system.'

In Assyrian representations, the King is seen in adoration only before one emblem of the sun-god—the figure with wings and tail of a bird enclosed in a circle. The king is generally shown standing or kneeling before this figure, one hand uplifted in sign of worship. The Sacred Tree is before him, but only, it may be supposed, to give further emphasis to the Life thought. This symbol—the winged circle—is never represented over a person of inferior rank and in its warlike aspect, as protector and guardian of the king in battle, the warrior within the circle is represented shooting an arrow with head shaped like a trident against the enemies of Assyria.

The Assyrians exaggerated the muscular, and gloried in the combative, masculine aspect of the sun. Their gods were always bearded.

Layard finds that the Persians adopted their religious symbols from the Assyrians, and that the form of the supreme deity—the winged figure within the circle—and the types of wisdom and power are precisely the same on the monuments of both people.

Ormuzd or Ormazd (Ahura-Mazda) all-wise, all good, the power of light is the Persian solar god. Ahrimanes, symbolised by a great *lizard* or *serpent* is the power of evil, darkness, sin. Mithra is the god of sunlight and bears the same relationship to Ahura-Mazda, the Supreme solar deity that Christ bears to God the Father. He is the messenger, the light of the world, the Mediator between Light and Darkness, the god of re-generation, the power of God made manifest. Ahura-Mazda, like Ra and Shamash is remote, awe-inspiring—a force that needs to be interpreted by a divine intermediary.

Mithra corresponds in his symbols and attributes to the Babylonian Marduk.

The highest deity among the Japanese is not heaven as in the religion of the Chinese but the sun. The symbol of the sun-god in Ise is a metallic *mirror* which the sun-goddess gave with a jewel and sword to Ninigi her grandson when he was about to descend to earth. In other temples also a mirror is the most common representation of the god.

The Egyptians, too, had the *Ank* or *Sacred Mirror* wherein every great deity contemplates perpetually his own image, representing the ideal and the material semblance of the ideal.

According to Aquinas the "universe exists in a twofold manner first ideally in the mind of God, and secondly materially, externally to him, so that in Creation the Almighty contemplates his own mind as in a mirror."

The Baals of the Canaanites were personifications of the sun. The Phœnician sun-god Melkarth was the Baal of Tyre. Baal signified the lord, the owner.

In the changing centuries, and as populations and political power shifted from one centre to another, younger gods displaced the older gods as leaders in the pantheon. In this change, the older god became the father, and the younger god his son.

In Egypt Osiris, less abstract with more human qualities than Ra, although an older god was called the son of Ra, and was raised to first place in the pantheon of gods. In this transformation there was evidenced a long step towards monotheism, in that Osiris a solar god should gradually absorb the functions and attributes of the other gods, while Isis, who is the moon, absorbs those of Neith the earth goddess and Nut the sky and water goddess.

"Ra is the soul of Osiris and Osiris the soul of Ra."

Horus, one of the oldest sun-gods, reappears as the youthful, ever gloriously young morning sun. Although older, he is now called the son of Osiris who has become the god and judge of the dead.

In the Babylonian religion, Anu is the beloved father of Enlil. In the Ninib cult, Ninib is the son of Enlil and these become the two gods of sun and storm. "In this union of the two, Enlil is represented as the power behind the throne who hands over his attributes —symbolised by storm weapons—to his beloved son who proceeds to conquer the monster, i.e. chaos." [4] Marduk was called the son of Ea. In the Nebo cult Nebo becomes the son of Marduk.

It was an accepted and common form of the ritual

[4] Jastrow's "Religious Belief in Babylonia and Assyria."

for the two gods—father and son—to be invoked together.

In featuring this drama of the universe—which surely gives magnificent play to the imagination if one is to interpret it at all, the younger gods of vegetation, gods of fertility, storm, fire, gradually assume solar attributes and become the twice-born gods. They are the spring sun-gods and fire-gods. The Phrygian Attis, the youthful Tammuz of the Babylonians, the Greek Adonis and the Egyptian Osiris represented the yearly decay and the renewal of life—more especially the life of all nature and vegetation, which they personified as gods who died annually and then rose again from the dead. Dionysos is also a twice-born god of regeneration. In a painting at Pompeii Dionysos is depicted as a solar deity with his symbolic animal the panther. Again as a solar god he is pictured seated on a sun globe strewn with stars.

Mithra is also identified with the Greek god Dionysos and all the other twice-born gods of regeneration, and each is said to be born on December 25th, for it is then that the sun is born, the winter solstice is past and the "great luminary begins his revivifying journey northward."

In this mighty pageant the sun was represented as the Creator, the twelve months his attendants, the twelfth month his betrayer through whom he meets his doom. He descends into the abode of death only to rise again in the full glory of light and power for the eternal salvation of man.

'Dying to live' was, as we have seen, the keystone of all ancient religions and each year as spring returned all nature revived this faith in the immortality of life.

The Orphic and Eleusinian mysteries of the Greeks,

Photo. Alinari

Dionysos
(Museo Nazionale, Naples)

the Saturnalia of the Romans, the mysteries of the Babylonians, of Cybele and Attis as well as many others were originally vernal festivals in celebration of the resurrected life and generative powers of nature.

"In the mysteries of Mithra caverns and grottoes were consecrated to the world, the universe and the nymphs. One of the rites consisted in imitating the motion of the stars in the heavens. The initiates took the name of constellations and assumed the figures of animals. One was a lion, another a raven, a third a ram, etc. Hence came the use of masks in the first representations of the drama." [5]

This "Dance of the Stars" was the origin of the various forms of round dancing which is found among all races, just as the statelier dances go back to the circular worship of walking around trees and shrines.

The Egyptians had a festival in which men and women, representing the seasons, the months of the year and the different parts of the day walked in procession after the god of life.

In the mysteries of Ceres (Demeter) the procession was headed by a figure who was called the Creator, a torch bearer following him represented the Sun, the one nearest the altar was the Moon, and the herald of the procession was Mercury.

Some of the rites observed in these vernal festivals have still survived in our own Easter, in which the egg symbolising from time immemorial the hidden mystery of life, plays such an important part still.

In their spring time festivals it was the custom among the early Franks and Germans to make offerings of eggs and buns. The same custom prevailed among the Egyptians who impressed the cross, the em-

[5] Volney's Ruins.

blem of life upon the buns, as we do now upon our hot cross buns. Eggs and buns also figured in the Chaldean rites connected with the worship of Ishtar, the goddess who descended to and arose from the nether world.

It has been conjectured that these crossed cakes may have been a mystical allusion to the four rivers of Paradise flowing towards the cardinal points.

In Egypt the sacred bulls were fed upon a cake composed of flour, milk or oil and honey, upon which a cross was impressed. On high festivals priests and worshippers partook of these cakes.

The sacrament of eating bread and drinking wine was a part of the Eleusinian mysteries in celebration of the re-newed life of the sun. Here the bread was supposed to represent Ceres, the goddess of corn and harvest, and the wine Bacchus, god of the vintage and the cultivation of the fruits of the earth. Partaking of the body and blood of the gods of productivity in this symbolical way was a religious rite among all ancient peoples. And the idea of sanctifying one's self by assimilating a divine being may be traced back to this custom of a remoter period when the forces of nature typified Life.

It was but a step up to transform the symbol into the Christian sacrament of the Eucharist, which is merely the old idea sublimated, carried on like the octave. In the continuance of all these symbolical representations, one finds the physical idea interwoven with the nature idea into a myth which holds something "eternally and beneficently true"—a truth, which lost or disregarded for a time, is forever being discovered afresh and carried on into the new life of the spiritual ideal.

Fire plays a large part in the ritual and ceremonies

Photo Brogi

Ceremony in Honour of Demeter (Ceres)—Fresco from Pompeii

(Museo Nazionale, Naples)

of the sun worshippers. The belief that the sun died in winter only to be born again in the spring, led to the feeling that man, the recipient of all his blessings could and should aid the god who was the principle of life and light, in his struggle with the opposing principle of death.

Thus the religions of all these ancient civilisations became magical dramas in which were shown not only the natural processes which were to be seen on every side reflected in growth and decay, production and disintegration, marriage, death, re-production and re-birth —but also the artificial means which were used to assist the gods of light and life, vegetation and fertility.

Fire as a manifestation of heat and warmth on earth was worshipped as a secondary principle of solar creative force. The Egyptians saw in the glowing fire the "Creator spirit Ptah." Ptah was called 'the blacksmith' as was Vulcan (the Greek Hephæstus) who was the god of fire and forged the thunderbolts for Jupiter.

Although there are no traces of fire worship on the earliest monuments, there are abundant proofs of its prevalence at a later period in Assyria and Babylonia as well as in Persia. None of the fire-gods of Babylonia were so important, however, as Agni (ignis) the great god of India, "the moving flame" who was both destructive and beneficent. Nusku like Agni was the "messenger of the gods" and when Marduk was exalted to first place in the pantheon, it is Nusku who carries his messages to Ea. In this capacity Nusku may have symbolised the rays of the sun.

Perpetual fires were kept burning in honour of the sun-god who was light, power, life. As his forces began to wane at midsummer, great bonfires were lit to strengthen him.

These fire festivals that prevailed all over Europe down to the beginning of the nineteenth century, and that are still observed in some places, have the same general characteristics, differing slightly in different localities and at the different seasons, and as usual acquiring and taking on much that was undreamed of in the earlier conception.

Probably the purest and simplest form of sun adoration was manifested by the ancients in the altars placed on top of pyramids, built in triangular form (symbolic of fire), where fire was kept constantly burning in homage to the sun, the source of all light and warmth. This is a custom that is still carried out in the Catholic Church in the light that is never permitted to die out.

From this first form of worship there came the practical idea—ever dear to man's heart, with its overmastering appeal to the eternal busy-ness of him, to his mental as well as physical agility—which suggested utilising fire to aid the god, to show him that man understood that he, the mighty sun was struggling against fearful odds; to cheer him, put heart into him by the genial glow of the secondary creative force which had been magically delivered to man through the agency of the fire sticks. This was done absolutely selflessly at first, we may be sure. He was still single minded, until there came about quite fortuitously, the understanding that in giving assistance to the god he was incidentally helping himself, and that fire was a means of purification as well as worship, and fire festivals an occasion for merry making as well as prayer.

If this were not true, we would not have the simple beauty of the original idea. It must be that the first thought in every religion is that of disinterested worship—a pouring out of self without thought of return.

The secondary aspect, after this emotion has spent itself is the practical viewpoint of those less idealistically inspired, who without adoring, respect religion on the basis of what religion can do for them. So we get the eternal paradox which seems to puzzle antiquarians and archeologists—the outgoing and incoming aspect of all these ancient symbolic customs, which are as much a part of life as breathing—and both are true.

Fire festivals occurred most commonly in the spring or at Midsummer, although in some parts they were held at the end of autumn or during the course of the winter, particularly on Hallowe'en, Christmas Day and the eve of the Twelfth Day.

The spring fire festivals usually fell on the first Sunday in Lent, on Easter Eve and on May Day. In one of the French provinces the first Sunday in Lent is known as "Sunday of the Fire brands," and in Switzerland as "Spark Sunday." The Easter fire festival is still celebrated all over Northern and Central Germany, the fire being kindled in the various localities year after year on the same mountain. The eve of May Day is the notorious Walpurgis Night when witches are abroad everywhere, and kindling bonfires on this night was called "driving away the witches."

In the Central Highlands of Scotland the Beltane fires—a Druidical festival—were lighted with much ceremony the first of May. "Like the other public worship of the Druids the Beltane feast seems to have been performed on hills and eminences. They thought it degrading to him whose temple is the universe to suppose that he would dwell in any house made with hands." Their religious ceremonies and sacrifices were therefore held in the open air. The idea of a scape goat or human sacrifice is shown in the Beltane feast where whoever gets a particular piece of the Beltane cake was called "the Beltane *carline* a term of great reproach." In some places whoever draws the black bit "is the *devoted* person who is to be sacrificed to Baal."

Of all the fire festivals, however, that of Midsummer Eve, the 23rd of June (later called the Eve of St. John) or Midsummer Day the 24th of June ranked above all the others in importance.

It was a matter of knowledge to the ancient sun worshippers—who kept such a watchful eye on nature—and never failed to give them a certain feeling of solicitude that "the summer solstice or Midsummer Day is the great turning point in the sun's career, when after climbing higher and higher day by day in the sky the luminary stops and thenceforth retraces his steps down the heavenly road." The Midsummer fires were to help rekindle the dwindling light of the sun. Huge bonfires were built, and men and boys in procession carried lighted torches around the fields. It was customary to have the festival on a mountain, and in some places a great wheel made of straw was set fire to and sent rolling down the hill. The wheel rolling down from a high eminence typified the sun which now "having reached the high point in the ecliptic" was on the descending way. Frequently cartwheels were smeared with pitch then lighted and sent rolling down the hills. Sometimes an oaken stake was driven in the ground and a wheel fixed on it making the stake an axle. The villagers worked by turns to keep the wheel revolving rapidly until it was ignited by friction. Bayley's belief that this curious custom may have had its origin from the idea that the "oak tree symbolised the core, pole, or axis of Immaculate fire" is worth noting again. The regular method of producing these sacred fires was by the friction of two pieces of wood which were generally oak. Among the Celts, Germans and Slavs it was strictly commanded that the fire sticks should be of oak. In other words, there is here a blending of Tree worship and Sun worship, each symbolising life.

In many places the young people were in the habit of throwing blazing disks in the air. These were made of "thin, round pieces of wood a few inches in diameter with notched edges to imitate the rays of the sun or stars."

This is simply the crude beginning of the modern fire works with which the southern Italians celebrate Christmas, Easter and all the festas of the saints, and other nations use to celebrate patriotic events. The wheel of St. Catherine, the Catherine wheels of our fire works and the fiery disks of the ancients all have a common origin—all are seemingly derived from the solar wheel.

In some places the custom was adopted of putting a straw man in a hole and burning him. This was called the "burying of Death."

It was believed that the more bonfires there were the more fruitful would be the year. And the midsummer bonfire on the Eve of St. John was the most joyous night of the whole year. The people danced around the fires and young people hand in hand would leap over or through the fire.

In Norway and all over Bohemia the fires are still lighted on Midsummer Eve. In Brittany also the custom still obtains. Bayley quotes from Le Braz "that in every village hamlet and farm in Brittany on the night of the 23rd of June there still occurs the annual burning of the consecrated log." When the flames die down the assemblage kneels by the fire, "an old man prays aloud. Then they all rise and march thrice round the fire; at the third turn they stop and everyone picks up a pebble and throws it on the burning pile. After that they disperse."[6]

The Midsummer fire was sometimes called the "fire of heaven."

The *Yule log* was the counterpart of the Midsummer fire but, owing to the season, the ceremony was held indoors. This made it more of a private or family festival, contrasting in marked fashion with the riotous publicity of the Midsummer celebration. On Christmas Eve the "Yule-clog or Christmas-block" was lighted by a fragment of its predecessor which had been kept from the last Christmas for this purpose.

Besides these fire festivals which occurred at fixed dates, in many places the peasants were wont to resort to a ritual of fire in seasons of distress or epidemics among man or beast, or in times of drought. These were called *Need-fires* and were supposed to bring healing and welfare.

In the division of opinion as to the origin of these sacred fires, those who support the solar theory fall back upon sun charms and imitative magic, while others insist that the fire festivals were solely for purificatory purposes designed to destroy everything harmful—witches, evil intentions, vermin, disease—all that is foul and corrupt. As a matter of fact, the two theories are not irreconcilable once we admit that man is spirit plus matter, a sun worshipper first, who finds that fire worship and bonfires and ashes have a potent influence in driving away noxious things—that fire is a practical help as well as a means of evincing his glad impulse to be of service to the mighty Sun. And so he mingles the practical and the diverting with the ideal, and the fire

[6] "The Golden Bough," Frazer.

festivals become joyous ceremonials into which creep all sorts of little human customs and superstitions. These grow and grow until the main purpose is almost lost sight of and forgotten.

In the days when agriculture itself was a religious rite, the days before the satanic quality about machinery had impersonalised work and stifled all mirth—man intensified his work, identified it with the gods of storm and sunshine, prayed, feared, sang, danced with growth, fertility, fecundity, Life more abundant ever in mind.

There is a bit of this left in Sorrento. There are still the wine pressers in Sorrento and Capri—laughing youths who tread the grapes in the vat with their bare feet, singing the while the Italian folk songs, or "*Giovanezza*"—the ringing, joyous marching song of the Fascisti that all Italy is singing, humming, playing.

Fire was also a symbol of re-newal, purification, youth. In order that the reigning power, like the sun, might be ever young and glorious there came about the annual burning of kings or their effigies—or in many cases men were elected or chosen by casting lots to impersonate the king for the time being, and become the sacrifice. This, too, became a pageant. The beggar who was king for a day or two days or whatever period of time may have been decided upon, was given all the trappings and power of royalty. To make the sacrifice more impressive, he was frequently chosen for his beauty and physical perfection. All knees bent to him as if he were truly king. He has his moment—then passes on. Dramas are still fashioned out of this ancient motif. Anthony Hope's *Prisoner of Zenda* is merely an enchantingly told revival or development of this old theme of "King for a Day."

Most of the world's fairy stories that come down to us from remotest times, and that are found to be practically the same among widely scattered races are variants of old solar myths. Anatole France gives a delightful exposition of this in the latter part of *"Le Livre de Mon Ami."* Bayley finds that "Little distinction can be drawn between classic myth and popular fairy tale . . . and what is often supposed to be mere fairy tale proves in many instances to be unsuspected theology."

It has been said that every mythological figure contained a philosophical concept. And it is extraordinary how many things become clear and full of poetic beauty when interpreted as solar myths passed over to us from preceding civilisations.

Little Red Riding Hood and Cinderella—especially the Indian version of the latter as given by Ernest Thompson Seton under the Indian name of *Little Burnt All Over*—show marked solar influence. Bluebeard slaying his seven wives is the sun slaying the dawn, Prince Charming on the other hand is the Sun as lover waking the Sleeping Princess and the whole world to love and light. Bayley interprets the Song of Solomon most ingeniously as a "mythical and dramatic love duet between the sun and moon"—the moon typifying Wisdom, and maintains that the idea that Solomon was an inveterate sensualist originated from the "literalisation and misconception of the time honoured and poetic fancy that the Sun was the great fecundator and All Lover whose eye shone impartially upon the just and the unjust."

The Round Table of King Arthur typifies the Sun, the glorious King of Life; and the twelve knights are the twelve months or twelve signs of the zodiac.

Dido is the mythical bride of the sun. Siegfried, St. George, King Arthur, Horus—all the heroic dragon slayers enact the old story, play the old immortal part.

Whether or not one accepts sun worship as an explanation of much that would otherwise seem nonsensical and meaningless, it must be conceded that it gives a consecutiveness, a common origin to thought that is tremendously vitalising and illuminating.

Even now any story that elaborates upon this ancient idea of the sun as hero, protector, the Great Lover, the slayer of dragons, the redeemer, who destroys sin and chaos, who suffers for the sins of others, one who struggles with death and darkness only to emerge triumphant in the splendour of re-newed life and power—a story on any one of these themes goes along with Life—partakes of the eternal aspect. The hero may be a Parsifal or a swashbuckler like the immortal D'Artagnan, it doesn't matter, the eternally dramatic quality of heroic strife is there.

And so, too, with Cinderella, the little fire tender, the spirit of truth and service abused by the hateful sisters Pride and Selfishness and finally taken as his bride by the Prince of Light! It is simply charming the way young and old adore the fairy story of Cinderella. It is a notorious literary fact that you have only to give fresh costumes and new surroundings to the Cinderella idea and you have a successful story or play to your credit.

The *rays of the sun* were called by the old imagists the hair of the sun-god. The strength of the sun-god departs when he is shorn of his hair in winter. The Egyptians depicted the sun at the winter solstice as having but a single hair or ray. The Assyrians also had the same idea. The tuft of hair of the Mohammedans is derived from this ancient conception. The priest's tonsure represents the disk of the sun. The Arabs shaved their heads in a circle in imitation of the sun. Devotees of the sun would also voluntarily shave their heads to show their willingness to partake of the same sacrifice and undergo the same diminution of strength. The hair was sacred to the sun-god. Cutting the hair was a sacrificial offering. The priests of Egypt and India had shaven heads. Sakya-Muni when he retired from the world before becoming the Buddha cut off his hair. The hair as a source of strength in the biblical story of Samson and Delilah is clearly derived from this old fanciful conception of the rays of the sun. The story itself has been interpreted as a solar myth.

"Nothing can be more suggestive of Samson's solar character than the loss of his strength. . . . Apollo is called by Homer 'he of unshorn hair' which translated into Hebrew would mean Nazir. Samson's hair is put up in seven braids in the style of the sun-god who in one of the Mithraic monuments is represented with seven rays, characterising the mysterious power of the seven planetary gods. . . . The name of the traitress Delilah is symbolical and means the 'weakening or debilitating one.' Finally Samson is blinded (the sun loses his light) and when he dies he stands between the two pillars of sunset, at Gaza, the most western city in Danite geography." [7]

Sun worship led to all sorts of fanciful and poetic—even grotesque conceptions. The course of the sun through the heavens and the way he goes back again at night to his daily starting point appealed profoundly

[7] "The Story of Samson," Paul Carus.

Photo, Vivari

Apollo Belvedere

(Vatican, Rome)

to the imagination of the Egyptians, as to all other ancient races.

Sometimes they pictured him as a calf born each day of Hathor, the cow-goddess of the sky. Sometimes he traversed the heavens on the back of the sky cow in a boat such as was used by kings on the Nile. At evening he exchanged this boat for another returning to the East at night through the dark North quarter.

Again the sun is represented by a wild ass which was ever chased by the night serpent Hain as it ran around the mountains supporting the sky. Sometimes the sun is a great cat which fought with the night serpent Apep below the sacred tree at Heliopolis. Apep was represented in the form of a serpent with his back stuck full of knives.

The *Cat* because its eyes varied in form like the sun with the period of day, represented to the Egyptians the splendour of light. Thus the cat is frequently depicted cutting off the head of the serpent of darkness in the presence of the Sacred Three—Ra, Osiris and Horus, or the three phases of the sun.

The Egyptian Bast was a feline goddess and her car was drawn by cats. All feline goddesses represented the variable power of the sun.

Set—identical with Typhon—the red-haired god of pre-historic times, became the Egyptian Satan and was symbolised under various names as a black pig, a black serpent or red mythical monster.

The sun-god was sometimes represented seated at the helm of a ship, the ship resting upon a crocodile. The crocodile symbolised the human passions—these were not intrinsically bad when brought under subjection by the soul. "Thus the crocodile which attacked the departed before new birth is rendered divine in the regenerate form and held in high reverence by the Egyptians because it spoke of a time when man should regain the mastery of his passions and when the last barrier between himself and his glorious soul should be removed forever." [8]

The Egyptian *Cartouche* or oval in which the name of a royal person was enclosed was originally a circle symbolising the circular course of the sun about the universe. Inscribing the king's name inside a circle denoted his association as a being of majesty and dominion with the sun-god, that his power followed the course of the sun, and that he and those of his name like the sun would endure forever.

In Egypt teachers of the sun cult sold charms and received rewards so that the chosen worshippers might enter the Sun boat of Ra.

To reach the Island of the Blessed a river must be crossed, and the ferryman would only take those who were "righteous before heaven and earth and the island."

As sun worship extended, the ferryman became the boatman of Ra the sun-god, and the Island of the Blessed was transferred to the skies. The sacred texts, whether in the form of appeals or commands were chiefly concerned in persuading the boatman to ferry the king across the river, to induce the gates of the sky to open and the sun-god to take the king in his barge and set him upon the throne of Osiris.

It was also believed that the king mounts to heaven by the *ladder* which Ra and Horus provide for him. Among the ancient Egyptians it was believed that the sky was so close that one could climb to heaven on a ladder.

[8] "The House of The Hidden Places," W. Marsham Adams.

Sakya-muni was said to have descended from the Tushita heaven by a ladder brought to him by Indra. This ladder is often portrayed with the footprints of Buddha on the top and bottom rung.

In the mysteries of Mithra a ladder of seven steps composed of seven different kinds of metal representing the seven spheres of the planets by means of which souls ascended and descended, symbolised the passage of the soul. Small bronze ladders were placed in tombs. They were also used as amulets. The superstition that walking under a ladder brings bad luck may be a relic of this ancient superstition, typifying the sinister side, the refusal to climb, one who dodges, ignores the true way to salvation.

This is the same ladder, doubtless, of Jacob's vision showing that ideas travel if they do not multiply. *Stairs* were also a symbol of ascending to heaven. Osiris was called 'God of the Stairs.'

The Pythagoreans put it more exquisitely. They believed that the glittering motes dancing in a sunbeam were souls descending on the wings of light, and that in the same way the sun re-absorbed the souls of the dead.

Worship of the rising sun began with the dawn—"at the moment when its first rays struck the demons who invaded the earth in the darkness. . . . In temples thrice a day—at dawn, at midday and at dusk—a prayer was addressed to the heavenly source of light, the worshipper turning toward the East in the morning, towards the South at mid-day and towards the West in the evening." [9]

The Moslems still do this, and it is even now a part

[9] "Astrology and Religion among the Greeks and Romans," Franz Cumont.

of the liturgy for clergymen and priests to turn to the East when reciting the creed.

It was also and still is customary, I believe, to bury the dead so that upon the day of resurrection when graves yawn and the dead rise up they may look first to the East—to the rising sun of Light, Life, Majesty, Power.

The observance of Sunday, the day of the sun—as a day of rest and worship is also a survival of ancient solar worship.

Crowns worn by kings and emperors symbolised the sun's rays.

The sixty-five symbols on Buddha's sacred foot are nearly all solar emblems.

Amber because of its golden transparency was a symbol of the sun and is still worn as an amulet against evil and disease.

"The god of the world is in the light above the firmament and His emblems are upon earth; it is unto those that worship is paid daily."[10]

The symbols of the sun—the lotus, the winged disk, solar birds, solar animals, the scarabæus, the solar wheel have but the one purpose, that of reflecting the varying aspects of Creative Force, the multitudinous and bewildering ways in which it manifests itself—this surging, permeating, quickening, illuminating spirit of Life.

The Sphinx is a form of Horus. "Hence Horus is represented as the sphinx, whose face turned eastward is the radiant sun and whose body in the form of a lion is emblematic of his divine strength."[11]

The Sphinx with the head of a woman and the body

[10] "Maxims of Ani," now in Museum at Cairo.

[11] Goodyear's "Grammar of the Lotus."

Photo. Alinari

Sphinx with Woman's Head

(Museo Barracco, Rome)

Sekhebet

Ptah-Seker-Osiris

of a lion may have been used to symbolise the invincible power represented by the union of the masculine and feminine principles.

The lion typified the scorching, unrelenting midsummer heat of the sun. As the sun-god was believed to have the power of modifying solar heat, he is often represented, as in the Samson myth and the myths of all other solar heroes, as the slayer of the lion. Herakles of the Greeks wears the lion's skin.

The *Kara-shishi,* the Heavenly Dog, the Dog of Foo—Foo meaning Buddha is a form of lion found at the entrance to Shinto and Buddhist shrines. "They are given hideous grinning faces, curly manes and bushy, flame-like tails." They are placed in pairs before temples, palaces and tombs, the one male and the other female. The male has the mouth open, the female has the mouth closed. Usually one is green, the other blue. They are the protectors, the symbols of divine guardian-ship. Sometimes they are represented playing with the sacred ball or 'tama.' Depicted thus the Dog of Foo or lion becomes the defender of the sacred symbol.

Lions in pairs as guardians have played an immortal part in history. They have guarded the Sacred Tree, stood at door ways and before the temples of all ancient races, faced each other on the gates of cities, and with power still unabated, perform the same office of watchfulness at the entrance to large public buildings, or on monuments where courage is to be extolled even in the present day.

In the heraldic grouping of animals in Mycenæa *oxen and goats* were confined to trees or tree pillars, whereas lions were associated with altar bases or structural columns, just as in the religious art of Egypt one finds them "exclusively acting as supporters of the sun symbol on the horizon."

Layard found winged human headed lions and bulls, "magnificent figures guarding the portals of Assyrian temples" and believed that power was probably typified indiscriminately by the body of a lion or bull.

The lion seated showing whole figure was the emblem of courage; showing head and shoulders only it typified force; head only with eyes open, the lion symbolised vigilance.

The lion figures prominently in mediæval church architecture, at the doors of churches as the guardian of the sanctuary, and as a support to pulpits as in the duomos of Siena, Pisa, Ravello, Lucca and elsewhere in Italy. Its use thus being merely a time honoured extension of the historic idea. It was also given to certain saints. The symbol of St. Mark is a lion usually winged. St. Jerome also has the lion in allusion to a well known legend.

Among the ancients one cult or section identified the spirit of life or heaven with a *bull* and another with a *goat*. In Assyria the sacred bull and the wild goat are pictured together kneeling before the Tree of Life.

"The bull has always held a prominent place in the religious systems of Asia. The sacred bull of the Assyrians, the Apis of the Egyptians and the bull Nandi of the Hindus are evidently identical types. The Golden Calf of the Israelites will not be forgotten, and for the use of the bull as a sacred ornament by the Jews the brazen sea in the temple of Solomon may be cited." [12]

The bull in ancient religions symbolised the power residing in the sun. It also was a symbol of the humid

[12] Layard's "Nineveh."

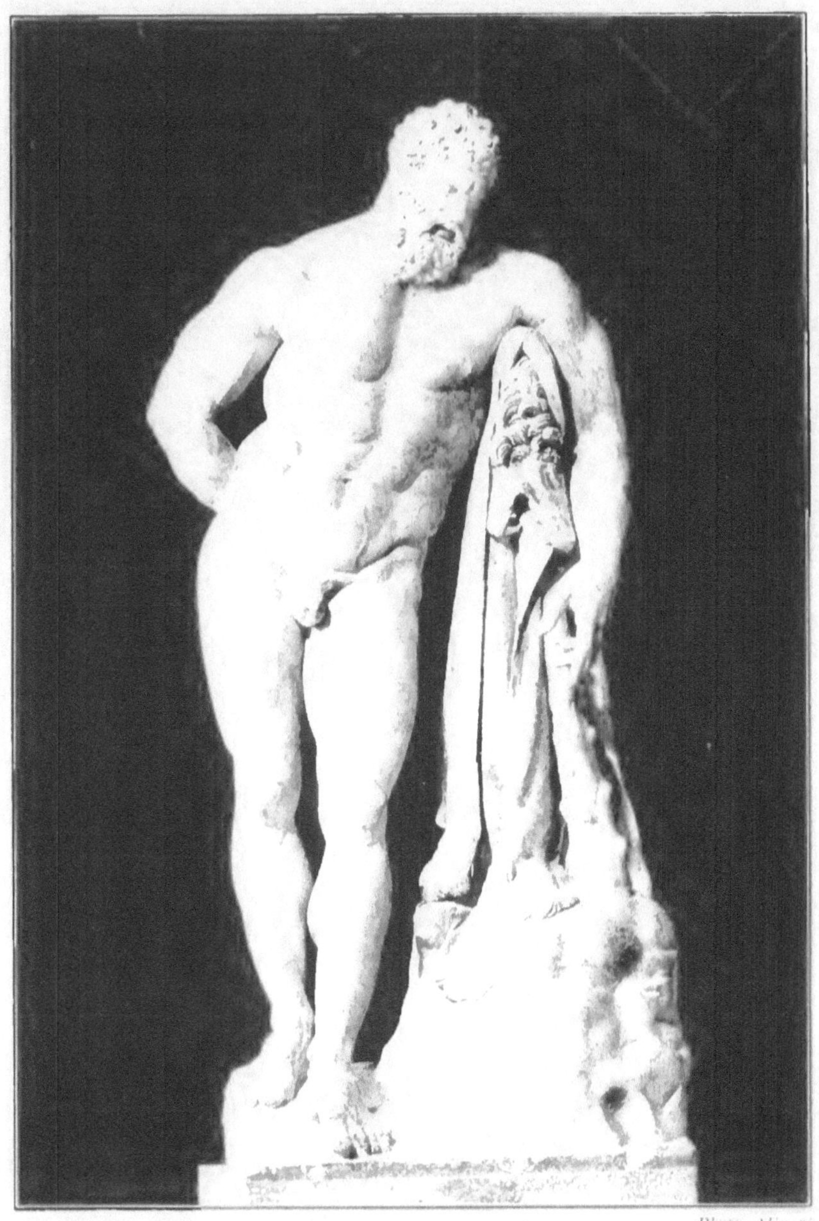

Photo. Alinari

HERAKLES (HERCULES)
(Museo Nazionale, Naples)

side of nature and was thus given to Osiris who besides being a sun-god represented also the river Nile and everything that was moist, beneficent and generative in nature.

The Bull god Apis of the Egyptians was believed to be an incarnation of Osiris, and an offspring of the sun-god Ptah of Memphis. As a symbol of creative force and reproductive powers this bull god Apis plays an enormous part in the early religious worship of the Egyptians. He was searched for, examined with meticulous care and recognised as the divine exponent by certain signs—these were a triangular mark on the forehead, a small lump shaped like a scarabæus (symbol of self-creation) under the tongue, and a mark in the form of an eagle (symbol of omnipotence) on the back.

In this reverence shown for the sacred bull there is found again that curious mixture of the ideal and the practical. Apis is also the *ox* into which the soul of Osiris enters "because that animal had been of service in the cultivation of the ground."

Osiris is identified with Dionysos, whom the Greeks not only regarded as a tree-god and god of wine but as the god of the whole humid nature. Thus the ox or bull was looked upon as an incarnation of the generative power of Dionysos by the Greeks, and the sacrifice and eating of the ox was a part of the cult of Dionysos. The sacrifice of the bull was also one of the leading features in the Mithraic rites.

The goat typified the masculine principle, the reproductive powers of the sun, "generative heat or the vital urge. Demi-urge is a gnostic term for the Deity meaning the Ever Existent Fire, the Solar en-urgy." (Bayley.)

The sacred Sumerian goat bore on its forehead the same triangular symbol as the Apis bull of Egypt.

The *Goat* is given to the Babylonian sun-god Marduk. It was the custom among the Babylonians, after having prayed to Marduk to take away from them all sin and disease, to release a goat and drive it into the desert. This resembles the Jewish scapegoat.

Tammuz as sentinel of the night heaven has the goat.

The goat in India was associated with Agni and Varuna. A goat was slain at funeral ceremonies to let the gods know that a soul was on its way to beg permission to enter heaven.

Thor, god of thunder and fertility had a chariot drawn by goats.

The Greeks gave Pan—the god of shepherds, huntsmen and all inhabitants of the country, Pan, who dwelt chiefly in Arcadia—the horns, ears, and limbs of a goat.

The Asp was identified with the solar gods and represented the hissing, seething heat of the sun. It was an Egyptian symbol of dominion. Among the Greeks it denoted protecting or benevolent power.

The creative tears of Ra, the sun-god descended as shining rays upon the earth. Osiris and Isis also wept creative tears. Kheperá, too, the father of the gods and creator of all things, identified with the rising sun and thus resurrection, was said to have gathered his members together and wept over them and "men and women sprang into existence from the tear that fell from my eye."

The god Kheperá has a beetle for his head. This is the *scarabæus* which was also called Kheperá by the Egyptians, and was a pre-eminently sacred symbol typifying the rising sun and eternal life.

The Scarabæus or Sacred Beetle symbolised divine,

Photo, Alinari

The God Apis, Serapeum (Saitic Period)

(Louvre, Paris)

Photo, Alinari

Lion of the Serapeum or Tomb of Apis

(Louvre, Paris)

self-created power. The early Egyptians believed that it had no female but deposited its generative seed in round pellets of earth which it rolled about by thrusting it backward as it moved, by means of the hind legs "and this in imitation of the sun, which while it moves from West to East turns the heaven in the opposite way." From this mysterious ball the beetle comes forth full of life after twenty-eight days of incubation by the moon. It was believed that the beetle was born anew from the egg which it alone had created, and thus it symbolised for the Egyptians self-existent being. It was so highly reverenced that the wings on the winged globe or sun disk—the sacred symbol of the deity—have been thought by some to represent the scarabæus instead of the falcon.

The Chinese regarded the sun as the concrete essence of the masculine principle and the source of all brightness.

Like the falcon, eagle and goose the *cock* is associated with the sun. The cock was sacred to Mithra, Zas and to nearly all the other solar gods of antiquity. The cock is the herald and announcer of Apollo. The Chinese symbolised the sun by a cock within a circle, and in their symbolic writings the cock is still the emblem of the sun, being frequently depicted as "clapping wings of gold while the sun rises behind him."

COCK AND LOTUS.
From Goodyear's *Grammar of the Lotus*.

The cock, the acknowledged emblem of the sun, who still loudly proclaims the rise of the God of Day, with the same assiduous watchfulness now as in the olden times, was also looked upon by the Chinese as an exorcising agency. De Groot quotes a Chinese writer as saying "The cock is the emblem of the accumulated *Yang* (the sun) and the South. Etherial things which partake of the *yang* element have the property of

COCKS ON LOTUS FACING DOUBLE LOTUS FLOWER.
Greek vase in Louvre.
From Goodyear's *Grammar of the Lotus*.

flaming up, hence when the *yang* arises above the horizon the cock crows because things of the same nature influence each other." As the spirits of darkness are identified with *yin* the passive or negative principle, the cock was used at funerals, because being imbued with *yang* matter, it would neutralise or dissipate the power of evil spirits. It was a cardinal belief also that, the spirits of darkness are put to flight each morning by the crowing of the cock.

The fish is also associated with the sun. It is one of the oldest and most widespread symbols of fertility. It also denoted knowledge, wisdom, intellect, water. In the first incarnation Vishnu returned as a fish. The fish thus becomes identified with a saviour. The fish as one of the symbols of Buddha indicated freedom—one who moves freely in all directions as a fish moves in the waters. Ea the Babylonian god of waters is typified by a goat-fish.

In early mythology the dolphin "strongest and swiftest of fish, called by Gregory of Ny-ssa 'the most royal of swimmers'" was supposed to bear the soul of the deceased across the sea to the Island of the Blessed. Thus the symbolical use of the fish on ancient tombs.

Among the Latins and Greeks the dolphin was venerated as the saviour of the shipwrecked. Thus Christ is frequently symbolised by the early Christians as a dolphin.

In the catacombs Christ is represented by two fishes. Two fishes are the zodiacal sign of Pisces. The Trinity was sometimes symbolised by three fishes typifying regeneration.

The fish because of its extraordinary fecundity was given to Venus, also to the Egyptian Isis and the Japanese Kwannon. The Christians gave it to the Virgin Mary. In the mystical *Vesica Piscis,* however, there is no reference except in name to the fish. The oval that surrounds the Virgin represents the almond, *mandorla* —symbol of virginity and self-production.

In Egypt, according to Plutarch, the fish is a phallic emblem.

It has been conjectured that the connection of the fish with the sun came from the ancient conception of creation which divided the waters above and below the firmament—the ocean and waters below the earth, and the waters of the clouds causing rain and floods above. The god of the sun passes through these as a fish, or in his sun barge.

The association of the fish, symbol of fecundity, water, the feminine principle, with the sun which typifies power, light, fire, the masculine principle, makes one suspect, however, that we are merely encountering another of the ancient devices for symbolising the union of sun and moon, fire and water, masculine and feminine. If this is the explanation of what otherwise would seem far fetched to the verge of absurdity, we are once more confronted simply enough, by that immortal combination which the ancients regarded as the inseparable accompaniment of Life.

In India "Surya is the sun seen in the sky who traverses the way prepared for him by Varuna in a car drawn by swift steeds, or flies across the sky like a great red bird, or he is the eye of Mitra and Varuna or Agni." [13]

In the Hindu pantheon Surya, the sun is shown drawn by seven horses with Aruna as charioteer. Another representation portrays the chariot of the great Aum drawn by seven *green* horses—green typifying renewal, eternal Life—preceded by Aruna the Dawn.

In Indian symbolism the *horse* is associated with the sun.

The chariot and horses of fire which bore aloft the prophet Elijah were presumably, the horses and chariot of the sun. Indra figures as 'driving a car of light and lustre.'

The *horse* symbolised knowledge, understanding, intellect, wisdom. The wooden horse introduced in the siege of Troy may have typified the conquering power of intelligence. *Four horses* denoted equity, justice. The ancients depicted the sun as a charioteer driving a team of four horses across the heavens. The chariot of Phœbus Apollo the Roman god of light and the presiding deity over poetry, music and eloquence is drawn by horses.

[13] Moore's "History of Religions."

Photo. Alinari

SPHINX (XIIITH DYNASTY)

(Louvre, Paris)

Pegasus the winged horse becomes the favourite of the muses.

Among the Greeks Neptune, god of the waters and the force and flow of life was typified by the horse which was to them "as a crested sea wave animated and bridled." Neptune (or Poseidon) is generally represented sitting in a shell-shaped chariot drawn by sea horses or dolphins, and holding his trident in his hand.

The Arabs likened the word Wisdom to a horse's bridle.

The White Horse, as we have seen under the heading of the unicorn, symbolised innocent, unblemished intellect and reason.

Buddha left his house to become an ascetic on a white horse. A white horse saves Buddha from the evil designs of the Rakshasa the cannibal demons. The white horse plays a notable part in Chinese Buddhism and is attached to all important Shinto shrines.

The Hindu Vishnu is supposed to come in one more manifestation for the salvation of the world appearing for the final time with drawn sword riding on a white horse.

The second coming of Christ on a white horse has also been prophesied.

The connection of the white horse with a saviour may explain the rather stale joke of looking for a white horse after meeting a woman with red hair, going back to the pre-historic Set, the red-haired god of destruction and the white horse as symbol of the sun, light, the Saviour.

St. John's vision of the Four Horsemen is never read without a feeling of fascinated terror.

"And I saw and behold a white horse; and he that sat on him had a bow; and a crown was given unto him;

and he went forth conquering and to conquer. . . . "And there went out another horse that was red; and power was given to him that sat thereon to take peace

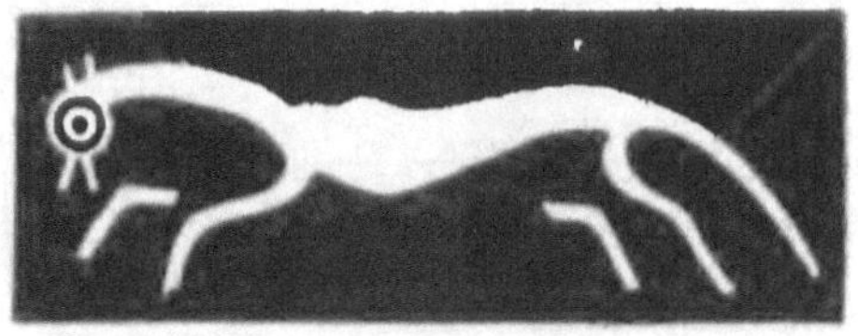

FACSIMILE OF CELEBRATED WHITE HORSE NEAR SHRIVENHAM, ENGLAND.
This same symbolic horse appeared on a British gold coin about 150 B.C.
Bayley, *Lost Language of Symbolism.*

from the earth, and that they should kill one another; and there was given unto him a great sword.

"And when he had opened the third seal. . . . I beheld and lo a black horse; and he that sat on him had a pair of balances in his hand. . . .

"And when he had opened the fourth seal. . . . I looked and behold a pale horse; and his name that sat on him was Death, and Hell followed with him. And power was given unto them over the fourth part of the earth, to kill with sword and with hunger and with death the beasts of the earth." (Rev. 6: 2-8.)

Goethe makes powerful use of this figure of Death in the Erl-King.

The enormous sale of Ibanez's *Four Horsemen of the Apocalypse* published the year of the Armistice which puzzled both critics and publishers, may possibly be explained on the hypothesis that its title appealed to some imperious, inherited instinct, touched some quivering, sensitive cord of association which for ages past had seen the Conqueror appear on a white horse, War on a red, Famine riding a black horse and Death seated on a pale horse. The one chapter on the Russian and the Four Horsemen lifted the book from the common-place and gave it its entrance into the enlarged field of universal human consciousness.

There could be no curvetting, prancing joy in the religion of life of the Hebrews. "A horse is a vain thing for safety."

The Jews worshipped the *ass.* To the Hebrew the horse typified the might and the oppression of the Egyptian and the Canaanite, while the ass by its adaptability to the needs of locomotion in a mountainous country, represented the attainment of peace and rest for the promised seed. The horse was identified with the worship of the sun, but the ass became the sacred animal of the children of Yahveh and the subject of special enactments of the Mosaic law.

Kings, judges and prophets rode on white asses.

The angel of the Lord endowed Balaam's ass with the gift of speech.

The ass was sacred to Dionysos "who is represented in many antique pictures and bas-reliefs as coming to mankind surrounded by his merry followers riding on a donkey."

Christ makes his entry into Jerusalem riding on an ass.

In mediæval times in southern France the ass or crier had a special mass in his honour, in which the congregation in place of saying amen brayed the responses.

I confess to a real affection for those patient little beasts of burden that I see so much of here in Italy—an affection so real that I know but one word for it—the donkey and I are *simpatica.* The donkey knows quite as well as his master that it is *"très difficile de contenter tout le monde et son père."* His bray says so much that I feel but cannot say. I have an inner conviction, truth to tell, that in an earlier civilisation he may have been my symbolic animal—or I the donkey. Thus I take distinct pleasure in recording here the fact, that in the Christian Church in Southern France back in mediæval days the donkey was held in such high esteem that he had a special mass celebrated in his honour.

The Wheel with its spokes of which 'none is the last' is one of the most ancient, and easily the most important symbol of the mystic power of the sun.

Anything that could be used to symbolise motion or endless creation seems to have entered into the very fibre of thought of the ancients.

The *solar wheel* is traced back to the sun disk crossed by the four cardinal points, and the development, ramifications and associations of this one symbol, which began with the circle and cross, are as mystical as they are enthralling.

"The wheel in India was connected with the title of *Chakravartin* from *Chakra* a wheel—the title meaning a supreme ruler or a universal monarch who ruled the four quarters of the world and on his coronation he had to drive his chariot or wheel to the four cardinal points to signify his conquest of them." [14]

It is related that "Buddha at his birth took seven steps towards each of the four cardinal points thus indicating the conquering of the circle or universe."

The wheel is associated with the lotus flower, the symbol of the solar matrix, the mysterious sanctuary.

[14] "The Swastika," Thomas Wilson.

The full bloom lotus with its centre surrounded by eight petals becomes the eight-spoked wheel of Buddhism. The eight spokes—or multiples of eight symbolise the eight-fold path of self conquest. The eight glorious emblems of Buddha are the lotus, fish, knot, conch-shell, umbrella, jar or sacred bowl, canopy and wheel.

Cakra or wheel in the days of the Veda typified the occult power of the sun. It represented unending, perfect completion. With the Buddhists it is the Excellent Wheel of Good Law "which turns twelve times or three revolutions for each of the four noble truths."

Buddha is the wheel king—the 'king whose wheel rolls over the whole world.'

The turning of the wheel symbolised the doctrine of perpetual cycles of existence.

Karma was called 'the wheel of fate that revolves relentlessly and unceasingly.'

The sun with rays becomes the 'thousand spoked wheel of victory.'

The Mahabharata tells of the Garuda bird's attempting to steal the Soma (ambrosia) of the gods. First the Garuda quenches the fire which protects the Soma. Then he sees a revolving wheel, "a wheel of steel, keen edged and as sharp as a razor revolving incessantly" which protects the Soma. The Eagle-giant passes through the spokes of the wheel only to encounter two great snakes of the 'lustre of blazing fire.' These the Garuda bird slays and snatches the Soma, which the gods later recover.

One of the symbols of Vishnu, who in later times superseded Varuna, the greatest of the gods of the Rig-veda, is the discus or fiery wheel which "revolves and returns to the thrower like lightning."

Among the Assyrians the solar wheel was a symbol of life and the god within the wheel not only was a god of war but of fertility. The life or spirit of the god was in the solar wheel. The spirit of Ashur, the great

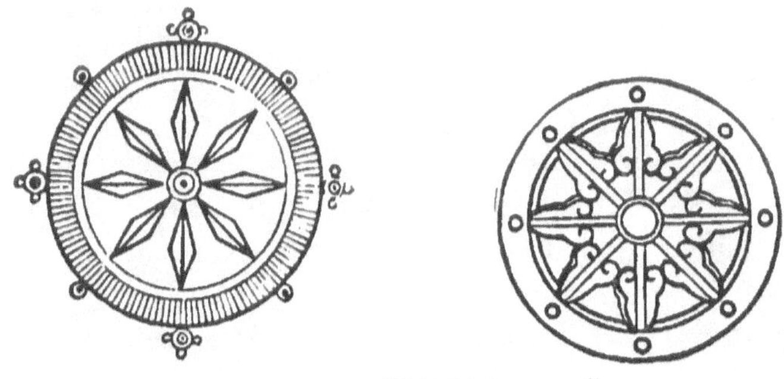

TYPES OF THE "ROUE DE LA LOI."
Gaillard, *Croix et Swastika en Chine.*

sun-god was thought to animate the wheel that brought the changing seasons.

Shamash the solar god of the Babylonians is shown seated on his throne with a sun wheel in front of him. The spokes of the wheel are shaped like stars with the three-fold rippling water rays.

The Vision of Ezekiel, so frequently quoted, testifies to the importance and prevalence of the wheel symbol. In the first chapter he describes the four living creatures that had the face of a man, the face of a lion, the face of an ox and the face of an eagle. "Their appearance was like burning coals of fire . . . and the fire was bright and out of the fire went forth lightning. And the living creatures ran and returned as the appearance of a flash of lightning . . . behold one wheel upon the earth by the living creatures with his four faces.

Photo. Alinari

THE VISION OF EZEKIEL—RAPHAEL

(Pitti Palace, Florence)

"The appearance of the wheels and their work was like unto the colour of a beryl; and they four had one likeness; and their appearance and their work was as it were a wheel in the middle of a wheel. . . . And when the living creatures went the wheels went by them; and when the living creatures were lifted up from the earth the wheels were lifted up, . . . for the spirit of the living creature was in the wheels."

And again in chapter ten in his vision of the cherubim, the Lord commands the man clothed with linen to "take fire from between the wheels."

"And when I looked behold the four wheels by the cherubim . . . one wheel by one cherub and another wheel by another cherub . . . as for their appearances they four had one likeness, as if a wheel had been in the midst of a wheel. . . . And their whole body, and their backs, and their hands and their wings, and the wheels, were full of eyes round about, even the wheels that they four had.

"As for the wheels, it was cried unto them in my hearing, O wheel." (Ez. 10:9–13.)

These are the four beasts of Revelation that were "full of eyes before and behind. . . . And the first beast was like a lion, and the second beast like a calf, and the third beast had a face like a man, and the fourth beast was like a flying eagle.

"And the four beasts had each of them six-wings about him; and they were full of eyes within; and they rest not day and night, saying, Holy, holy, holy, Lord God Almighty which was, and is, and is to come." (Rev. 4:7–8.)

These four living creatures become in the Christian religion the four conventional symbols of the four evangelists. St. Matthew is given the angel or man, St.

Mark the lion—usually with wings, St. Luke the ox, and St. John the eagle.

One can only speculate as to the origin of these four mysterious creatures. Their meaning is lost in obscurity. That there was a meaning of high import attached to them seems obvious, however.

Layard found that a man, a lion, an ox and an eagle were constantly portrayed on the sculptured walls of Nineveh.

Mackenzie points out that in an earlier stage, before the gods of Babylonia and Assyria were given human form, Nannar (Sin, the moon-god), Ninib (Saturn the old sun) and Enlil were symbolised by the bull, while Nergal a tribal sun god was given the lion. The eagle was represented by the Zu bird which symbolised storm, fertility and a phase of the sun.

In the moon cult the god Sin is depicted as an old man with flowing beard.

The Hebrews have been accused of being "a people who never invented anything, yet produced the greatest sacred literature in the world." So, too, the Hebrew prophets were greatly given to utilising "for their poetic imagery the characteristic beliefs of the peoples to whom they made direct reference." A method which resulted in a picturesque and turgid way of making a direct, telling and unanswerable appeal.

It is highly probable, therefore, that when he described the four living creatures and the wheel, Ezekiel was simply making use of Assyrian symbolism which he had seen again and again when the Jews were in captivity.

If this be the case, then there is no mystery. And we are merely encountering an ancient symbolic representation of the old forces of life—the old factors, fire and water, sun and moon, combined with the silently moving, orderly revolution of the universe, typified by the solar wheel.

The *nimbus, aureole or glory* which is used in Christian art to distinguish holy personages is derived from the solar disk which was given to emperors and kings in ancient art to express their divine origin and their association with the life and power of the sun.

The cruciform nimbus found its first inception in the wheel cross.

The rosette so extensively used in decorative art and architecture is a solar emblem derived from the lotus.

The umbrella or *parasol,* an emblem of royalty and power, universally adopted by Eastern nations, and carried over the heads of emperors and princes in times of peace and sometimes in war, is derived from the solar wheel. The umbrella is placed over the head of Buddha to signify power.

Knossos on the island of Crete was the seat of the great sun worship of the pre-historic Greek civilisation, and the legend of the Minotaur is supposed to be the mythical marriage of the sun and moon. Excavations in recent years have unearthed the palace of King Minos called the Labyrinth or 'Palace of the Axe'—from the old word *labrys* which signified axe or double axe. The *two-edged* or *Double Axe* is found throughout the palace, outlined on the walls as a religious symbol of the sun or the "power of Light."

Among the Egyptians also the axe was a symbol of the sun and was called the 'Clever One,' the 'Cleaver of the Way.' The battle axe as a symbol had the same meaning as the hammer, sword or cross.

The *sacred double axe* as a religious symbol of the sun is, however, pre-eminently associated with the island of Crete.

MYCENÆAN VASE.
Old Salamis.
Evans, *Mycenæan Trees and Pillar Cult.*

Evans finds the double axe set in the ground between pairs of bulls, the bulls having a double axe also between their horns, and adds that "the appearance of the divine double axe between two bulls and the connexion of the God of the Double Axe with the animal is shown again and again and takes us back to Crete and to the parallel associations of Zeus-Minos and the Minotaur." [15]

Curiously enough the woodsman when he marks a track through the forest with his axe still speaks of it as 'blazing a trail.' A decade or so ago a popular novel of the Michigan forests by Stewart Edward White was called *The Blazed Trail.*

It was the Chaldeans, those wise and learned men of the East—astronomers, astrologists, diviners—who de-

[15] "Mycenæan Trees and Pillar Cult," A. J. Evans.

veloped the primitive worship paid to the sun, the moon and certain stars, into a lofty system of theology in which the Sun Lord of Life held supreme sway. Sun worship was now pantheism become scientific, which saw the gods as cosmic energies. It was the "logical result of paganism steeped in erudition." Even in this new religion, however, which was to spread later to Greece and Rome, the Babylonian theology never quite broke with the primitive reverence which all the Semitic tribes bestowed upon the mysterious forces that surrounded man, and they continued to combine in their worship the old festivals of nature with the ideas derived from astrology.

Cumont quotes from Jastrow, "An astral theory of the universe is not an outcome of popular thought, but the result of a long process of speculative reasoning carried on in restricted learned circles."

When therefore the "Greeks conquered Mesopotamia under Alexander they found above a deep substratum of mythology a learned theology founded on patient astronomical observations." [16]

Although the "whole spirit of the Hellenic religion, profoundly human, ideally aesthetic . . . was opposed to the deification of celestial bodies," the belief that the heavenly bodies were divine appealed profoundly to the Greek philosophers, notably Plato and Aristotle. It influenced the stoics who in turn did much to reconcile it with popular beliefs. The Romans, who were said to know all religions while preferring none, ended by transferring their pagan worship to the skies. The Roman emperors lent it their interested support. They based their claim to divine rights upon the sun. It was believed that the monarch's soul descended from heaven

[16] "Astrology and Religion among the Greeks and Romans," F. Cumont.

by grace of the sun who bestowed upon it its own sovereign power. Among the numerous symbols of the sun, that of *Sol Invictus*, a circle with rays, was used by the Roman emperors and later adopted by Louis XIV *(Le Roi Soleil)* of France.

Even after our era the cult of Mithraism or sun worship vied with Christianity in popular favour. In 274 A.D. Aurelian created the new cult of the "Invincible Sun." A century later Diocletian officially recognised Mithra as the protector of the restored empire. The Christian emperors Constantine and Constantius were not wholly blind to the advantages of a form of worship that bestowed upon them so 'illustrious a descent.' Constantine, indeed, was strongly suspected of leanings toward Mithraism.

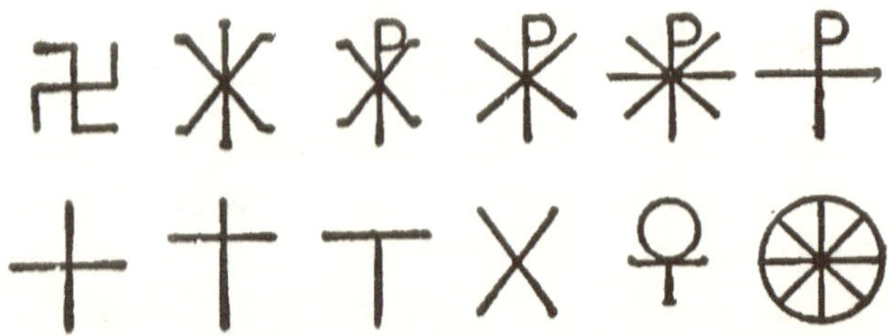

VARIOUS FORMS OF CONSTANTINE'S MONOGRAM OR CROSS.

The famous labarum of Constantine's according to Bayley "was a symbol used long ages before Christianity and probably stood for X the Great Fire and P *pater* or *Patah.*" Other writers have looked upon it in its older form as an adaptation of the solar wheel. It can hardly be denied that the various forms of Constantine's monogram or cross would indicate either catholicity of belief or religious philandering—or, perhaps one might better say, a profound respect for the great symbols of Life.

In the fourth century Julian the Apostate, the last pagan to occupy the throne of the Cæsars attempted to revive sun worship, but the growing power of the Christian religion had become too strong to be set aside. "The Invincible Sun, conquered at last passed on its sceptre to the new religion of Life."

It was not until sometime between 354 and 360 A.D. that the Church adopted the 25th of December, the birthday of Mithra and other twice-born gods, as the date of the Nativity of Christ, the new Sun of Righteousness in whom mankind saw again embodied the old, tenaciously held, mystical idea of 'Dying to Live.'

XIII

THE SWASTIKA

The Wheel is the emblem of creative motion because "Manifesting Force is rotary, being, in fact, the 'Wheel of the spirit of Life' involving the whole system of the universe."

"A constantly moving something circling about a pure central point."—Goethe.

"Repetition, being a law of the cosmos and manifesting itself in the movements of the stars and of atoms, in biology, ties of mankind—will continually occur because the Law of Series is at work."—Paul Kammerer.

"The Sun which is as a bridegroom coming out of his chamber and rejoiceth as a strong man to run a race."—Ps. 19: 4.

XIII

THE SWASTIKA

ARISTOTLE said "Life is movement." The *Swastika* with its 'bent arms poised for flight' has been saying the same since time began. Revealing also a further truth, to those with eyes to see, that all harmonious movement must necessarily spring from a central source.

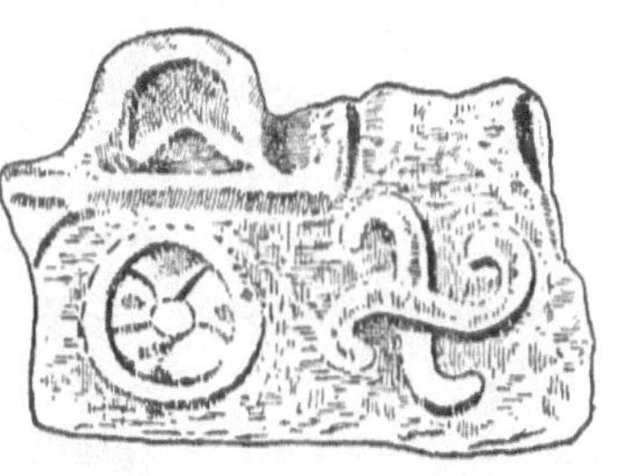

FRAGMENT OF STONE SLAB FROM THE ANCIENT MAYA CITY OF MAYAPAN.
Ogee Swastika (Tetraskelion).
Wilson, *The Swastika.*

Less awe-inspiring than some of the other life symbols, the Swastika has been looked upon from earliest times down to the present day as a charm or amulet that brings good luck, long life, fortune. It is a happy, re-assuring, friendly symbol, suggesting not movement alone, but movement that is orderly progression, movement that is planned, guided by an eternal law.

Swastika is a sanskrit word composed of *su,* good and *asti,* being, with the suffix *ka,* and is the equivalent of 'It is well,' or 'That it may be so,' or 'So be it,' implying, under no matter what circumstances, complete resignation—or perhaps acceptance is a better word for a sign that was used to denote life, movement, pleasure, happiness, good luck.

The swastika was reverenced in India more than three thousand years before the Christian era, and is still used by the Hindu women as a charm against evil. Among the Chinese it carried the idea of perfection. It stood for a great number, infinity, many blessings. It was the key to excellence. Enclosed in a circle it was the word for the sun. It was known in Japan under the name of *Mang-ziou* (the sign of 10,000 years). It is stamped on archaic vases and pottery found in India, Persia, China, Italy, Greece, Cyprus; it is found on ancient bronze ornaments in England, France, Etruria; it appears on bronze objects found in the Swiss lake dwellings and on ceintures of bronze, also on weapons and various articles of dress and ornament in Germany and Scandinavia; it is graven on sculptured stones and Celtic crosses in Ireland and Scotland, and is found in pre-historic burial grounds in Scandinavia, Mexico, Peru, Yucatan, Paraguay and the United States. It was used before the Aryans commenced their migrations, and has been called the oldest Aryan symbol. Apparently it was never adopted by the Phœnicians, Babylonians, Assyrians, or Egyptians, yet it has been found in Egypt, the inference being that it was brought there by the Greeks. Wherever it appears, like the wheel it was considered to be an image of the sun and was thus honoured. The heraldry of the Middle Ages blazoned it on shields. In modern heraldry it is given

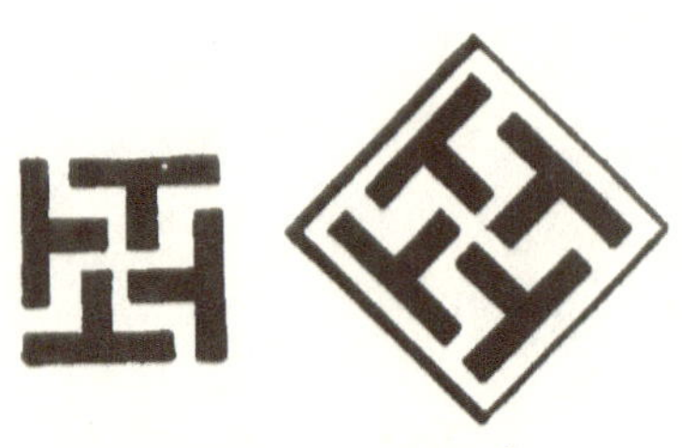

SWASTIKA OF FOUR T'S.
Gaillard, *Croix et Swastika en Chine.*

the name gammadion or *crux gammata* from its resemblance to a four-fold repetition of the Greek gamma.

It was a symbol of high religious import among both Brahmins and Buddhists. It has been called the monogram of Vishnu and Siva.

It was the cross of the Manicheans and was their sole symbol. The only form of the cross of which the Christians made any use during the second and third centuries was the swastika.

ARCHAIC GREEK VASE WITH FIVE SWASTIKAS OF FOUR DIFFERENT FORMS.
Athens.
Wilson, *The Swastika*.

In Great Britain it was called *fylfot* from the Anglo-Saxon *fower-fot*—four footed or many footed.

The symbol of Thor the Scandinavian god of thunder was a solar wheel, and his weapon the hammer. Thor's hammer has a confusing record. Some authorities call it the fylfot cross, others the *crux ansata* and others again liken it to the Chinese Y. This, perhaps, because the swastika itself has been connected with the cross, the circle and the Y.

The swastika has been given as an emblem to sun-gods, sky-gods, rain-gods; it is the sun chariot of Agni; it is found in the footprints of Buddha; it is the especial

FOOTPRINT OF BUDDHA AS CARVED ON THE AMARAVÂTI TOPE.
From Schliemann's *Ilios*.

symbol of the esoteric doctrine of Buddha; Buddha is sometimes depicted in the 'swastika posture'—with legs crossed and arms cross-wise over chest; in Japan it is the symbol of Buddha's heart and is frequently displayed on his breast. It has been given a phallic meaning by some, while others believe that it typified the generative or feminine principle, justifying their belief by its appearance on statues of various nature goddesses—Ceres, Astarte, Hera and notably upon a leaden statuette of Artemis Nana of Chaldea found at

Troy, where the swastika is shown on a triangular shaped shield. Wilson in his book on *The Swastika* cites the fact that the aboriginal women of Brazil wore a triangular shield or plaque made of terra-cotta suspended from the waist in front of the body by cords, and that one of these, which is in the U. S. Museum at Washington, is decorated with two swastikas, which he thinks "may have been a charm signifying good fortune in bearing children," and that as children were believed to be God's greatest blessing, its symbolism may well have been extended, may also have represented the desire of man to raise up 'heirs of his body' and preserve the continuity of Life. He finds that the male aborigines used a somewhat similar covering and comments upon their resemblance to the "*Ceinture de Chasteté*, specimens of which are shown privately in the Musée de Cluny at Paris and are said to have been invented by Françoise de Carara of Padua, Italy," and applied to all the women of his seraglio.

The same authority says "Of the many forms of the cross the swastika is the most ancient. Despite the theories and the speculations of students its origin is unknown. It began before history and is properly classed as pre-historic." [1]

It is not unreasonable to believe, however, that its origin may have been—doubtless was, simple enough. "Starting with the sun's disk as a circle and wishing to represent its motion sometimes they gave it wings, again they depicted it as a wheel, while motion in one direction was indicated by taking away part of the rim of the wheel leaving only sufficient to show its course. Thus came the swastika of the Hindus and the fylfot of the Northern races, one of the most

[1] "The Swastika," Thomas Wilson.

universally diffused of all the mystic emblems of sun worship." [2]

Some attribute its origin to the Hittites, while others contend that it was used in the Bronze Age which was prior to the Hittites or the Aryans.

It has always been a matter of keen conjecture how the swastika came into North America, reviving stories of the lost island of Atlantis, the lost tribes of Israel and the migration of Buddhism from Asia. Nothing is known, however, except that the swastika is there at the beginning of history, and that it was also a favourite symbol in Mexico, Peru, Yucatan and Paraguay.

Brinton in *The Taki, the Swastika and the Cross in America,* says "When the symbol of the sun and the four directions was inscribed within the circle of the visible horizon we obtain the figure representing the motions of the sun with reference to the earth as in. . . . the wheel cross, as distinguished from the ring cross."

Taking the Aztec figure of the year cycle—which is reproduced here from the Atlas of Duran's *"Historia de las Indies et Nueva España"*—Brinton traces the development and primary signification of those world-wide symbols, the square, the cross, the wheel, the circle, the swastika—the illustration of the Aztec figure shows the beginning of the latter in the elements of the broken circle—and he finds it easy to see how from this figure was derived the "Nuhuatl doctrine of the . . . Four Motions of the Sun with its accessories of the Four Ages of the World," and adds that "the Tree of Life so constantly occurring in Mayan and Mexican art is but another outgrowth of the same symbolic expression for the same ideas."

[2] "Origin of Triads and Trinities," John Newton.

The Druids were said to have shaped their trees in the form of the swastika or fylfot cross.

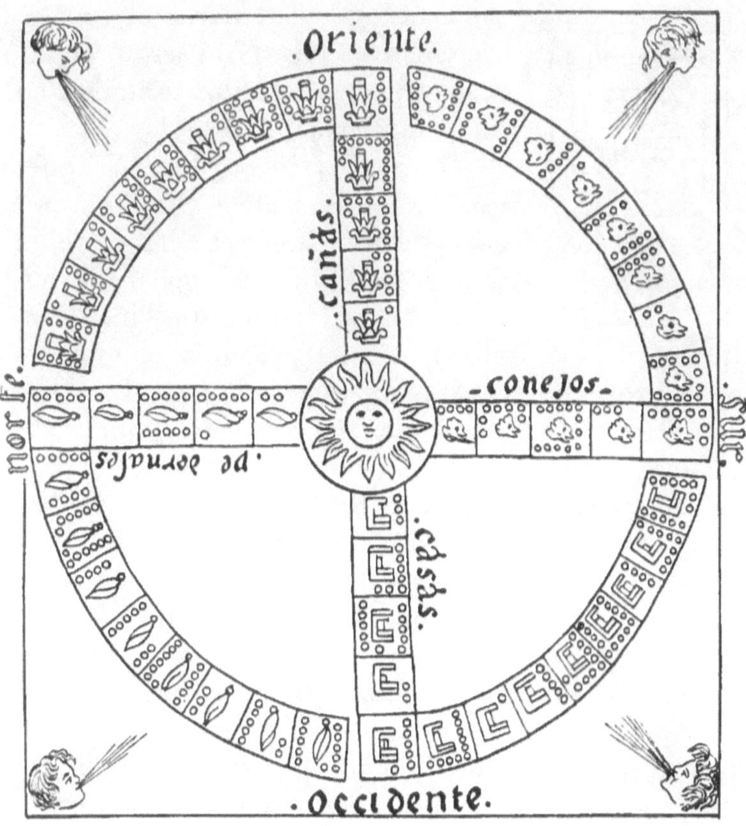

AZTEC FIGURE OF THE YEAR CYCLE.

In the opinion of Count Goblet d'Alviella no symbol has given rise to so many interpretations "not even the trisula of the Buddhists."

The figure of a swastika enclosed in a square with radiating lines for the corners has been called the seal or mark of a deified saint of the Jains of India, also a "sacred temple or edifice, a species of labyrinth, a garden of diamonds, a chain, a golden waist or shoulder belt, and a conique with spires turning to the right."

Goodyear considers the swastika the equivalent of the lotus, of the solar diagram, of the solar rosette, of the centre of the rosette, of concentric rings, of the spiral scroll, of the geometric boss, of the triangle and of the anthemion.

NANDYAVARTA.

A third sign of the footprint of Buddha.

Gaillard speaks of the *"X de fer Chinois"*—also called St. Andrew's cross—which becomes a sceptre in the hands of thunder gods, the emblem of royal power for kings, emblem of the two pillars or dual principles, and when crossed or re-duplicated becomes a sign of good omen—a variation of the swastika or the conquering sun or the *"roi de la roue."* [3]

The swastika is persistently connected with the *sacred fire sticks.* Agni was the god of the fire stick (the swastika) and it was he who was the author of divine heat which was the 'efficient cause of life both in heaven and earth.'

"The Samidhs or kindling sticks are said to represent Spring. They are to be used in lighting the sacrificial fire and are ordered to be applied to light the three enclosing sticks (*paradhi*) which are placed in the form of a triangle around the firewood. These enclosing sticks are said to be the three former Agni (fire gods) who were struck down by the thunderbolt of Indra. These gods are (1) the Lord of the Earth, (2) the Lord of the Universe, and (3) the Lord of Living Things, or, the old triad of Mother Earth, the Phallic god the Father and the vital power animating both." These enclosing sticks or fire gods are "kindled by the two *samidhs* which are the swastika or fire

[3] *"Croix et Swastika en Chine,"* Louis Gaillard.

sticks which when rubbed together produce the flame. They are said to represent the heavenly and earthly fire. With the first the priest kindles the middle enclosing stick at the base of the triangle which represents the vital and creative power which animates both the mother earth and the universal father and binds them together. He then kindles with it the fire material which the triangle encloses. He thus kindles the three former gods and the sacred central fire, the emblem of the divine power in the latent heat, the creative force of which was greater than that of the old gods. With the second *samidh,* or the earthly fire which he puts on the burning fire wood he kindles the Spring and the whole productive year. The functions of the *Samidhs* . . . clearly represent the vivifying power of heat which kindles into life the old generating gods of the popular triad, and these when they receive the requisite impulse from the animating heat kindle the earth into life in the Spring. . . . Thus the *Samidhs* are the 'productive pair' which typify the union of heaven and earth under heavenly influences." [4]

If one becomes bewildered by the number of meanings attached to this one symbol, on the other hand there is this to be said, too, that no symbol brings home more forcibly a fact that the modern is apt to overlook, and that is how much was formerly expressed by a few symbolic lines.

As we have said before, the ancients were not specialists. Their best loved symbols were as inclusive as life itself.

This marvellous symbol of motion, good fortune, long life seems to have touched everything and everywhere, vivifying whatever it touched. It is the skele-

[4] Hewitt's "Early History of Northern India."

ton symbol of the solar wheel or whirligig, its bent arms or rays indicating motion, universal movement;

THE LOTUS AND SWASTIKA WITH SOLAR GEESE AND SOLAR DEER.

Goodyear, *Grammar of the Lotus.* Pl. 38, p. 251.

it is connected with the labyrinth; it typified the four cardinal points, the pre-Christian cross, the revolution of the wheel of life; it was the representation of zigzag lightning and the double hatchet or axe; it could signify "rain, storms, lightning, sun, light, seasons;" and it could also be the fire sticks, fire wheel, sun chariot and a symbol of fecundity.

How derived, and whatever else it may have typified, the swastika stands out pre-eminently as the symbolical representation of solar energy.

Goodyear finds its solar significance proved by Hindu coins of the Jains and that it "appears with solar deer, solar antelope, the symbolic fish, the solar ibex, the solar sphinx, the solar ram and the solar horse. Its almost constant association is with the solar bird." [5]

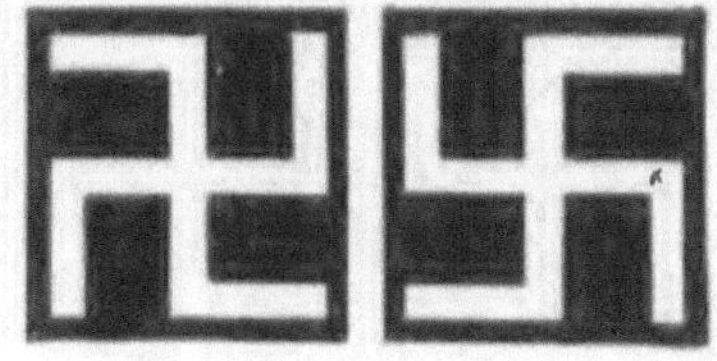

The Greeks associated the swastika with the cult of Apollo.

Max Muller believed that the swastika with hands pointing to the right was originally a symbol of the sun, perhaps the vernal sun, and he called the other with arms bent to the left the suavastika or the autumnal sun.

The Hindus are said to have given the 'right handed' swastika to the god Ganesh representing the masculine principle or light, life, glory, the sun—and the 'left handed' to the goddess Kali or the feminine principle typifying the subterranean course of the sun or darkness, death, destruction.

It is more generally conceded, however, that no distinction was intended to be expressed by the way in which the arms were bent whether to the right or left.

[5] Goodyears' "Grammar of the Lotus."

The *swastika* and the *triskelion* seem to have originated from a single symbolic idea.

"Different forms of the swastika, i.e. those to the right, left, square, ogee, curved, spiral and meander,

TETRASKELION (FOUR-ARMED.)

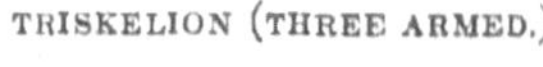

TRISKELION (THREE ARMED.)

FIVE OR MANY ARMED. OGEE SWASTIKA WITH CIRCLE.

Wilson, *The Swastika.*

triskelion and tetraskelion have been found on the same object showing their inter-relationship." [6]

The *triskelion*, a variation of these whirling symbols of the sun, is found on ancient Greek shields and Roman coins, its rays sometimes taking the form of legs, thus indicating conclusively the idea of motion, energy, victory. The triskelion proceeds apparently from the same symbolic idea of the swastika, its branches usually curved radiating from a centre on a solar face. The well known trinity of legs with bent knees has been used from the most ancient times as the arms of Sicily and the Isle of Man. The triskelion is found also in Ireland and in North America. It has many variants. Sometimes two, three or four arms or rays proceed from a central hub or dot conveying the idea of circular motion.

[6] "The Swastika," Thomas Wilson.

Perrot and Chipiez speak of the *triskelis* or *triquetra* as a name derived from three serpent's heads which "usually figure in the field much after the fashion of those supporting the famous tripod at Delphi consecrated by the Greeks to Apollo after the battle of Platæa."

SICILIAN COIN.
Waring, *Ceramic Art in Remote Ages.*

The number of heads was not constant, but the three rayed design seems to have been the more accepted form and gradually superseded the others.

It has been suggested that the swastika on Buddha's breast is the equivalent of the uræus snakes of the Egyptians "two in number and known as the winged sun."

Brinton associates the three legs diverging from a centre with the ancient *triquetrum* or *triskeles* which is seen on the oldest coins of Sicily and Lycia, Asia Minor, and also on Slavic and Teutonic vases "disinterred from mounds of the bronze age or earlier in Central and Northern Europe." The triquetrum is a figure with three straight or curved lines springing from a central point and surrounded by a circle. In the figure with curved lines he finds the "precise form of the Chinese *Tai-Ki* a symbolic figure which plays a prominent part in the mystical writing, the divination and the decorative art of China." The *Tai-Ki* is properly translated the Great Uniter. (*Ta* great, *Ki* to join together, to make one, to unite.) "As the Chinese believe in the mystic power of numbers and as that which reduces all multiplicity to unity naturally controls or is at the summit of all things, therefore the *Ta-Ki* expresses the completest and highest creative force."[7]

[7] "The Taki, the Cross and the Swastika in America," D. G. Brinton.

Yang and *yin*, heaven and earth, masculine and feminine, are thought to be 'brought into fructifying union by *Ta-Ki*.' And thus to the symbolic representation of the 'pair of opposites'—a circle divided by two arcs with opposite centres and called the Chinese monad—is added a third arc from above, the ***Ta-Ki*** which unites the two.

The *triquetrum* with three straight lines springing from a central point and surrounded by a circle is the same as the Chinese Y without the circle, a symbol of untold antiquity that conveyed precisely the same meaning of unity or productive union.

The *triquetrum* the 'three comma shaped figure' is the same as the Japanese *mitsu-tomoe* and has been associated with the ancient spiral which denoted thunder. The Chinese *triquetrums* differ somewhat from the Japanese yet the whirling motion is evident in them all.

Besides everything else the swastika was always ornamental, and from it have been developed some of

the most exquisite running and interlacing designs. You find it on old bits of pottery, or on rugs or fabrics, where it is cunningly woven into labyrinthine forms that are without beginning or end. In Italy these were called 'Solomon's Knots' and were supposed to typify divine inscrutability.

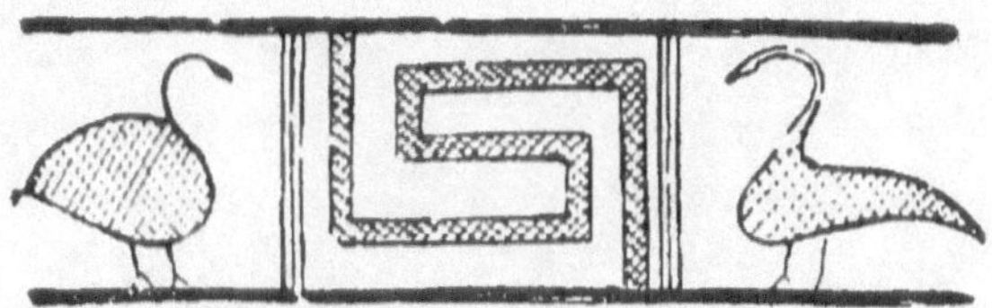

MEANDER DETAIL WITH SOLAR GEESE.
Greek "geometric" vase in the Louvre.

"It was Kipling who suggested that Bok should name his Merion home 'Swastika.' Bok asked the author what he knew about the mystic sign:

'There is a huge book (I've forgotten the name but the Smithsonian will know)' he wrote back, 'about the Swastika (pronounced Swas-ti-ka to rhyme with 'car's ticker'), in literature, art, religion, dogma, etc., I believe there are two sorts of Swastikas . . . one is bad, the other good, but which is which I know not for sure. The Hindu trader opens his yearly account books with a Swastika as an 'auspicious beginning' and all the races of the earth have used it. It's an inexhaustible subject and some man in the Smithsonian ought to be full of it. Anyhow the sign on the door or the hearth should protect you against fire and water and thieves.' "[8]

[8] "The Americanization of Edward Bok."

XIV

THE ZODIAC

"Those (literal ones) who make Bacchus wine and Vulcan flame are like men who would make cable, sail and anchor of a ship the pilot, or take yarn and web for the weaver. One who hath bought the books of Plato we say has bought Plato."—Plutarch.

"The celestial 'circle of necessity.'"

XIV

THE ZODIAC

A BABYLONIAN creation myth relates that Marduk, who brought order out of chaos, 'set all the great gods in their several stations' and created their images in the stars of the zodiac. The early astronomers of Babylonia believed that the "sun travelled from West to East along a broad path, swinging from side to side of it in the course of a year. This path is the zodiac—the celestial 'circle of necessity.' "

One can only touch upon these zodiacal symbols which are so closely inter-allied with the hours, days, weeks, months, seasons; with the gods and goddesses of light, power, fecundity, productivity, sterility, decay, death and resurrection; with the heavenly bodies and with the earth; with man's toil, and with the symbolic animals that typify the generative aspects of the sun. The attempt to connect man and his destinies with the planets as guiding forces represented a gigantesque religious conception based upon the idea of a divine cosmic law which not only influences, but unites and dominates everything that lives and moves and breathes, everything that grows or enters into decay, sometimes for good, sometimes for ill.

"At Babylon a *number* was a very different thing

from a *figure*. Just as in ancient times and, above all, in Egypt, the *name* had a magic power, and ceremonial words formed an irresistible incantation, so here the number possesses an active force, the number is a symbol, and its properties are sacred attributes."[1]

The revolving year with its recurring seasons, marked into twelve periods of time or months by the new moon, the twelve hours between sunrise and sunset,—the Chinese as well as the Babylonians divided the day of twenty-four hours into double hours believing that it bore a definite relationship to the twelve signs of the zodiac and the twelve mansions of the elliptic—the four

[1] Cumont's "Astrology and Religion."

cardinal points, the four seasons, the seven days of the week made the numbers 4, 7 and 12 for thousands of years sacred numbers of highest significance.

The Four Ages were originally the four seasons. The sun-god was associated with the Spring—the Italian *primavera* is a most lovely and expressive word for the season that brings to view once more the association of the mighty sun with the re-awakening of nature. The moon belonged to the summer, Venus presided over the autumn months and Mars was the god of winter. The Greeks, however, gave to their Aphrodite (Venus), goddess of love and beauty the month of April—*aperilis*—the opening, the germinating month.

The sun, moon and five planets became the 'sacred seven.' The five planets like sun and moon "traversed the constellations of the zodiac," and in Babylonia were identified with the great deities. "Jupiter whose golden light burns most steadily in the sky" was assigned to Marduk, Venus was one of the forms of the goddess Ishtar, Saturn fell to Ninib, Mercury to Nebo and Mars to Nergal, the god of war.

The seven days of the week belong to the "sacred seven." Sunday is the day of Mithra the sun-god. Monday (Ital. *lunedi,* Fr. *lundi*) belongs to Diana the moon goddess. Tuesday (Ital. *martedi,* Fr. *mardi*) is the day of Mars. Wednesday (Ital. *mercoledi,* Fr. *mercredi*) belongs to Mercury. Thursday (Ital. *giovedi,* Fr. *jeudi*) to Jupiter (Jove), the Teutonic Thor. Friday (Ital. *venerdi,* Fr. *vendredi*) to Venus. Friday also corresponds to the German *Freitag* the day of Fria or Freya the Teutonic goddess of love. Saturday (Ital. *sabato,* Fr. *samedi*) is the day of Saturn.

These planets were the tutelary deities, not alone of the days but of the hours, years, centuries and even the thousand of years. To each planet was ascribed a plant, a stone and a metal. These derived peculiar and miraculous powers under this benign and celestial protection.

The Babylonians gave the following colours to the sun, moon and five planets:—The Sun, gold; the Moon, silver; Jupiter, orange; Venus, yellow; Saturn, black; Mars, red; and Mercury, blue.

Later on in Greece the planets become the stars of Hermes, Aphrodite, Ares, Zeus and Kronos.

In the earliest days in Babylonia the moon was masculine and to the ancient astronomers Sin, the moon-god was a more powerful divinity than Shamash, the sun, and before the duration of the year was known, time was reckoned by the phases of the moon. The people of India also used the lunar year for ages before the solar year became the official measure of time.

"The magic idea of a power superior to man was connected from the very beginning with the notation of time."[2]

Thus the centuries, years and seasons—as related to the four winds and four cardinal points,—the twelve months presided over by the twelve signs of the zodiac, the seven days of the week, day and night, the twelve hours were all "personified and deified as being the authors of all the changes in the universe."

The hours were goddesses and the months gods. Infinity of time was exalted as the Supreme Cause.

Sacred calendars regulated religious ceremonies and civil life according to the course of the moon. These calendars were of high religious import in star worship, their most important function being to record the days and hours or periods of time which would be auspicious or inauspicious.

[2] "Astrology and Religion," Cumont.

Photo. Alinari

Ares (Mars) in Repose (after Lysippus)

(Museo Ludovisi Boncompagni, Rome)

Among the Mithraites Time was represented as a huge monster with the head of a lion to show that he

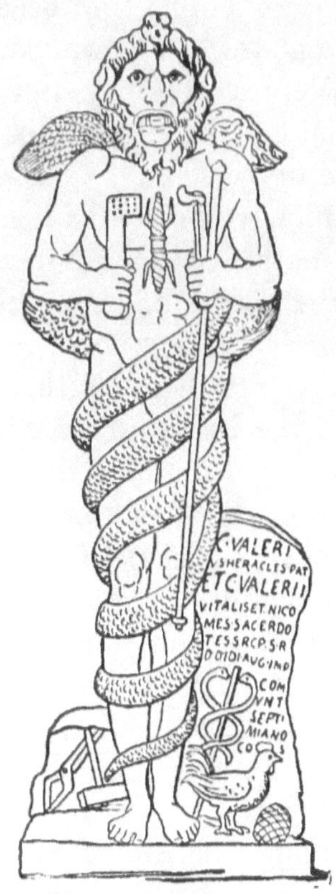

LION-HEADED FIGURE OF THE MITHRAIC KRONOS OR BOUNDLESS TIME.

The body is entwined six times by a serpent, and four wings having the symbols of the four seasons spring from the back. A thunderbolt is engraved on the breast. In the left hand is a key and in the right a key and sceptre or long rod the emblem of authority. At the foot of the statue are the hammer and tongs of Vulcan, the cock, the sacred cone and the wand of Mercury typifying that the power of all the gods is embodied in the Mithraic Suturn.

Cumont, *Mysteries of Mithra.*

devours all things. Again Time is shown helping Truth out of a cave.

Numbers were held sacred, but unlike Time and all its divisions were never deified.

The Chaldeans placed the planets in the following order, Saturn, Jupiter, Mars and the Sun, Venus, Mercury and the Moon. The Sun occupies the fourth place, having three above it, Saturn, Jupiter and Mars and three below, Venus, Mercury and the Moon. In other words, the sun has the central position among the seven circles of the universe.

This system no longer presented itself as a "learned theory taught by mathematicians but as a sacred doctrine revealed to the adepts of exotic cults which have all assumed the form of mysteries. . . . The mysteries of Mithra imported into Europe this composite theology, offspring of the intercourse between Magi and Chaldeans; and the signs of the zodiac, the symbols of the planets, the emblems of the elements appear time after time on the bas-reliefs, mosaics and paintings of their subterranean temples."[3]

Nor did this symbolism die out with the advent of Christianity but instead, was incorporated—unconsciously, perhaps, as a graphic representation of the eternal flux of life.

The worship given to the sun, moon and five planets was also extended to all the constellations of the firmament, and especially reverenced were the twelve signs of the zodiac to which were attributed a powerful influence over the life and destiny of all mankind. Each of the zodiacal signs was divided into three decans and "a god imagined for each of these thirty-six compartments." The Druids also recognised these thirty-six divisions which they called the thirty-six gates of the Great House of Heaven.

Among the Babylonians Sin, Shamash and Ishtar were the three great rulers of the zodiac. The Sun,

[3] "Astrology and Religion," Cumont.

Moon and Venus were distinguished from the other planets and Venus as the powerful Ishtar was called the 'rival of the sun and moon.'

A Latin couplet gives the names of the zodiac:—
"*Sunt Aries, Taurus, Gemini, Cancer, Leo, Virgo, Libraque, Scorpius, Arcitenus, Caper, Amphora, Pisces.*"

The symbols of the zodiac begin with the opening of spring.

1 Aries (the ram or lamb) ....Mar. 20—April 19.
2 Taurus (the bull) ....April 20—May 19.
3 Gemini (the twins) ....May 20—June 19.
4 Cancer (the crab) .... June 20—July 19.
5 Leo (the lion) ....July 20—Aug. 19.
6 Virgo (the virgin) ....Aug. 20—Sept. 19.
7 Libra (the balance) ....Sept. 20—Oct. 19.
8 Scorpio (the scorpion) .....Oct. 20—Nov. 19.
9 Arcitenus (Sagittarius the Archer) ....Nov. 20—Dec. 19.
10 Caper (Capricorn the goat) .Dec. 20—Jan. 19.
11 Amphora (Aquarius the vase or waterman) ....Jan. 20—Feb. 19.
12 Pisces (the fishes) ....Feb. 20—Mar. 19.

The sky was deified in its whole and in its parts. The two portions, light and dark, were worshipped under the form of the Dioscuri. These twins shared in turn life and death and were identified with the two hemispheres. Gemini, or Castor and Pollux are represented in the Chinese and Hindu zodiacs as a man and a woman.

To the Greek imagination the "Ram was the famous ram of the Golden Fleece . . . or it might be the ram

SIGNS OF THE ZODIAC AS GIVEN IN THE FAMOUS "ZODIAC OF DENDERA."

Now in the Bibliotèque Nationale, Paris.
Budge, *Gods of the Egyptians*. Vol. II, p. 315.

which guided the thirsty company of Bacchus to the wells of the oasis of Ammon."

Cancer the crab is called the scarab in the Egyptian zodiac.

The dolphin takes the place of Caper or Capricorn in the Chinese zodiac. It will be recalled that the Babylonian water god Ea was symbolised by a goat-fish. Both the goat and the fish are symbols of fecundity.

Volney gives an interesting interpretation of the ancient's ingenious method of generalising and transferring their ideas to everything that seemed in any way analogous. Thus the Egyptians, having noticed that the return of the inundation was constantly signalled by the appearance of a very beautiful star towards the source of the Nile, compared it with the fidelity and the watchfulness of a dog and called it 'Sirius, the dog, the barker.' In the same manner they called "stars of the crab, those which showed themselves when the sun having reached the bounds of the tropics, returned backwards and side wise like the crab or *cancer;* stars of the wild goat those when the sun having arrived at its highest altitude . . . imitated that animal who delights in climbing the highest rocks; stars of the balance those when the days and nights being of the same length, seemed to observe an equilibrium like that instrument; stars of the scorpion those which were perceptible when certain regular winds brought a burning vapour like the poison of the scorpion. . . . Thus in time those same animals which the imagination had raised to heaven descended again to earth . . . decked in the livery and invested with the attributes of stars." [4]

What was first looked upon as a talisman or har-

[4] Volney's "Ruins."

binger was later, when the original meaning was lost, adored as a fetich.

These sacred animals became symbols of power. The *ram* which figures as Aries in the zodiac, symbolis-

THE SKY WAS CONSIDERED THE ABODE OF THE GODS AND CERTAIN MYTHICAL CREATURES, WHO WERE GIVEN DEFINITE PLACES IN THE HEAVENS, AS HERE INDICATED BY STARS AND CIRCLES ON THE FIGURES.

FROM A WALL-PAINTING IN THE TOMB OF SETI I, IN THE VALLEY OF THE KINGS. DYN. XIX (ABOUT 1300 B.C.)

CHART OF THE STARS IN THE REGION OF THE NORTH POLE

(Metropolitan Museum of Art.)

ing the renewal of solar energy, creative heat, became the *celestial ram,* the deliverer, or again the lamb who sacrificed himself for the sake of the world, the one who releases the heavens from the evil and malevolent spirits, who saves the world from cold and desolation, who conquers the serpent of sin and darkness or Satan.

The *bull* like the sun was the great fecundator of nature who in the spring revives vegetation and brings back abundance. The celestial ram is the one who opens the way to renewed life, who breaks down the icy clutch of winter, and Taurus and the Sun plow the blue meadows of the heavens, signifying the eternal productive pair. The bull Apis of the Egyptians, the golden calf of the Jews, the Assyrian winged bull, the bull of the Apocalypse with wings, the bull sacrificed in the mysteries of Mithra symbolise not so much the sun itself as the companion force which unites with the sun to produce life. In ancient religions the bull typified the power residing in the sun. In the flood myth of the Mexicans the deluge was caused by the 'water sun' which suddenly discharged the moisture it had been drawing up from the earth in the form of vapour through long ages.

In the *"Recherches sur le Culte de Venus"* Lajard finds that the two principal attributes of Venus both in the Orient and the Occident are the lion and the bull. The *lion* symbolised the sun, heat, light, the active, generative power. The bull was the symbol of the humid power, the passive power. When the two animals are given together to Venus they typified the hermaphroditism of the goddess.

The symbolism of the ox, the bull and the cow was carefully differentiated. The *cow* was sacred to the Great Mother. The Egyptians gave it to Hathor and to Isis as a symbol of productivity. The cow was also worshipped by the Hindus and it is still revered in India. The ox typified strength, renunciation, patient, unremitting toil. Thus this sign of the zodiac, the bull of heaven, found its counterpart on earth in the ox who represented in the early days the spirit of agriculture, the slow, plodding labour of upturning the earth, planting the seed, releasing the powers of nature.

The zodiacal sign of Leo represented the midsummer splendour and raging heat of the sun. This sun, called 'master of double strength' by the Egyptians was represented by the hieroglyph of two lions, or sometimes two lions are seated back to back supporting the globe of the sun. Plutarch affirmed that the Egyptians honoured the lion and put lions' heads at the entrance to temples because the Nile rises when the sun enters the zodiacal sign of Leo.

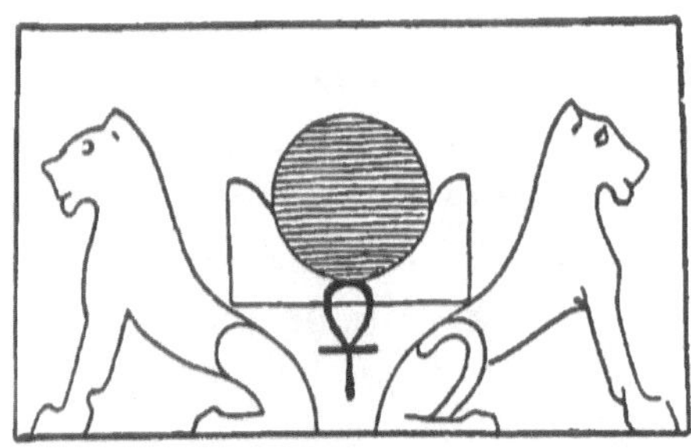

The *scorpion* was associated with drought, disease, disaster, death. It was a malignant enemy, a hurtful force, the very opposite to growth. "Their torment was as the torment of a scorpion when he striketh a man." It was believed to 'pour out his venom upon earth' causing the destruction of all things, and in the zodiac the scorpion is placed in opposition to Taurus symbolising the period of the year when winter approaches and all nature loses its productivity.

The signs of the zodiac gave immense play as well as a fixed limitation to the imagination. Innumerable stories are set going only to be arrested, kept in form by the sacred number twelve.

Many Assyriologists consider that the twelve tablets of the Izdubar (or Gilgamesh) epic were founded on the sun's passage through the twelve signs of the zodiac. The hero begins his career in Aries as a king. The ram, typifying creative energy and force thus becomes associated with kings who are called 'bell wethers or leaders—the rams of their people.' The Gilgamesh epic is the great mythological poem of Babylonia. "Like all solar deities—like the sun itself—the birth and origin of Gilgamesh is wrapped in mystery. He is,

GILGAMESH AND THE LION. SARGON'S PALACE, KHORSABAD

(Louvre, Paris)

indeed, one of the 'fatal children' like Sargon, Perseus or Arthur." [5]

The Round Table of King Arthur and his Twelve Knights typify the Sun the mighty King of Life, the round table is his disk, the twelve knights are the twelve months or twelve signs of the zodiac. Twelve is a number of tremendous importance. There are the twelve labours of Herakles who is called a solar hero—one who "never gained victories for himself"; the twelve prophets, twelve tribes of the children of Israel, twelve disciples, a jury is still composed of twelve persons.

The Odyssey is said to "reflect the myth of the sun's migrations. It is a myth changed into a saga."

[5] "Myths of Babylonia and Assyria," Mackenzie.

XV

HORNS AND THE CRESCENT MOON

"Tanūanpat or Summer, the moon god, the impulse which gives life to the three heavens, earth, air and sky is called the 'rippling one who flies through the wide heavens wetting his horns.'"—Hewitt.

"Representations of the sun by a disc or radiating face, the moon by a crescent, water by fishes or wavy lines, air by birds do not belong to any definite region or race but are common to all humanity."—D'Alviella.

XV

HORNS AND THE CRESCENT MOON

THE moon cult preceded sun worship. As we have seen the earliest germ of a creation myth represented night as parent of the day and water of the earth.

"At the beginning naught save darkness and water. The spirit of night the Great Mother and her first born the moon child."

"Out of darkness and death came light and life. Life was also motion. When the primordial waters became troubled life began to be."

One finds a close connection between moon worship, earth worship and water worship—all three representing the feminine or passive principle in nature. The moon was supposed to exercise a generative influence on nature, and the light of the moon on growing crops was believed to be more beneficial than the scorching rays of the sun. It was also thought to be the source of all moisture and that everything from the sap of plants to the blood of all beings and animals was vitalised by the water of life which the moon controlled.

So pronounced has been this age-long connection between the moon and water that even now it is not uncommon to hear the weather-wise speak of a wet moon or a dry moon, basing his dictum upon the position of the crescent moon in the skies. When a new moon ushers in rain, it is also a common saying that rain will continue until the moon changes into the next quarter.

Strangely enough although the moon is thought to have represented originally the "feminine power which gave life to mother earth and her offspring" and the moon itself is a symbol of the Celestial Mother,—and the crescent moon of virginity—the moon god was masculine.

LOTUSES AND THE MOON GOD.

Assyrian Seal.

Goodyear, *Grammar of the Lotus.*

In Egypt, Assyria and throughout most of the ancient world the moon god was called the 'father of the gods' and the 'friend of man.' The god of the moon was believed to control nature by his fertilising power causing trees and grass and crops to grow. By his mild and beneficent light he also robbed the serpent of darkness of much of his power and helped to dispel the terrors of the night.

Sin the moon-god of the Assyrians is the god of wisdom. The moon cult was associated with astrology and it is Sin who reads the signs of the heavens.

Tanūanpat the moon-god of ancient India was called self-created, "the heavenly fire, offspring of himself." Narasamsa (beloved of men) was also another name of the moon-god and both seem to have been used to typify the moon-god as summer, or the visible symbol of life-giving and productive energy which manifests itself in the warmth and glow of summer. The moon as summer becomes the uniting bond between spring the time of inception and autumn the time of garnering. The harvest moon is the moon which ripens.

According to Plutarch the Egyptians called the moon the mother of the world and believed her to have both the male and the female nature, "because she is first filled and impregnated by the sun and then herself sends forth generative principles into the air, and from thence scatters them down upon the earth."

In Babylonia as well as in Egypt opinions differed as to the origin of life. The worshippers of Ea believed that the essence of life was to be found in the liquid element. Blood was the vehicle of life and the worship of rivers and wells was connected with a wide spread belief that the blood of a god flowed in the sacred waters. Rivers were thus looked upon by the Babylonians as the "source of the life blood and the seat of the soul." In India it was common to speak of sap as the 'blood of trees.'

The idea prevailed that no remission of sins was possible without shedding of blood. It was also a cardinal belief from remotest times that inspiration—a fresh access of life was derived from drinking blood or fermented liquors made from the 'blood of grapes' or the sap of plants.

The custom of drinking was originally a highly ceremonious function of a deeply religious character. In the East water was vitalised by the sacred juice of the Soma plant which filled with religious fervour and ecstasy the hearts of those who drank of the precious liquid. Thus "He that . . . drinketh my blood, dwelleth in me and I in him" perpetuates, gives living assurance to an ancient belief founded on nature worship or the worship of life. Nor need one doubt that the devout believer in Jesus Christ assimilates the characteristics of Christ—which were all spiritual—when he partakes of the symbolic bread and wine. Nor is it any reproach that the Church has merely given new meaning, lifted to the higher needs of the soul a form of religious worship as old as man himself.

In the vibration of religious thought which gave supremacy first to the moon and then to the sun, Mackenzie thinks it possible that the belief obtained "even among the water worshippers of Eridu that the sun and moon which rose from the primordial deep had their origin in the everlasting fire in Ea's domain at the bottom of the sea. In the Indian god Varuna's ocean home an 'Asura fire' (demon fire) burned constantly; it was bound and confined but could not be extinguished. Fed by water, this fire it was believed would burst forth in the last day and consume the universe. A similar belief can be traced in Teutonic mythology." [1]

Here again one finds the intimate, mystical, yet highly practical association between fire and water, and always the unquenchable desire to discover the origination of life. Is it to be found in the 'everlasting fire at the bottom of Ea's domain' which at the last day bursts forth and consumes the universe?

Speaking generally one could almost say even now that the world divides itself between the sun worshippers and the water worshippers—those who sit by the tranquil stream of life and those who exult in the heat and fury of it. And always the few Great Adepts who, standing above passion and desire, see that sun without water and water without sun are destructive forces. One scorches from intensity until it dries up the springs of action. The other drenches with the sentimental, the meaningless until force and energy evaporate.

The *moon* was called the 'Awakener and Assembler of the stars.'

[1] "Myths of Babylonia and Assyria," Mackenzie.

Photo. Alinari

Artemis (Diana)
(Vatican, Rome)

The moon attended by stars is still perpetuated in the arms of Turkey and Egypt. The former has the crescent with one star and the latter the crescent and three stars.

"All over Europe rays of the sun and the crescent moon seem to have typified horns. Pan had pyramidal horns tapering from earth to heaven, Moses was represented with horns or two shafts of light springing from his forehead. Thus horns were a symbol of light. The branching antlers of the buck were likened to the rising of the sun." [2]

The moon god Sin was depicted as an old man with flowing beard. Upon his head was a cap with the horns of the moon.

A *cap with upturned horns* symbolised divine power.

The winged figures of Assyria are depicted wearing the horned cap.

Horns typified the 'call of the spirit.'

Horns as a symbol of divinity and power go back to the moon cult.

In Egypt Khensu, who was associated with Amen-Ra and Mut in the Theban triad, was the god of the moon and was portrayed with the head of a hawk surmounted by the lunar disk and crescent. The Egyptian goddess Hathor the "ubiquitous, universal mother" is given the head of a vulture surmounted by a disk and horns.

Thoth, the scribe of the gods and the measurer of time is also in one aspect the god of the moon and is given the head of an ibis and above it rests the crescent.

The *crescent moon* was also given to Isis, Ishtar, Diana and the Virgin Mary.

[2] Bayley's "Lost Language of Symbolism."

"All people have understood the horns to be a symbol of power. The Israelites were, of course, quite familiar with horns upon the heads of the gods of Egypt, and fresh from the land of bondage they would readily believe that their great law giver had become divine, that he had miraculously received the mark of divinity and of kingly power. The belief that Moses actually descended with solid horns upon his head was devoutly held and has continued to be believed down to the Middle Ages." [3]

The crescent was given the name of the horned moon. Later the symbolism was developed realistically and the horns of animals were used. The horns of the bull or cow typified honour, power. Those of the ram or goat signified fecundity, fertility.

In the early Minoan worship the "horns of consecration" occupy a prominent position along with the other religious symbols such as trees, stones, pillars, cones and the double axe.

On a painted sarcophagus from Hagia Triada now in the Metropolitan Museum of New York and which is estimated to date from the Late Minoan II or the beginning of the Late Minoan III period, or about 1400 B.C., there are scenes depicted representing funerary rites. On one side, among other figures, a woman is shown pouring a libation into a large vase which stands between two posts or pillars surmounted by double axes and sacred birds. On the other side is an altar upon which are placed the "horns of consecration" and a pillar which is also surmounted by the sacred double axe and the sacred bird—the customary Cretan symbols of life.

A. J. Evans considers that the Mycenæan "horns

[3] "Horns of Honour," F. T. Elworthy.

Dove Shrine in Gold with Four Horns on Top and the Columns in the Three Openings Springing from the "Horns of Consecration"

(Schliemann, *Mycenæ*)

of consecration" suggest the horns of the altar of the Hebrew ritual, and that this may relate to the sacrificial oxen whose horns were set upon the altar as a part of the ritual of primitive worship, "but it is more likely to have been derived from Egypt and to represent the lunar cult—the horns of the crescent moon."

He finds that the "horns of consecration" are of a portable nature, they are superimposed on the summit of the 'dove shrines' of Mycenæa, surmount archways, are found at the foot of sacred trees as well as on the roof of shrines and are equally associated with sacred pillars. He adds that "this distinctive piece of Mycenæan ritual furniture" occupies the same position in relation to the double axe that it does to the tree and pillar form of divinity indicating that the double axe also represented the indwelling place of a divinity. He also makes the interesting suggestion that the double axe was more than a symbol of the sun—that it represented the "conjunction of the divine pair—a solar and lunar deity."[4]

The illustrations on pages 84 and 254 of lion supporters of the Egyptian solar disk shows the conventionalised sacred horns of the crescent moon.

The emblem came to be regarded as in itself powerful and was used as a badge of victory, of royal dignity. The crest and the *panache* of heraldry and the plume of modern days were used originally to convey the same idea of strength, power, triumph that the ancients expressed by horns on the head.

> "Soon as Aurora drives away the night
> And edges eastern clouds with rosy light,

[4] "Mycenæan Trees and Pillar Cult," A. J. Evans.

> The healthy huntsman with the cheerful horn
> Summons the dogs, and greets the dappled morn."

The horn of Diana was an emblem of the chase as well as typifying the moon-goddess.

Horns in all ages were a symbol of luck. They were looked upon as protective amulets and were placed on tombs and over doorways of houses to ward off the evil influences of the unseen.

Horns over doorways may still be seen in the vicinity of Sorrento showing that this ancient belief in the efficacy of horns obtains in certain parts of Italy even to this day.

The Italians, also, to protect themselves against a person suspected of bringing the *iettatura*—bad luck, misfortune, one who was possessed of the *mal occhio,* the evil eye, employed the *mano cornuta*—the middle fingers closed and the fore and little fingers thrust out like horns. Nor was the use of the *mano cornuta* wholly confined to Italy. The same gesture was also resorted to as a protection against evil forces in England and the north countries.

The Italian of today will admit half laughingly to the gesture, although professing not to believe in it. It is a matter of instinct now, done secretly with the hand at the side, in order not to mortify the person under suspicion.

Some of us still avoid walking under ladders. Some of us are inexplicably comforted for a moment when, glancing up at the sky, we see the crescent moon, the new little moon, over the right shoulder for good luck, and are, in spite of all reason, a bit cast down when we have the bad fortune to see it for the first time over the left.

The *cornucopia* or *Horn of Plenty,* a horn in which are displayed flowers and various fruits, symbolised peace and prosperity, and was associated in Greek art with the great nature goddesses and the gods of vegetation and the vintage.

The cornucopia is the equivalent of the *calabash* or *gourd* which the Chinese placed on a tripod as a symbol of blessing and fertility. The calabash typified the creative power of nature. Druggists kept medicines in gourd shaped bottles. For the same reason the Elixir of Life was stored in a calabash.

According to Frazer the South Slavonian peasant crowns the horns of his cows with wreaths of flowers on St. George's day—the 23rd of April—in order to guard the cattle against witchcraft.

XVI

THE TRISULA

"The plasticity of the Trisula is only equalled by its power of absorption. It borrows from the vegetable kingdom as well as from man and the moon and the sun or flames."—D'Alviella.

"Throughout the symbology of Egypt life was the centre, the circumference, the totality of good. Life was the sceptre in the hand of Amon; life was the 'richest gift of Osiris.' 'Be not ungrateful to thy Creator' says the sage Ptah-Hotep, in what is perhaps the oldest document in existence, 'for he has given thee life.'"—W. Marsham Adams.

"Tranquillity according to His essence, activity according to His nature; perfect stillness, perfect fecundity, this is the two-fold character of the Absolute."—Ruysbroeck.

XVI

THE TRISULA

THE *trisula* (*tri*-three, *sula*-point,) and the thunderbolt are forms of the trident.

Like the swastika the ramifications of the trisula are almost endless. It has "alternately been considered to be an equivalent of the thunderbolt, a form of the Sacred Tree, a contraction of the scarab, a combination of the solar globe and crescent, connected with horns—symbolical of divine power—and the Asherah stake entwined with bandelets." [1]

There is a strong resemblance between the trisula and the conventionalised *fleur de lis.* Sceptres in the West were frequently surmounted by the *fleur de lis* or flower of light, an ancient emblem of the Trinity or three in one.

The trisula has been called the caduceus of India.

The original form of the caduceus—a rod or the sacred tau surmounted by a circle or disk upon which rests a crescent—is significant. The classic form a winged rod encircled by two serpents is thought by some to have been used by the Greeks to symbolise the combination of the two forces, or hermaphroditism.

In some places the trisula seems to represent the "Siviat emblem of the *lingam* between two serpents."

[1] "The Migration of Symbols," D'Alviella.

The *linga* is the flame in the lotus or the form in which Adi-Buddha manifested himself at the beginning of the world. The flame symbol is also seen issuing from the centre of a moon crescent indicating the union of fire and water or the active and passive principles.

"*Vajrasattva* in some of the Nepalese writings is identified with the first Buddha who manifested himself on Mt. Sumeru in the following manner. A lotus flower of precious jewels appeared on the summit of Mt. Sumeru which is the centre of the universe and above it arose a moon crescent upon which supremely exalted was seated *Vajrasattva*. It is not probable that the image of the god is here meant but the *symbol* which designated him, a linga-shaped flame. If the moon crescent which arose above the lotus flower is represented with the flame symbol in the centre instead of the image, it forms a trident." [2]

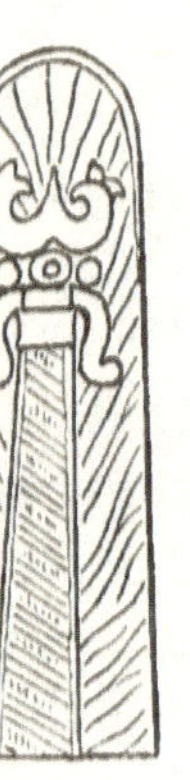

THE MONOGRAM OF BUDDHA.

The trisula placed upon a pillar surmounted by flames is the monogram of Buddha. It is also the emblem of the Tri-ratna or Three Jewels.

The Assyrian gods are represented holding the trisula or trident with zigzag shaped points to typify lightning.

The *Sacred Trident* is an ancient symbol of the heavenly triad. Thus the trident of Poseidon (Neptune) may have symbolised the third place the sea holds after heaven and air, but it is also here a "sceptre endowed with marvellous power."

In Egypt the trident or trisula is associated with the winged globe.

[2] "The Gods of Northern Buddhism," Getty.

Photo. Alinari

Poseidon (Neptune)

(Lateran, Rome)

As the *vajra*—"diamond or that which is indestructible"—usually translated *thunderbolt*, the trisula becomes the 'sceptre of diamonds' of Indra the storm god.

The *trisula* is one of the principal symbols of Siva, who is generally represented with a sceptre in his hand surmounted by a trisula. In the temples of Siva the trisula was placed, not above the entrance, but on the *sikhara* or spire where it is still to be found to this day.

In Buddhism the trisula is given a prominent place along with the stupa, the Sacred Tree of Life, the swastika and the 'Excellent Wheel of Good Law.'

The symbol was given a high place in the worship of Vishnu, and signified male and female, or Rama or Sita. It was combined of the two colors white and red, the outer and lower parts white and the central line red.

The thunderbolts given to Zeus with forked lightning projecting from either side bear a strong resemblance to the trisula.

The *vajra* or *thunderbolt* has sometimes been likened to the discus, the weapon of Vishnu. As both the *vajra* and the discus, like the celestial two-headed mallet or the double hammer of Thor were weapons of the gods, symbolising lightning, rain and thus life and fertility they are probably only variant symbols of divine power.

"The discus of Vishnu goes by the name of *chakra* and although not represented as a wheel it is doubtless the same symbol. . . . Viswakarma like the Greek Hephæstos the architect or artificer of the gods was said to have formed the discus of Vishnu, the trisula of Siva and the *vajra* or thunderbolt of Indra, making them from parings of Surya the sun which he put in a lathe and turned. Here we get the solar origin." [3]

Buddha is believed to have wrested the *vajra* from Indra changing the symbol by closing the points of the dart.

The *vajra* is a sceptre as well as a weapon in the hands of the thunder gods. It is a symbol of royal power for kings and an emblem of the two pillars or dual principles.

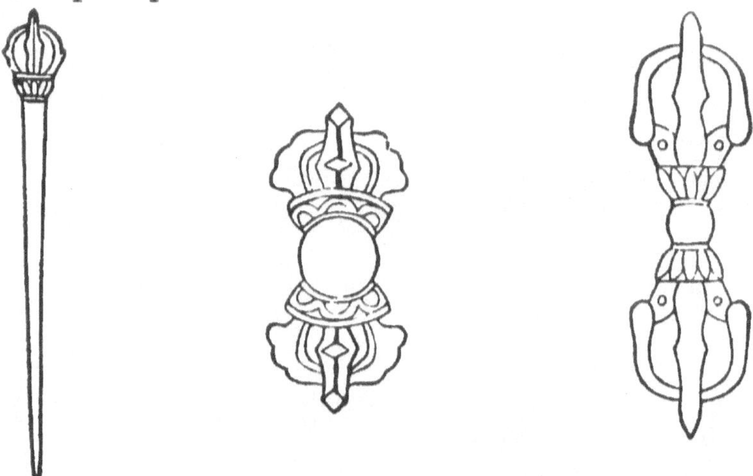

SCEPTRE AND DIFFERENT FORMS OF THE DORJÉ.

The Lamas of Thibet have a small sceptre about six inches long with a trident at each end. It is made of brass and called the *dorjé*. Occasionally the ends are composed of two or four tridents arranged like a "whorl."

The gods of Mesopotamia carried a double trident.

The *Surya* (sun or sun disk) surmounted by a trident is called *surya-mani* or sun jewel. Issuing from the lotus it represents Adi-Buddha at the creation of the world.

[3] "The Trisula Symbol," William Simpson.

D'Alviella considers that this emblem—the trident on the wheel—is its most rational form and that it represents a flash of lightning, is the image of a three tongued flame and when coupled with the disk is a symbol of fire or solar radiation.

Simpson, on the other hand, does not believe that it was originally connected with the wheel. He classifies it as an universal symbol and one of the most important of the ancient world—a symbol so ancient and so widespread that its first origin has been lost. "That the trisula is a development of solar and lunar forms as symbols of creative power, would explain its universal application." This, he believes is the most tenable explanation of its sacred character—that it grew out of a combination of solar and lunar symbols. "These two symbols representing the dual creative or re-creative power of the universe—the power which continues all life both animal and vegetable—their conjunction became a fit emblem of the divine energy which preserves and rules. It expressed the power which produced the cosmos out of chaos." [4]

According to Plutarch the trisula typified the idea of Being—the Eternal and Ever Living as opposed to the constant change, the alternate death and resurrection of nature.

Thus it was a symbol of life not only in its inception but in its continuance—it not only symbolised the mystery of life but was the emblem of Life Everlasting. With this interpretation of the trisula in its sceptre form the sceptre ceases to be a meaningless adjunct of royalty and becomes instead a high and potent symbol of creation, power, life.

In its sceptre form the trisula has been associated

[4] "The Trisula Symbol," William Simpson.

with the pillar with a globular break in the middle and two uræus serpents curving up on either side. This symbol is seen frequently in the hands of the Babylonian Ishtar. These pillars with the break were sometimes double cones, but the meaning is always the same and typified the dual cult. "In the primal principle this duality was considered androgynous or bi-sexual." The divided column or sceptre thus expressed the ancient Semitic conception of a bi-sexual god-head.

1. EGYPTIAN URÆUS PILLAR. 2 and 3. CYPRO-MYCENÆAN COMPARISONS. 4. DUAL URÆUS STAFF OF ISHTAR.
Evans, *Mycenæan Trees and Pillar Cult.*

"The Babylonian religion shared the trait so common in all Semitic cults of the combination of the male and female principles in the personification of the powers that controlled the fate of man." (Jastrow.)

In its trisula form it is supposed to have been derived from the juxtaposition of the solar emblem or flame within the crescent and thus also is the equivalent of the "old androgynous notion . . . which was simply a personification of creative power."

The Assyrians frequently represented the disk of Shamash the sun-god within the crescent, "Sin the moon-god of the Assyrians was depicted standing in the centre of the crescent. The old legend of the 'man in the moon' placed there as a punishment for gathering sticks on Sunday gains new significance. The golden hand of the sun resting in a crescent becomes a form closely approximating the trisula." [5]

The trisula was used as an amulet or charm, and like the lotus, *fleur de lis* and swastika was also used as a decorative motif.

[5] Simpson's "The Trisula Symbol."

XVII

FATHER GODS AND MOTHER GODDESSES

"The gods might die annually. The goddesses alone were immortal."

"The unnamable beginning of heaven and earth, the namable mother of all things."

"There must be in every centre of humanity one human being upon a larger plan, one who does not 'give her best' but gives her all."—Chesterton.

"God made man and man returned the compliment."—Voltaire.

XVII

FATHER GODS AND MOTHER GODDESSES

CLOSELY interwoven with the dual conception of sun and moon, fire and water, light and darkness, which were personified by various gods, is found "another and more philosophical duality representing the male and female principles."

Wherever the sun cult prevailed there were also goddesses who represented the Great Mother Earth.

"The earth bringing forth its infinite vegetation was regarded as the female principle rendered fruitful by the beneficent rays of the sun. 'Dust thou art and unto dust thou shalt return' illustrates the extension of this analogy to human life which in ancient myths is likewise represented as springing into existence from mother earth." [1]

The Mediterranean races, the neolithic tribes of Sumeria, Arabia and Europe whose early religion had not yet taken the form of temple worship but was a part of their daily life, made worship of the mother goddess the predominant part of their religion.

Worship of the Great Earth Mother was one of the most prominent features of the Babylonian religion. The Egyptians reverenced and exalted motherhood both in religious and social life. Among all the Semit-

[1] Jastrow's "Religious Belief in Babylonia and Assyria."

ic races the Great Goddess—Virgin and Mother, seems to have been looked upon as the dispensing agency of life, prolific and wasteful or destructive by turns—a force accurately reflecting nature "under her two-fold aspect of cruel and beneficent." Wherever the Semites settled this conception of the Great Mother as the symbol of the Earth is found to exist and to enter largely into all the sacred rites and rituals of their religion.

The Aryans and the Germanic tribes were *father worshippers.* Indeed, among all the wandering tribes, wherever life was rugged and hard, wherever the prowess of the male had to be relied upon to obtain the food supply, the masculine gods of force and strength were exalted, and the foremost deity of the pantheon was the Great Father, the Baal, the 'lord of heaven.' He was Rammon, 'the Rimmon of the Bible,' a hammer god imported by the Semites from the hills. He was Indra, Thor, Jupiter, Tarku and other gods of the sky. He was a god of rain, thunder, fertility and war who finally takes on solar attributes. Yet, when in the shift of political power the god fell or was displaced, 'The Great Mother lived on, being the goddess of the land.'

And when on the other hand the worshippers of Father gods appeared as conquerors, having invaded the kingdoms of Mother worshipping races and set up their gods to be worshipped, they found themselves powerless to dispossess the Mother goddesses. "The Aryan Hellenes were able to plant their Zeus and Poseidon on the high hill of Athens but could not overthrow the supremacy of Athena."

In Egypt the land of ancient mother deities the primeval deities appear to have been grouped in four

Photo. Alinari

Zeus (Jupiter)

(Vatican, Rome)

pairs symbolising the reciprocal principles of nature. This seems to have been the case also in Babylonia. The female in the first pair was more strongly individualised than the male.

The typical Great Mother was a virgin goddess self-created and self-sustaining. She represented the feminine principle and her fatherless son the masculine principle. Her associations varied in different localities. In one it was the earth, in another the sky and again water. She was worshipped as the World Mother, the 'giver of all good things,' the 'Preserver' and also the 'Destroyer.' It was a cardinal belief among the ancients that the Great Mother of the Universe was undecaying, eternal.

While recognising the male, the mother worshippers reverenced the Great Mother as First Cause, and women held a high social status wherever the goddess was worshipped. Whenever also the political power of her worshippers became extensive the attributes of the Great Mother grew correspondingly. She became the Great Lady. Her power was felt and worshipped in all the relations of life. "Not a few of the Pharaohs reigned as husbands or sons of royal ladies." Among the Hittites also succession to the throne was regulated by female descent.

The most universal and sacred symbol—the symbol *par excellence* of the feminine principle is the *Ark*.

The *ark* represented the Holy of holies, the consecrated receptacle of life and was one of the most important symbols in the religious rites and ceremonies of the ancients. The ark of the Egyptians held the symbols of the creative forces of life, the phallus, typifying the sun, the masculine principle, the active creator; the egg, symbol of the preserver, the passive or feminine principle; and the serpent, symbolising the destroyer or the reproducer. This ark, the sanctified repository of the divine symbols of life was the most sacred of all images connected with the worship of Osiris.

"The evidence which connects ships and Mother worshippers most closely together is the great reverence paid to the sacred ark—the *Din* or *Christa,* the receptacle of the law which was no less sacred to the Zoroastrians than to the Jew. This sacred ark . . . was originally among the Sumerians of the Euphrates valley the ship of the gods in which they were carried in procession." [2]

The *Cista* is the mystic chest in which were kept the various symbolic images of life used in the mysteries of Dionysos and Demeter.

The word ark is Egyptian, meaning a covered chest or box.

The arks of the Old Testament are Noah's ark in which the righteous were saved, the ark in which Moses was hidden and the Ark of the Covenant.

The finding of Moses has been likened to the finding of Sargon. The bulrushes are identified with the papyrus, used probably by the mother of Moses because the plant being sacred to Isis would protect the child from crocodiles. Isis was said to have concealed her son Horus among the papyrus plants so that he might not be found and destroyed by Set. In the legend Isis when searching for the scattered portions of her husband's body "makes use of a boat made of the reed papyrus in order the more easily to pass through the lower and fenny parts of the country. For which reason say they, the crocodile never touches any persons

[2] Hewitt's "Early History of Northern India."

who sail in this sort of a vessel, as either fearing the anger of the goddess, or else respecting it on account of its once having carried her." (Plutarch.)

The Egyptians still believe that the papyrus plant is a protection against crocodiles.

"The *Ark of the Covenant* was a chest (not a boat) made of shittim wood overlaid with gold, on the lid of which was placed the golden 'mercy seat' over which two cherubim extended their wings." In it were placed and preserved the two tables of stone on which was engraved the Covenant between God and His people. It contained also by divine command an omer of manna, Aaron's rod which sprang into life and budded, and the books of the Law.

This Jewish ark of the covenant bears a close resemblance to the sacred ark of the Egyptians and as a feature in the religious life and worship of the Israelites its importance and the reverence it inspired can hardly be overstated.

Among all ancient races the ark was a symbol of salvation, its preservation implied safety, sanctifying the nation who honoured it as the abiding place of divine wisdom and power.

The Great Mother, goddess of nature and fertility was worshipped under many names. In Egypt Mut was the Universal Mother who represented 'Nature the mother of all things.' Neith was the Libyan Great Mother and was goddess of the earth. Nut was goddess of the sky. Hathor represented the feminine principle in nature and was called 'Hathor of Thebes,' 'lady of the Sycamore' 'mistress of the gods.' These goddesses are depicted holding the *crux ansata* in one hand and the sceptre in the other. Hathor, as goddess of maternity, is given the head of a vulture surmounted by the moon crescent or horns, and the solar disk. Again she is represented as a cow. Bast another Egyptian goddess was given the head of a cat, Nazit was a serpent goddess, Hekt a frog. (The frog was an Egyptian symbol of fertility and abundance).

In time all these sacred animals were associated with the great Egyptian goddess Isis who absorbed the attributes of the other goddesses who were looked upon as her manifestations.

Ishtar was the great nature goddess of the Babylonians. At Comana in Pontus the Great Mother was known as the goddess Ma a name which may have been as old as the Sumerian *Mama* (the creatrix) or *Mamitum* (goddess of destiny). Anaitis was the Great Mother of Armenia. Ate of Cilicia, Artemis (Diana) of Ephesus, Astarte of the Phœnicians with her great sanctuary at Byblus and who is a form of Ishtar and identical with the biblical Ashtoreth are all nature goddesses. The worship of Aphrodite among the Greeks is said to have originated in Cyprus where traces of the Astarte cult are found. Atargatis was the Syrian Astarte of Hierapolis. The Phrygian Cybele, the Mother of the Gods, was the great Asiatic goddess of fertility.

In Crete the chief divinity was a great nature goddess generally known as Ariadne. She was a serpent goddess and is usually depicted holding snakes at arms length or with serpents coiled about her. In Asia Minor the Great Mother goddess is associated with a lioness. Among the gods and goddesses worshipped in the Babylonian temples Layard identifies Rhea and Hera as part of a triad whose statues were of beaten gold. Rhea seated on a chair of gold had two lions

Photo. Alinari

Artemis (Diana) of Ephesus
(Lateran, Rome)

at her side, and near her were large silver serpents. Hera stands erect holding a serpent by the head in her right hand and a sceptre studded with precious stones in her left. "In the rock tablets of Pterium she is represented standing erect on a lion and crowned with a tower or mural coronet which we learn from Lucian was peculiar to the Semitic figure of the goddess. To the Shemites she was known as Astarte, Ashtoreth, Mylitta and Alitta." [3]

Mylitta is the Assyrian Venus.

Venus in Cyprus was known as 'my lady of Trees and Doves.' The Scandanavian Freya like the Egyptian goddess Bast was associated with the cat, her car was drawn by cats. "All feline goddesses represented the variable power of the sun."

Cybele the mother goddess of Phrygia is best known as the mother of Attis who is associated with Osiris, Mithra, Dionysos, Adonis, Tammuz and other twice born gods of vegetation, while Cybele is simply another form of Aphrodite, Ishtar and Isis.

The two distinct kinds of Supreme deities, the Great Father and the Great Mother and her son, was an early conception developed and adhered to tenaciously by peoples of widely divergent origin and totally different habits of life. In Egypt finally, under a highly centralised government, these opposing worships were merged and ultimately brought about a fusion of religious beliefs which in turn developed into a highly complex and very fascinating mythology. The Great Father then became the husband of the Great Mother, or the son-god was worshipped as the 'husband of his mother.' Isis was mother, wife and sister to Osiris, Ishtar mother and wife to Tammuz, Aphrodite is

[3] Layard's "Nineveh."

mother and wife of Adonis. The Great Mother goddess played all parts. She was mother, daughter and wife of a god, sister, wife and servant—friend and adviser, 'cruel and beneficent,' 'mighty queen of all gods.'

This complex relationship spread from Egypt to other countries.

Although some legends call Attis the son of Cybele, others represent him as a fair young herdsman or shepherd whom the goddess loved, and condemned to a life of celibacy. Attis was a tree spirit as well as a god of vegetation and after his death he was said to have been changed into a pine tree.

The great seat of worship of Aphrodite and Adonis was Paphos. "The sanctuary of Aphrodite at Old Paphos (the modern Kuklia) was one of the most celebrated shrines in the ancient world."

The image of Aphrodite was a white cone or pyramid.

"A cone was also the emblem of Astarte at Byblus, of the native goddess whom the Greeks called Artemis at Perga in Pamphylia, and of the sun-god Heliogabalus at Emasa in Syria. Conical stones which apparently served as idols have been found at Golgi in Cyprus and in the Phœnician Temples at Malta; and cones of sandstone came to light at the shrine of the 'Mistress of the Turquoise' among the barren hills and frowning precipices of Sinai." [4]

Some of the 'specialised Mother goddesses' whose attributes corresponded to the thought and moral as well as political development of the states they represented, were brought into Egypt—the land where mother deities had been reverenced from most ancient

[4] Frazer's "The Golden Bough."

times—during the Empire period by the Rameses Kings.

Of these imported goddesses Astarte the goddess of love was the most popular. Astarte is the 'goddess of evil repute' whom the Bible refers to as Ashtoreth. Kadesh another form of Astarte was called 'mistress of all the gods' and represented the "licentious phase of Ashtoreth." The Egyptians depicted her as a moon goddess standing naked on the back of a lioness. She holds lotus flowers and what appears to be a mirror in one hand and in the other two serpents. Astarte is sometimes given the head of a lioness.

The Oriental cults were gradually adopted by Rome. Cybele and Attis, who had become a solar god as well as a god of vegetation, were transported from Phrygia, Isis and Serapis from Alexandria and Mithra from Persia.

The worship of Cybele the Great Mother goddess of the Phrygians was adopted by the Romans in 204 B.C. when the small black stone in which the great goddess of fertility was embodied was brought to Rome, as their long struggle with Hannibal was approaching its end. The prophecy revealed in the Sybilline books that the presence of the goddess would drive out the invader was fulfilled the following year. Harvests, too, were abundant. "A further step was taken by Emperor Claudius when he incorporated the Phrygian worship of the sacred tree and with it probably the orgiastic rites of Attis in the established religion of Rome." [5]

The great spring festival of Cybele and her youthful son or lover was now celebrated at Rome.

The Great Mother goddess who personified all the reproductive powers of nature was thus worshipped

[5] Frazer's "The Golden Bough."

under various names but the myth and ritual were practically the same. Associated with the goddess was a lover, or perhaps a succession of 'lovers divine yet mortal' with whom she mated year after year, "thereby ensuring the fruitfulness of the ground and the increase of man and beast."

The worship of Cybele, the Asiatic goddess of fertility and her lover or son, was very popular under the Roman Empire, surviving the establishment of Christianity by Constantine. "In the days of Augustine her effeminate priests still paraded the streets and squares of Carthage with whitened faces, scented hair and mincing gait, while like the mendicant friars of the Middle Ages they begged alms from the passers by. . . . The religion of the Great Mother, with its curious blending of crude savagery with spiritual aspirations . . . by saturating the European peoples with alien ideals of life gradually undermined the whole fabric of ancient civilisation."[6]

It seems nearer true, however, to say that it was not the worship of the Great Mother but the prostitution of this worship that contributed largely to the fall of ancient civilisations.

It is significant that worship of the Great Mother goddesses was more prominent among highly civilised races who had established themselves in luxurious surroundings in large communities and cities, while the Father gods were worshipped in the solitude of the mountains or the lonely deserts by wandering nomads. As civilisations became more advanced the worship of the father gods receded until the masculine principle was nearly lost sight of as an object of worship. Again and again the male has had to be rescued from extinc-

[6] Frazer's "The Golden Bough."

Photo. Alinari

HEAD OF CYBELE

(Museo Nazionale delle Terme, Rome)

tion—rescued from himself. It is the male apparently who forgets the purpose of life and prostrates himself to the goddess, who is no longer the Great Mother but the goddess of love. She has become Venus, Aphrodite, Astarte—the Ashtoreth of the Bible the 'mistress of all the gods' and ceremonies associated with the worship of the great goddesses of nature and love are as elaborate as they are indecent. In this periodic evolution of nations, when the shift goes to cities, Mother Earth is no longer reverenced, children are denied and religion itself dies out. The cult of the feminine principle flourishes, however, and love is exalted. Life is refined, beautiful, made a matter of exquisite sensation, but productivity is no longer the ultimate meaning of love, and grossest licentiousness prevails.

Seemingly it is the force of inertia that brings about the sway of the feminine principle *per se*—and as such dissociated from the principle of growth.

Always pre-eminent, a force to be reckoned with, the history of ancient civilisations shows this constant oscillation between the Supreme Mother goddess cult and the Father cult—the swing from the brute to effeminacy. In this age-long struggle to adjust the problem of sex, one is struck by the marvellous insight of the ancients. Was it gained empirically—by experience, or was it revealed?

"The earlier generations saw God face to face; we through their eyes." (Emerson.)

The oldest records show that the malign influence of these forces when used against each other, or when either was allowed to have supreme power seems to have been clearly understood, and that it was the constant effort of the ancients, in all soundly conceived and healthy civilisations, to harness these two absolutely antagonistic principles and make them travel together. Their whole symbolism reflects this.

The recognised principle of balance, the modern idea of fifty-fifty may well have been the underlying reason for their androgynous gods.

In India also, there was the same swing. There was the Universal Mother Ida. Then Idah the rains, the plural of Ida, which apparently means the two Idas who as "male and female were the ancestors of Nahusha the great serpent father of the royal families of the snake race." In time the feminine principle was overshadowed by the masculine and the male god Pushan reigned supreme. Various systems of religious belief followed. The Aryans gave exclusive worship to Agni god of fire, the masculine principle. Ushas the virgin goddess of the dawn was the only feminine divinity until Krishna exalted the feminine principle which again came into power, as civilisation in India grew more refined and as a consequence less virile. The Idah, representing the masculine and feminine principles were still worshipped, however, as Ardhanari the combined figure of Siva and Parvati.

In both China and Japan the masculine principle is regarded as of first importance since no woman, unless she gains masculinity through repeated incarnations, can be received in Sukhavati the Western Paradise presided over by Amitabha, the Buddha of Infinite Light.

Ho-Hsien-Ku, who was the only woman among the eight immortals of the Taoist faith to gain immortality, achieved the masculine principle as well as the feminine.

The Buddhist or Taoist conception of immortality is the ultimate union of the two dualistic forces into one—thus representing completion instead of negation or annihilation.

The fundamental principle of the Yoga system is the union of the individual with the universal spirit. The whole system being built upon the union of Spiritual and Material—the "Oneness of the Two Parts."

In spite of their philosophy which recognised that displacement, continual displacement rather than ultimate balance and union is the law of the universe, and that Life is not a mould but a living, changing thing, the Chinese yielded to the hunger for union in their goddess Kwanyin—identical with the Japanese Kwannon—who was worshipped as both masculine and feminine. She was the feminine form of the god of mercy Avalokitésvara and was worshipped not as the consort but as the feminine manifestation of the god. Although worshipped as masculine by the priests and the educated classes, the feminine form was more generally favoured both in Japan and China. She was worshipped by some as sex-less and by others as bi-sexual. To the common people Kwanyin was the goddess of infinite mercy and compassion—the goddess of many arms. "She of a thousand arms." Kwanyin is depicted in Buddhist art sometimes seated upon a lotus and again with many arms. To those who look beneath the surface, it is not the grotesque image but the thought behind the image that brings assuagement, "She of a thousand arms!"

Traces of this androgynous notion of the deity are found in Egypt, India and Greece as well as scattered over many other parts of the ancient world. The androgynous form was simply a way of personifying creative power, which in the primal principle was believed to be androgynous or bi-sexual. Hermaphrodite represented the union of Hermes and Aphrodite. The Syrian goddess Atargatis is believed by some to have been bi-sexual, Dionysos was given a two-fold nature.

Each male deity had a female śakti or energy symbolising the reciprocal principles of nature who, if painted takes his colour but of a paler shade. The symbols representing the union of the two elements took various forms in the East. As we have seen one of the most wide spread symbols was the flame rising from the lotus or the crescent moon. A flame was also depicted issuing from the *Kalaśa*—the vase which was supposed to contain the Waters of Life. This is precisely the same symbolism—the union of fire and water. In China it is sometimes typified by a willow in the *Kalaśa* and in Japan by the *vajra* or thunderbolt; in Tibet the Aśoka branch was placed in the sacred vase. The Aśoka was called the Tree of Consolation and Buddha was born between the Aśoka and the Bod-hi tree. The feminine Kwanyin is frequently depicted holding the Kalaśa or with it at her side. A willow branch with which she sprinkles the waters of Life is either in the vase or she holds it in her hand. The masculine form of Kwanyin often has the lotus bud in the Kalaśa.

Both in China and Japan the most important symbol typifying this mystic union is the *great monad* or circle divided by a wavy line.

There is no doubt that in the earlier periods these symbols of the reciprocal powers of nature or Life, that in a later and more profligate age became gross, were in their inception frank, simple, true.

On the other hand, it is possible that the 'bearded Aphrodite' which has shocked posterity, may have been a despairing effort against decadence, a desire to bring

Photo. Alinari

The Youthful Bacchus
(Museo Nazionale, Naples)

home in a visible, objective way to those too brutalised or indifferent to grasp it, the subtler meaning conveyed by the sceptre, the twin pillars, the ankh cross, the 'jewel in the lotus' and all the other religious emblems of life.

There are those who believe that the present age is verging toward, if it has not arrived at one of those periodic intervals when sex is worshipped and Life forgotten. The tools of expression have changed. Where the decadent Romans amused themselves with phallic images, the modern writes phallic novels.

But does the modern phallicist amuse? He shows sex obsession, but is it worship? Someway the interest seems too academic, too studied to be real. One can't help suspecting that the motive back of this pre-occupation with sex is not so much worship as it is a scientific curiosity that wishes to tabulate sex, explain it, label it, broadcast it.

Given the proper perspective sex is a supremely interesting thing. It is one of the most elemental facts of life, however, that to be alluring at all it needs the quality of the elusive, the vanishing, the escaping, the mysterious—and the modern with his tiny microscope, who would know all, say all has forgotten this.

Sex resists to the death the microscopic investigator. To those who would profanely penetrate its mysteries, it transforms itself like the dragon into something hideous. It defies the literal ones, those who would approach it scientifically, as much as religion does.

Life, which is all paradox, insists upon the *equivoque*, the *double entendre*.

Even in the illustration of the great nature goddess Atargatis, the Syrian Astarte of Hierapolis, whose statue goes back thousands upon thousands of years, one finds expressed to perfection precisely what the modern lacks.

You look at it! The goddess may be encircled by the serpent of life, productivity. She is a nature goddess and all nature goddesses had the serpent. Or again it may be the serpent of sexual passion, sensuality. It must be admitted that the expression suggests the latter. The statue erect, shameless, brazen seems to mock at modern lasciviousness—and alas! the reputation of the goddess is all against her—but who knows? Who can say positively what the complicated serpent says and unsays as he winds and glides through life?

Nature, you may say what you will, is never bald. There may come rents and fissures, but she covers them, if only with gaudy weeds as soon as she decently can.

The realist, in his eagerness to strip life bare to the bone, strips off also the serpent of life and all that the serpent implies. His morbid curiosity leaves us cold. And here, perhaps, instead of being dangerous the modern phallicist is after all an instrument of grace, the very one who is going to save our civilisation for us. Back of every myth lurks unsuspected theology. Concealed in the modern phallicist is the unsuspected and unsuspecting moralist.

The truth is, he is making phallicism a bore.

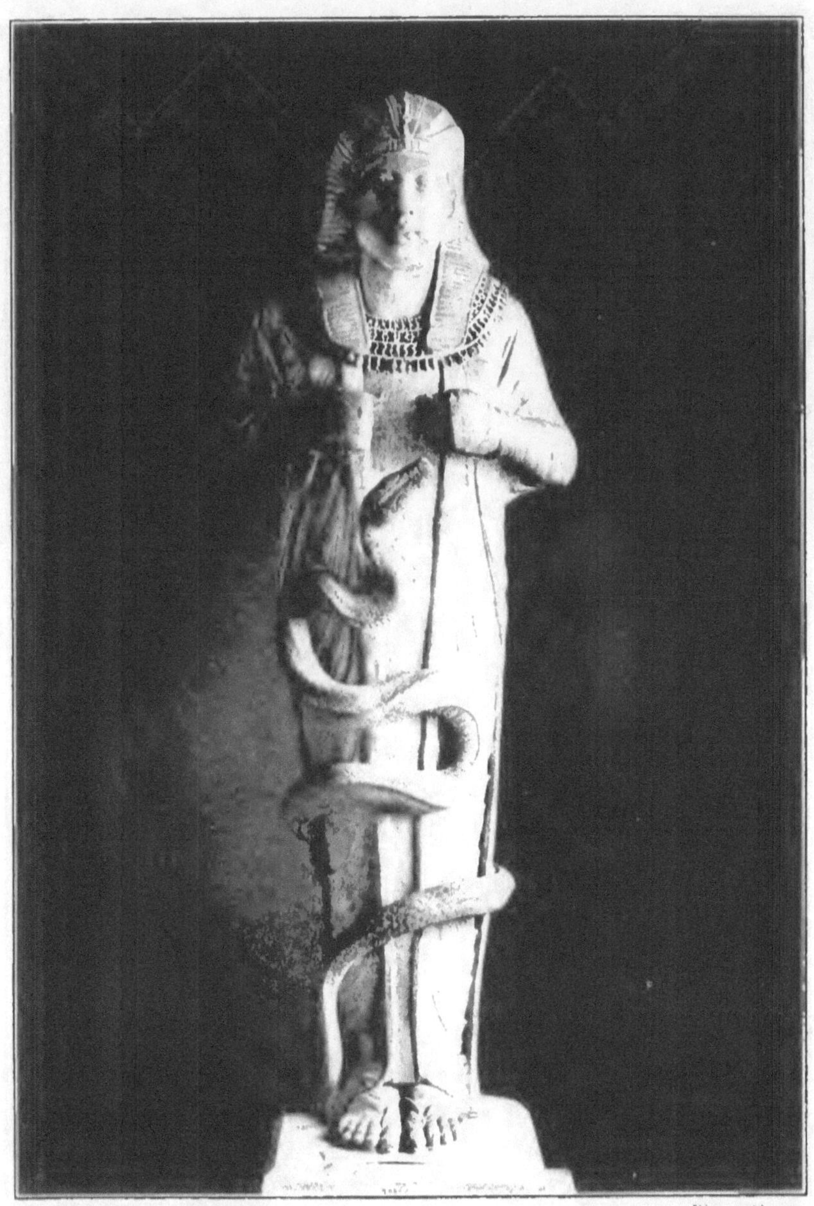

Photo. Alinari

Atargatis

(Museo delle Terme, Rome)

XVIII

LEGEND OF ISHTAR AND TAMMUZ

"Over and over again as Being and Becoming, as Eternity and Time, as Transcendence and Immanence, Reality and Appearance, the One and the Many—these two dominant ideas, demands, imperious instincts of man's self will re-appear, the warp and woof of his completed universe." Evelyn Underhill.

"God according to the Person is Eternal Works but according to the Essence and Its perpetual stillness He is Eternal Rest."—Ruysbroeck.

XVIII

LEGEND OF ISHTAR AND TAMMUZ

FROM the remotest periods of history Ishtar the great nature goddess of the Babylonians, stands out pre-eminent, supreme. Whatever god headed the pantheon the Babylonians never failed to include the 'powerful and potent Ishtar,' who, when associated with Shamash or Marduk partakes of their attributes, precisely as when with the solar god of the Assyrians, Ashur—who is war-like, a god of battle, Ishtar is also goddess of war. Under the astrological system of the Chaldeans Ishtar is associated with the planet Venus and thus becomes 'Queen of Heaven.'

"Appearing under manifold designations she is the goddess associated with mother earth, the great mother goddess who gave birth to everything that has life animate and inanimate. The conception of such a power clearly rests on the analogy suggested by the process of procreation which may be briefly defined as the commingling of the male and female principles. . . . Ishtar is the goddess of human instinct or passion which accompanies human love. She is the mother of mankind—but also she who awakens passion." [1]

Thus Ishtar was worshipped as the great mother

[1] "Religious Belief in Babylonia and Assyria," Jastrow.

goddess of fertility, as the goddess of war and the goddess who awakens love.

She was accused by Gilgamesh of abandoning her lovers—was said to desert them like *"La Belle Dame sans Merci"* but nature is as pitiless as it is sometimes kind. It is Ishtar who destroys the youthful Tammuz who dies with the dying vegetation. It is Ishtar, too, who descends into the nether regions of death and decay searching for her lover Tammuz.

The myth has lent itself to various interpretations that are full of charm and poetic imagery. In its original form it is simply another variant of the solar epic, Tammuz personifying the sun as well as vegetation, and Ishtar mother earth. Their representation as lovers or as husband and wife was the customary way of expressing the idea of life, and these two, Ishtar and Tammuz, stand out for all time as closely related figures symbolising vegetation, or the combination of the two forces whose conjunction brings about life and whose separation death.

The first act of Tammuz is to slay the demons of frost and cold. The festival of Tammuz was celebrated just before the summer solstice. His death was annually mourned. Dirges were chanted over an effigy of the dead god which "was washed with pure water, anointed with oil and clad in a red robe, while the fumes of incense rose into the air as if to stir his dormant senses by their pungent fragrance and wake him from the sleep of death."[2]

In the early days when agriculture was intimately associated with religion, the whole process became a dramatic pageant which was entered into emotionally, with joy and reverence as well as with fear and awe.

[2] Frazer's "The Golden Bough."

There were weeping ceremonies as well as rejoicings. The gods of vegetation were 'weeping deities who shed fertilising tears.' When the seed was cast into the ground 'to die,' it was done ceremoniously the sowers enacting the rôle of mourners.

The angel of the Hebrew God brought Ezekiel to the "door of the gate of the Lord's house which was toward the north; and behold, there sat women weeping for Tammuz." He is shown further and "greater abominations." Ezekiel is brought into the inner court of the Lord's house and behold, men "with their backs toward the temple of the Lord and their faces toward the east; and they worshipped the sun toward the east." (Ez. 8: 14-16.)

Tammuz was called Adôn, the Semitic word for 'lord' by the Semitic peoples of Babylonia and Assyria. The myth passed over to the Phœnicians and then was adopted by the Greeks who are thought to have derived their name Adonis from the title given to Tammuz by the Babylonians. Jastrow finds that the story of Adonis and Aphrodite may easily be traced back to Tammuz and Ishtar and that the weeping for the lost sun-god and the rejoicing when nature awakens to new life are again embodied in the story of the crucifixion and the resurrection of Christ. "The Son of God is slain to re-appear as the risen Lord just as in the Phrygian story of Attis and Cybele and in the Egyptian tale of Osiris and Isis we have another form of the same myth symbolising the change of seasons." [3]

In one of the more dramatic forms of the myth Tammuz is beloved by two goddesses Ishtar, the Queen of Heaven and Erishkigal, the queen of the Nether world. As the summer season wanes and the dearly

[3] Jastrow's "Religious Belief in Babylonia and Assyria."

loved Tammuz, god of vegetation and solar radiation dies, Ishtar descends to the nether regions of death and decay searching for him. The gradual passing of summer into winter is symbolised by the ornaments and articles of clothing that Ishtar is obliged to give to those who guard the seven gates that lead to the presence of the grim and wrathful goddess Erishkigal. At the first gate she is forced to yield up her crown, at the second her earrings, at the third her necklace of precious stones, at the fourth the ornaments from her breast, at the fifth her waist girdle studded with gems, at the sixth gate the bracelets are wrenched from her arms and ankles, and at the seventh her robes are stripped from her body, and Ishtar is brought naked before the Queen of Hades. By this time nature is bare, vegetation has disappeared, the god of winter is in full possession of the earth. Ishtar is still proud, and arrogantly demands the release of Tammuz. Whereupon Erishkigal, her sister and rival orders the plague demon to strike her with disease in all her body. The effect is disastrous upon earth. Ishtar is kept a prisoner by her jealous sister and all life and fertility cease on earth. The gods mourn. Shamash the great sun-god laments. Finally Ea creates a mysterious being Asushu-namir—clearly a counterpart of Tammuz the solar god of spring—and sends him to the nether abode of Erishkigal to reclaim Ishtar, who is first sprinkled with the water of Life. As she passes out through the seven gates each jewel and ornament and article of clothing is returned to her, and Ishtar comes forth with the spring from the nether world of disease and death, in all her old time beauty and splendour.

In the Greek version Adonis the beloved of Aphrodite is hidden as an infant by the goddess in a chest which falls into the possession of Proserpine, queen of the nether world, who refuses to give him back to Aphrodite. Zeus finally settles the dispute between the two goddesses of love and death by permitting him to spend six months with each. Other versions say that Adonis was killed in hunting by a wild boar, or by the jealous Ares who assumed the likeness of a boar in order to slay his rival, and that Proserpine restored him to life on the condition that he spend six months of the year with her. This decree that Adonis shall spend part of the year under ground and a part above ground is simply a variant of the annual disappearance and re-appearance of Tammuz.

As time goes on Tammuz becomes a shadowy, elusive figure, beloved for his youth and beauty but no longer dominant, and is gradually superseded by Ishtar in the official ritual of the temple.

The powerful goddess of nature lives on. Seven centuries after the religion of Assyria and Babylonia had passed out leaving hardly a trace, and when faith in the Greek and Roman gods had also lessened, the Romans brought Cybele, the mother goddess of Phrygia to Rome and built a temple in her honour. "It was Ishtar of Babylonia transformed to meet changed conditions. The same great feminine principle of nature in its various manifestations of mother earth, the source of all fertility, at once 'the loving mother of mankind and of the gods.' "

XIX

LEGEND OF ISIS AND OSIRIS

"Tout ce que les Grecs ont dit de Jupiter et de Junon est placé en Egypte sous la responsabilité d'Isis et Osiris. . . . Osiris est auteur de toute civilisation dans son pays; Isis invente l'agriculture. Osiris est considéré . . . comme le soleil dont les vicissitudes périodiques et annuelles sont exprimées par les phases de son histoire légendaire; Isis est donc la lune dont les rapports avec lui sont si frappants et si connus. L'un est la chaleur, l'autre est l'humidité. . . . Tous deux ont leur functions à part mais concomitantes dans la création et la conservation des êtres. Cette création est désigné par l'œuf auquel les deux époux avaient eu une égale part, qu' Isis fendit de ses cornes de vache et duquel sortit l'univers."—Auber.

Isis veiled: "I am all that has been, all that is, and all that will be and no mortal has drawn aside my veil."

XIX

LEGEND OF ISIS AND OSIRIS

WHILE the other gods of Egypt were worshipped each in his own locality Osiris and Isis were adored in all.

It has been said that one may speak of the religious ideas of the Egyptians, but not of an Egyptian religion. Highly complex and divergent as were these ideas, they seem gradually to have centred, and found their fullest and most enduring expression in the mystical cult of Isis and Osiris.

Osiris and Isis became the mightiest of the Egyptian gods and were also joint creators of the world.

Osiris represented the river Nile—everything that was moist and generative in nature. He was a god of life like the Greek god Dionysos. He was a solar god, a moon-god, the god of agriculture; he was the earth spirit, the "Apis bull of Memphis, the ram of Mendes, the reigning Pharaoh," fused with Ra the sun-god he died each day as an old man, appearing in heaven at night as the constellation Orion which was his ghost.

Osiris is "he that bringeth three to the mountains."

From the death and resurrection of Osiris the Egyptians drew all their hope of eternal life. Of the dead they said "Thou hast not gone dying thou hast gone living to Osiris." Every one who shared the fate of Osiris might also return to life. "As Osiris lives, so shall he also live; as Osiris died not, so shall he also not die; as Osiris perished not so shall he also not perish."

We are told that the Egyptians held a festival of Isis at the time when the Nile began to rise. They believed that the goddess was then mourning for the lost Osiris, and that the tears which dropped from her eyes swelled the impetuous tide of the river.

The symbols of Osiris are the eye and the sceptre typifying providence and power. He has the head of a hawk or a man and holds the *crux ansata* the symbol of life in his hand. As god of the dead he wears the *atef* crown with plumes and holds in his hands the crook, sceptre and flail, symbols of rule, sovereignty and dominion. Osiris is usually represented, however, as a mummy holding in his hands the crook, the sceptre, the flail and the *crux ansata.*

In a series of bas-reliefs the dead god is first depicted lying swathed as a mummy; in each scene he has raised himself higher and higher until in the final representation he has left the bier and is seen erect with the devoted Isis a little behind him, while a male figure holds up before his eyes the *crux ansata* the symbol of life. The resurrection of the god is even more graphically portrayed in another representation where the dead god is shown with stalks of corn springing from his body which a priest is watering from a pitcher that he holds in his hand. Here Osiris is the corn god who produced corn from himself. 'He gave his own body, to feed the people: he died that they might live.' The inscription reads 'This is the form of him whom one may not name, Osiris of the mysteries, who springs from the returning waters.'

Osiris has been called the son of Isis. Originally

Photo. Alinari

Osiris, Isis and Horus
(Louvre, Paris)

Isis was a Virgin Mother and Horus her fatherless son. She is a nature goddess, the Great Mother, the daughter of Nut the sky. Isis and Osiris are twin brother and sister. Her marriage with Osiris and his adoption of Horus is a later adaptation. Set the principle of evil is also her brother as well as the brother of Osiris. Set marries Nephthys his sister and sister of Osiris and Isis.

Isis absorbs the attributes and functions of the other goddesses, of Nut the sky and water goddess, of Neith the earth-goddess who typified growth. She is the moon goddess, she is all things. She is given the lotus and the horns of the crescent moon and sometimes the solar disk encircled by the uræus snake. All the sacred animals are associated with Isis.

In the age of Osiris and Isis "laws stern and inexorable as nature disciplined the people and promoted their welfare."

Isis as a mythical figure differs essentially from the powerful Ishtar, the capricious goddess who abandons her lovers, makes war on earth, descends into Hell and queens it in the skies. She differs, too, from Venus the queen of beauty who scatters love, beloved by all. Nor was she ever associated with Astarte in any of her degenerate manifestations or representations under different names. Isis has been likened to Ceres, but except as a goddess of nature there the relationship ends. Isis stands above, apart. It has been said that but for her presence in Egypt the world would never have known a madonna. Her cult obtained a great hold upon the Romans, and its influence upon the later religion of Christianity was profound. "Spiritualised by ages of religious evolution" the goddess becomes the refined and exquisite type for all the ages of the "true wife, the tender mother, the beneficent queen of nature, encircled by the nimbus of moral purity, of immemorial and mysterious sanctity."

"In that welter of religions which accompanied the decline of national life in antiquity her worship was one of the most popular at Rome and throughout the empire. . . . In a period of decadence when the fabric of empire itself, once deemed eternal, began to show ominous rents and fissures the serene figure of Isis with her spiritual calm, her gracious promise of immortality appeared to many like a star in a stormy sky . . . and roused in their breasts a rapture of devotion not unlike that paid in the Middle Ages to the Virgin Mary. . . . Her stately ritual with its shaven and tonsured priests, its matins and vespers, its tinkling music, its baptism and aspersions of holy water, its solemn procession, its jewelled images of the Mother of God presented many points of similarity to the pomps and ceremonies of Catholicism." [1]

We are indebted to Plutarch for the only connected account of the story of Isis and Osiris. The legend which follows is given as he relates it only in abbreviated form.

At the time of the murder of Osiris by his brother Set (whom the Greeks called Typhon), Osiris had become king of Egypt and by his wise rule had brought Egypt to an idyllic state. His people had so greatly benefitted by his discipline and care for their welfare, by his instructions in the arts of husbandry and his laws to regulate conduct and induce reverence and worship of the gods, that his brother Set (or the principle of evil) saw that his power over the minds of men was

[1] Frazer's "The Golden Bough."

gone, that these happy, trustful people could no longer be reached by evil unless Osiris himself could be entrapped and overthrown.

Thereupon Set with seventy-two others concocted a plot to rid the world of Osiris. Having stealthily taken the measurements of Osiris's body, Set caused a most beautiful chest to be constructed of the same size, and which was set off with all manner of ornaments to attract and please the eye. This chest was brought into his banquetting room, and at a great feast given to Osiris where all the conspirators were assembled, after the chest had been much admired, Set promised jestingly to give it to the one whom it should fit. Amid much merriment various ones tried it but found it too short or too long. At length Osiris was persuaded to lay himself down in it, whereupon the conspirators instantly clapped down the lid, fastened it with nails, sealed it with melted lead and carrying it to the river side they sent it out to sea "by way of the Tanaïtic mouth of the Nile, which, for this reason is still held in the utmost abomination by the Egyptians and never named by them but with proper marks of detestation." Accounting the sea abominable the Egyptians prohibited the use of salt (or Typhon's foam) at table. They would also make the picture of a fish to denote hatred.

The death of Osiris was "thus executed upon the 17th day of the month Athôr, when the sun was in Scorpio in the 28th year of Osiris's reign; though there are others who tell us that he was no more than twenty-eight years old at this time."

The rest of the legend relates to the search made by the disconsolate Isis for her husband's body.

Isis wanders everywhere all over the country mourning and seeking for Osiris. Seven scorpions accompany her in her flight through the papyrus swamps of the Delta. A child is stung to death by one of the scorpions. Her heart, touched by the mother's grief, Isis "laid her hands on the child and uttered her powerful spells; so the poison was driven out of the child and he lived."

After a wearisome time Isis receives definite news of the chest. She learns that it had been carried by the waves of the sea to Byblus on the coast of Syria and "there gently lodged in the branches of a bush of Tamarisk, which in a short time had shot up into a large and beautiful tree, growing round the chest and enclosing it on every side so that it was not to be seen; and further, that the king of the country, amazed at its unusual size, had cut the tree down, and made that part of the trunk wherein the chest was concealed a pillar to support the roof of his house. These things, say they, being made known to Isis in an extraordinary manner by the report of demons."

Isis goes immediately to Byblus, where in humble attire she sits down by a fountain and refuses to speak to any one except the queen's women who chanced to be there. "These she saluted and caressed . . . plaiting their hair for them and transmitting into them part of that wonderfully grateful odour which issued from her own body."

Hearing of her from her hand maidens and attracted by the divine perfume which still clung about them, the queen sent for Isis and made her nurse to one of her sons.

At last disclosing herself, the goddess requests that the pillar be given to her which was accordingly done "and then easily cutting it open, after she had taken out what she wanted, she wrapped up the remainder of the trunk in fine linen and pouring perfumed oil upon it, delivered it into the hands of the king and queen . . . then she threw herself upon the chest, making at the same time such a loud and terrible lamentation over it as frightened the younger of the king's sons who heard her out of his life."

Isis sets sail with the chest for Egypt.

"No sooner was she arrived in a desert place where she imagined herself to be alone, but she presently opened the chest and laying her face upon her dead husband's embraced his corpse and wept bitterly."

Isis leaves the chest in a lonely, unfrequented spot and goes to her son Horus who was being nurtured by Leto in the marshes about Buto. Here Set, who was hunting by the light of the moon accidentally finds it. Breaking open the chest he cuts the body of Osiris into fourteen pieces and scatters these over the length and breadth of the land.

Once more Isis sets out searching sorrowfully everywhere for the scattered fragments of her husband's body, and using a boat made of the reed papyrus "in order the more easily to pass through the lower and fenny parts of the country." The legend relates that Isis found all the pieces of Osiris's body—save one.

Isis buried each part of Osiris wherever she found it, erecting a temple over each to the memory of her husband, which accounts for the number of tombs of Osiris in Egypt. Others say, however, that Isis fashioned images of Osiris which she buried in different cities and localities instead of the real body, doing this, not only that the homage paid to his memory might be more extended, but also that she might hope thereby to elude the malignant Set who finding so many sepulchres would be confused and distracted from any further attempt to find the true one.

After being thus entrapped, murdered and dismembered by Set and partially restored by Isis, Osiris becomes King of the Nether World where he judges men according to their deeds. "Whatsoever a man soweth that shall he also reap."

Horus is now the reigning king. Desiring to take vengeance upon Set for the injuries done to Osiris and Isis, Horus engages Set in battle. The battle lasts for days. In the end Horus is victorious, right and justice triumph over evil, and having made Set prisoner, Horus gives him over into the custody of his mother Isis.

Isis, instead of putting Set to death, loosens his chains, and lets him go.

"And the majesty of Horus was enraged against his mother Isis like a panther of the south, and she fled before him. On that day a terrible struggle took place, and Horus cut off the head of Isis; and Thoth transformed this head by his incantations and put it on her again in the form of a head of a cow."

This briefly is the famous legend which has had so many mystical interpretations and led to so many philosophical deductions.

According to Plutarch "Isis is the power in matter which becomes everything and receives everything, as light and darkness, fire and water, day and night, life and death, beginning and end, so given all colours, many hues. Osiris is without shade, untempered, unmixed, the first principle or light." [2]

He considers that "Osiris and Isis typify all that is orderly and good. Typhon (Set) typifies excess, in-

[2] Plutarch's "Isis and Osiris," trans. by Goodwin.

temperance, disorder. In the legend Typhon is subdued but not destroyed, for the 'principle opposite to moist must not be entirely destroyed.' Although Osiris is 'lord of all the best instincts' it is impossible to do away utterly with evil—but the better is stronger. Typhon is that part of the soul that is unreasonable, passionate, uncontrolled; in the material world that which is perishable, diseased, violent—such as bad crops, drought, earthquakes, floods. Typhon invariably stands in the way of right development and the course of things. Osiris represents the true doctrine which Typhon scattered and Isis gathered again inviting her followers to join with her in the search. Osiris is the god of knowledge and Typhon the god of ignorance. Osiris is the soul, intellect, reason, Typhon is everything that is brutish in man or nature.

"Typhon's symbols are the ass, the stupidest of all domestic animals, and the crocodile and hippopotamus, the most brutal of wild beasts. In a statue at Hermopolis Typhon is represented as a hippopotamus upon which has alighted a hawk—which signifies power and rule—contending with a snake. Typhon often comes into possession of this power through violence and does not cease troubling himself and others.

"Now Isis is the female in nature and receives all generation and is therefore called by Plato the nurse and all receiver, but by the common people the many sided, the goddess with the thousand names—because under the influence of reason she receives all forms. And she has an inborn affection for the first principle of all things—which is the same as good—and she longs for it and pursues it. On the other hand, she flees the evil principle and thrusts it away, although she is space and matter for both. However, she always inclines to the better and freely offers herself to it for the reception of its effluxes, and for the reproduction of its likenesses in which she rejoices. For generation is an image of true being presented in matter and that which is born is always an imitation of that which exists.

"Therefore they do not improperly recount in the myth that the soul of Osiris is imperishable, but that Typhon often tears asunder and hides his body, while Isis wanders about until she has found it and fitted together the parts."[3]

The myth emphasises in Isis the receptive, the likeness to Mother Earth which receives good seed and bad, is incapable of discrimination, of eliminating, of discarding—and although preferring the good, must depend upon the intelligence and responsibility of the sower to obtain it.

The vitality of the story—its continued fascination for us probably lies in the fact that it is so soundly and universally conceived that it covers every phase of life. It is far more than the old contest between good and evil, light and darkness. It is primarily the story of man and woman. Isis, the leading figure is the eternal feminine who lacks the creative impulse yet completes creation,—who is negation, growth, multiplicity, inertia, form. If man makes Life for her, she in return makes him—but only so much as he is capable of being. She re-acts—one must never forget that, nor that matter is tool in the hands of the master builder.

The history of all womankind centres in her. To

[3] The above translation of Plutarch's *Isis and Osiris* is taken from a volume of miscellaneous pamphlets bound together under the title of *The Triangle* and belonging to the Isaac Myer Collection presented to the Public Library of New York.

understand Isis is to understand all women. She has all the virtues and all the faults. She is blind, far-seeing, wise, foolish. She tries to overcome the ravages and desolation occasioned by evil—and when evil is captured and put in her charge she pities and lets it go. The goddess mourns over the death of Osiris, makes untold sacrifices, searches for him everywhere, demeans herself, becomes a servant to mortals in order to recover his body. Having accomplished this, she leaves it to go to her son Horus. In her absence the spirit of evil again takes possession of Osiris and this time dismembers his body and scatters it to the four winds of heaven.

Having permitted the havoc to be wrought by her own negligence, Isis starts forth again, and with incredible toil and patience and faithfulness she at last succeeds in finding all the parts of Osiris—*save one*.

The myth relates that of the fourteen parts that Set the destroyer had scattered, Isis found everything but the creative, energising force. Concealing the loss, covering up the lack, Isis made substitutes and set up imitations which she asked the world to worship. In spite of all she could do, however, she could only imitate, she could not supply the creative force, and thus having lost the life giving power, Osiris inevitably ceased to be the god of the living and sank into the nether realm of darkness where he became god of the dead and his son Horus, the solar god of the morning light reigned in his stead.

XX

THE SISTRUM OF ISIS

"The intellect so skillful in dealing with the inert is awkward the moment it touches the living."—Bergson.

"The advance of knowledge is an infinite progression towards a goal that forever recedes."—Frazer.

"Wisdom is more moving than any motion; she passeth and goeth through all things by reason of her pureness . . . she is the brightness of the everlasting light, the unspotted mirror of the power of God."—Wisdom of Solomon 7:24, 26.

Photo. Alinari

Isis

(Museo Nazionale, Naples)

XX

THE SISTRUM OF ISIS

ISIS the immortal, the goddess of Life, the Eternal Feminine has many symbols, but only one weapon, one instrument to play upon when she wants to change conditions, to startle us into consciousness, to make us see the meaning of our habitual acceptances, and that's the *sistrum*—an instrument that now as ever is a particularly valuable feminine adjunct.

"The *sistrum* shows that whatever exists ought to be shaken and never cease from movement, but should be aroused and agitated as if it were asleep and its life quenched. For they say that by the sistrum they drove Typhon away; by this they set forth that destruction binds and halts, but by means of movement generation frees nature." (Plutarch.)

"Whose voice then shook the earth; but now he hath promised, saying yet once more I shake not the earth only, but also heaven.

"And this word yet once more signifieth the removing of things that are shaken as of things that are made, that those things which cannot be shaken may remain." (Hebrews 12:26-7.)

XXI

THE TRIANGLE

There are "three fundamental principles of the universe, the **Unity**, *the* **Duality** *and the* **Trinity**. . . . *The three great principles into which all forms of manifestation may be analysed—the* **Masculine, Positive** *or generating principle; the* **Feminine, Receptive** *or formative principle; and the* **Neuter** *or* **Mathematical** *principle, which by determining the proportional relations of the other two, gives rise to the principles of variety and multiplicity."*—Troward.

"The **Trinity** *was first shown in man, for Adam was first formed from the earth, then the woman from Adam. Afterwards was man created from both and so there is therein a* **Trinity**."—Durandus.

"Ethical idealism by which is here meant a high sense of duty and a noble view of life is possible only, so it would seem, under two conditions, either through a strong conviction that there is a compensation elsewhere for the wrongs, injustice and suffering in this world, or through an equally strong conviction that the unknown goal toward which mankind is striving can be reached only by the moral growth and ultimate perfection of the human race, whatever the future may have in store."—Jastrow.

"That a quest there is and an end is the single secret spoken."—Underhill.

XXI

THE TRIANGLE

The Triangle, the geometrical emblem of three things, one above two, the two lower uniting to produce the higher, or the union of the positive and negative forces to produce the third is the most complex and mystical as it is the most uncompromising of all the life symbols. None other holds within itself so much of the hidden meaning of that mysterious thing called Life. It is in very truth the symbol of the inexorable Law of Life. And it is no exaggeration to say that much of man's checkered career has been spent in struggling with the triangle—if not actually, then metaphysically.

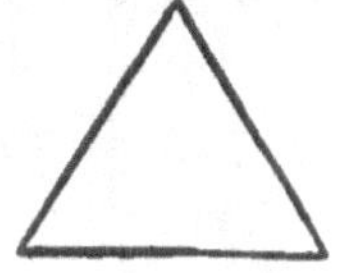

Beginning with chaos, then unity or the self-created, there comes duality. And man's thoughts are no sooner ensnared by that—for he is so made that he loves his opposite—than a third force presents itself, and this force is the result—or life. "*—Père, mère et fils* (*essence, substance et vie*)."

From earliest times primitive man appears to have grasped the idea of the three-fold nature of the universe —the divine, the human, the natural world and that he himself was the image or mirror of the macrocosm, composed of three things—body, mind, soul or spirit. There seems hardly to have been a time since history began when the idea of a unit of three in one was not a part of man's consciousness. In addition to the obvious dualism of nature he saw everywhere a third and higher aspect evolved by the union of these two opposite forces, and the triangle was used by primordial man at first presumably as a race symbol, signifying the family—father, mother, child. "The Egyptian Temples were dedicated to three gods. The first the male principle, the second the female, and the third the offspring of the other two, but these three are blended into one."

From the trinity of the family and the multitude of triads in nature arose, it is assumed, the conception of a trinity of gods. It is significant that the most ancient religions contain such trinities or family groups.

Set, Horus and Shu were the primary Egyptian Trinity symbolised by a triangle enclosed in a circle. In the earlier mythology Horus was the Water Season. Set his brother was the Drought, the Destroyer. Between these two was eternal conflict. Shu the Reconciler and Mediator was the god of winds and equinoctial storms. Shu was the god who first lifted up the heavens from the earth in the form of a triangle, and he is depicted standing on seven steps within a triangle.

The symbol of Set god of the South was the equilateral triangle. Horus god of the North had the triangle reversed. The two powers were symbolised thus: ⧗ This was called the Double Pyramid or Hand of the Egyptians and signified the union of fire and water.

When Horus became the Supreme Deity the triangles were merged into the five pointed star. This became the symbol of the Celestial world or the House of Horus.

Two interlacing triangles represented the "Double Horizon of Horus."

In one of the innumerable Egyptian triads Nut is heaven, Seb the earth and Shu the air and space which separates them. The most popular triad, however, and the one that more nearly epitomised Egyptian thought was Osiris, Isis and their son Horus. Osiris first cause, Isis receptive and Horus the result, or "Osiris, father or spirit, Isis, the material or matrix and Horus the sensible world." Osiris represented soul, intellect, reason. Horus, born of the union of reason and matter, was the "sensible image of the mental world."

The majority of these triads personified the powers of nature under various groupings such as, Heaven, earth, water. Fire, water, air. The sun, moon, Venus. The fire, light, ether of the Zoroastrians, and fire, light, spirit or air of the Hebrews.

In the Babylonian religion, to the gods of storm and sun, or fire and water was added a third representing the earth, fertility, productivity, or heaven, earth, water. Anu originally the sun becomes the god of heaven, Enlil starting as a storm-god becomes god of the earth and is sometimes called Bel or Bel-Enlil 'Lord of many lands.' To these are added Ea god of water. In time these transfer their powers to other triads but the forces symbolised, remain unchanged. Under whatever names the triad typifies heaven, sun, or fire, the power of moisture showing itself in storms and rains, and the power of fertility, fecundity personified by the earth.

Later "influenced by theological speculations which betray the astrological tendency" the Babylonians worshipped another triad which represented the three great divisions of the universe. This triad gave first place to Sin, the moon-god followed by Shamash and the goddess Ishtar as the planet Venus. "These deities again summing up the chief manifestations of divine power in the universe. Sin as leader of the hosts of the mighty heavens, Shamash the beneficent power of the sun and Ishtar in her original attribute as goddess of the earth, mother of life and source of fertility."

Hewitt finds that in India worship began first to Mother Earth, then to the Father and Mother of all things then came triads in the following order (1) The father, the life-giving bi-sexual power, and the mother earth. (2) The father, the moon-goddess, the mother earth. (3) The self-producing fire, the moon goddess, and the mother earth.

When Indra worship came into being the system was altered, material agents were no longer recognised and the god of the water of life, the god who makes rain became the father of all things. Worship of Indra succumbed to Vishnu, who was substituted for Varuna as third person of the triad, while Siva re-appeared as phallic god at its head. In this triad Pushkara the moon "meaning the divine lotus or the mother of the earth resting on the sanctifying waters" is the ruling god. It is thus seen that the popular 'trimurti' typified the "varying aspects of the mystery of creation."

The triad or 'trimurti' of the Brahmins are Brahma, the Creator, Vishnu, the Preserver and Siva, the Destroyer or Apathy.

The Tri-ratna, the 'three precious Tri-ratna' or the Buddhist triad are Buddha, intelligence, soul, the generative power, Dharma, matter, the body, the productive power, and Sangha the union of the two. From this union, or as the result of this union Sangha becomes the author of creation.

The mystic syllable *Aum* also signified the Tri-ratna or Three Jewels.

The *triangle* was a symbol of the tri-ratna and "according to the secret doctrines of certain sects represented the 'yoni' from which the world was manifest," or the source of all things.

As we have seen, at the beginning of the world Adi-Buddha was said to have manifested himself in the form of a flame rising from a lotus. Sometimes the stalk of the lotus is depicted rising from a triangle.

The Buddha discoursing on the symbol of three dots arranged in the form of a triangle, one dot above two, used the triangle as a symbol of the embodied form of the *Tathāgāta* or he who will have no more re-births. The Tathāgāta is also used to designate the Tri-Kaya or the three-fold embodiment, or living in three worlds at one time.

In the mystic doctrine of the Mandala of Two Parts of the Yoga system, the fundamental principle of which is the union of the individual with the universal spirit, the Mandala is the mystic circle that has for its centre an eight leaved lotus flower representing the heart of beings, the 'solar matrix,' the mysterious sanctuary to which the sun retires each night to be re-born. The eight petals typify the four Dhyāni-Bodhisattvas who have created the four worlds, and their four spiritual fathers or Buddhas. Above the lotus symbol is a triangle resting on its base and which here typifies Adi-Dharma or matter.

The six elements which when united produce the "six-fold bodily and mental happiness" are the five material elements of which man and the visible world are believed to be composed, earth, water, fire, air, ether—and the sixth element *manas* (mind), a particle of the essence of Adi-Buddha. This represents the diamond element or complete Enlightenment and is symbolised by the triangle (or tri-kona) the point below. The matrix or embryo element, the Material world which is "likened to the womb in which all of the child is conceived"—body as well as mind—contains the universe which it cares for and nourishes. The matrix element is composed of reason or form and the five elements and is symbolised by the triangle with the point above. The two elements—the spiritual and the material—are "one for 'Wisdom cannot exist without Reason nor Reason without Wisdom'."

The *triangle* among the Hindus represented also the generative power of the earth.

Although the Chinese divided nature into two great parts *yang* the masculine principle and *yin* the feminine principle, it was by the co-operation of these two principles that Life or the third or neuter principle was evolved.

The Taoist's triad was heaven, *yang* and *yin*. It was their belief that the union of the three alone embodied creative force. This was also called the 'union of the Three Powers.'

The Chinese trigrams contain three powers, heaven, earth, men. These three are one and the same. When doubled into the hexagrams the three powers unite and are one.

In the Zoroastrian triad Ahura Mazda (Ormuzd) is the Sun, or power of good, life, light, heaven. Ahrimanes is the power of darkness, evil, death, the earth or matter, and Mithra is the sunlight, the power of Truth, the Mediator between heaven and earth.

The triune conception represented a very early phase of Greek religion.

In the tree and pillar cult are found trinities of trees and pillars. These trinities were supposed to be the abode of a single divinity visualising the idea that "groups of two or three pillars could be the embodiment of a single divinity, a conception which lent itself to the idea of a triune god. The dove shrines of Mycenæa also supply a similar parallel. These shrines have three openings in each of which is an aniconical column which have at their base showing their divine character the 'horns of consecration'." [1]

The three sons of Saturn were Jupiter, the king of heaven and the soul of the world, Pluto, god of the nether regions and Neptune, god of the waters.

The Orphic trinity was Metis, Eros and Ericapeus or Will, Love and Life-giver or Phanes the Creative force which includes the three powers Light, Life, Energy.

According to Plutarch, Hesiod makes the first cause of all things Chaos—earth, hell, love. Isis is the earth, Typhon (Set) is hell and Osiris is love. Thus Osiris or love is First Cause, Isis is the faculty of reception and Horus is the result.

Plutarch divides the divine nature into three parts, the intelligible part, matter, and that which is made up of both "which the Greeks call Cosmos—trimness or order—and which we call the world."

Plato believed in the self-activity of an intelligent first cause, and that the world was made up of two forces one beneficent, and the other the opposite, with a third nature between resting upon the preceding forces. He called the first the intelligible part or the father, the second, matter, the mother, nurse, receptacle of generation, and the third is that which springs from both, the offspring or production.

[1] "Mycenæan Trees and Pillar Cult," A. J. Evans.

Triplicity has been called the very soul of astrology, magic, divination.

Agni, the fire god of India was worshipped as "displaying thine eternal triple form—as fire on earth, as lightning in the air, as the sun in the heaven."

To the Egyptian sun worshippers dawn, noon and sunset represent the three-fold aspect of the sun typified by Horus in the morning, Ra at noon and Osiris at night.

The goddess Hecate was called Luna in heaven, Hecate in hell and Trivia at crossroads. Diana was also worshipped as Trivia and statues of her were usually placed wherever three roads met. Diana was in turn identified with Hecate and the moon and was thus called Triformis.

Some sects of the Buddhists not only believed in the three-fold embodiment but also that a Buddha may live in three separate spheres at one and the same time.

The number three is mysterious, mystic, magical. "Even its use is three-fold, one definite showing intrinsic value, the other symbolic, esoteric and the third indefinite signifying many."

Three is the primitive plural. Many times and thrice are equivalents in the Greek.

Aristotle looked upon the "triad as the number of the complete whole, inasmuch as it contains a beginning, a middle and an end. Nature herself has provided us with this number for use in the holy service of the gods."

The importance of the triad conception and the hold it had and still has, for that matter, on the imagination, not only is shown in the ancient triad of gods or the tri-une god—carried on into the Christian religion as Father, Son and Holy Ghost—but by the way thought instinctively groups itself in threes. Sun, moon, stars; birth, life, death; heaven, earth, water; the three fates, three furies, three graces. Various fabulous monsters that had three heads—Chimæra had the head of a lion, a dragon and a goat and continually vomitted flames, Cerberus was the three headed dog of Pluto who guarded the entrance into hell, Hydra was said originally to have had three heads. There are the three dimensions, the three parts in every sequence of thought, Hegel's three aspects of truth—thesis, antithesis and synthesis. We demand three cheers. We speak of the 'world, the flesh, the devil' as opposed to the 'good, the true, the beautiful.' Goethe puts it "From the useful, through the true, to the beautiful." The former, however, expresses better the 'three in one' idea which is the very cadence, the haunting, mystical quality, the superb truth contained in these various groupings.

The mystics symbolise "the Trinity as Light, Life and Love:—

"*Light,* the perfect symbol of pure undifferentiated Being.

"*Life,* the Son, the hidden Steersman of the Universe, the Logos, Fire or Cosmic soul of things. This Life is the flawless expression or character of the Father, the personal and adorable Object of the mystic's adventure.

"*Love,* the principle of attraction. If we consider the Father as the supreme Subject and the Son as the Object of His thought, the personal Spirit of Love is the relation between the two and constitutes the very character of the two.

"The love wherewith we love is the Holy Spirit." [2]

[2] "Mysticism," Evelyn Underhill.

The *triangle* among the Japanese is a flame symbol typifying fire or the third element. From the days of the stupa the triangle has represented fire.

Three triangles or rays typifying the three-fold light of the world are found among the Mexicans, Egyptians and many other ancient races. Among the Chaldeans Eusoph the Light of Life was given the symbol of the equilateral triangle.

The triangle was the symbol of the great Aum 'dwelling in the infinite.' It was the emblem of heaven in three divisions.

The triangle was the primary form of the pyramid, which was typically the pyramid of heaven. The pyramids with their triangular sides were universally recognised "not alone as tombs for the dead, but as monuments to the Great Sun the Giver of Life and Light." Many had an altar on the apex in which the fire was never permitted to die out. The Chaldeans built palaces as well as temples in the form of a pyramid. Temples and monuments in pyramidal form are found correctly orientated in India, China, America, Java and the Polynesian Islands.

"The great pyramid of Cheops was built on lines ascertained by astronomical observations. It faces the four cardinal points and the tunnel which pierces its northern slope is in reality a telescope forever turned to the point of the heavens touched by the polar star in its lowest declination. A crystal lens has been discovered on the site of Nineveh and a few Egyptian priests are believed to have known and used the telescope." [3]

In an ancient papyrus Isis is referred to as the ruler of the pyramid.

[3] "Symbolism and Science," Lloyd P. Smith.

"The form of the pyramid enters into the hieroglyph of the star Sothis or Sirius. For the Grand Orient or position of the star when its rising forms the immediate harbinger of dawn was, as is well known, the great starting point for the age-long cycles of Egyptian reckoning. And whereas the figure employed to denote the pyramid embraces both edifice and platform on which it is built, the hieroglyph of Sothis represented the masonic portion alone. . . . , viz, the structure, representing to the Egyptian mind Eternal Light apart from its earthly support." [4]

A recent book on *The Mysterious Science of the Pharaohs* by the Abbé Moreux, director of the Observatory of Bourges, discusses the pyramid of Cheops "as a manifestation of the marvellously exact mathematical and geographical knowledge of the ancient Egyptians," adding that "we glorify acquisitions as our own which were known at least 6,000 years ago. The savants of antiquity had measured the earth! They had determined our distance from the sun! They had traced an ideal meridian! All that presupposes an advanced science and a very able technique."

The Egyptians called the nature of the universe the fairest of triangles.

The triangle was the delight of the Greek philosophers. Pythagoras adopted it as the most perfect geometrical figure inasmuch as it was the first form complete in itself.

Plato used the triangle as a symbol of marriage. In this triangle he makes the perpendicular equal 3, the base 4 and the hypothenuse 5. The perpendicular represents the male, the base the female and the hypothe-

[4] "The House of the Hidden Places," W. M. Adams.

nuse their offspring. This is Osiris, the first principle, Isis, the matrix and Horus the completed world, for "three is the first odd number and is perfect, four is a square that has an even number—two—for its side, and five is in some respects like each parent for it is the sum of three and two." In this diagram of marriage Plato calls the son 'that which is better.'

Plutarch calls the "area within the triangle the 'Plain of Truth' in which the Reason, the forms and the pattern of all things that have been and shall be are stored up."

St. Augustine expressed his obligation to Plato for enabling him to understand the doctrine of the Trinity.

The Druidic Harps were made in the form of a triangle. "Their strings were three and their turning-keys had each three arms."

The famous abracadabra, a cabalistic word which was believed to have curative powers and when worn as an amulet was supposed to ward off evil was depicted in the form of a triangle reversed. It is one of the mystery words which played such an important part in the secret rites of the early mystics. Its root is *abraxas* the Greek letters of which as numerals amounted to 365. It was thus adopted by the Egyptian Gnostic Basilides to signify the Supreme Deity as ruler of the 365 heavens of his system. Another authority speaks of it as "one of the numerous mystery words coined to express mathematically the unspeakable name of the Supreme Spirit . . . and accepted as the mystic equivalent of Mithras."

The well known Hexagram or Solomon's Seal with which he was said to have worked miracles warded off danger and curbed rebellious spirits was made of two equilateral triangles interlaced forming a six

Coloniae,
Ioan. Soter excudebat. MDXXXIII

Bayley, *Lost Language of Symbolism*

pointed star. Sometimes the lower triangle is dark and the upper one light, signifying the union of the spiritual and the material or spirit and matter.

SOLOMON'S SEAL.

THE PENTACLE.

The Pentacle or five pointed star, an ingenious elaboration of the triangle, was used by the Pythagoreans and others as a mystical emblem of perfection or of the universe. "Among the followers of Pythagoras the triple triangle typified Light and was an emblem of health."

The American Indian used the triangle reversed, duplicating it thus as a symbol of growth, expressing by a sign the same idea that Bergson advanced a few thousand years later, that the tendency of Life "is to develop in the form of a sheaf, creating by its very growth divergent directions among which its impetus is divided. . . . If . . . the unity of life is to be found solely in the impetus that pushes it along the road of time, the harmony is not in front but behind . . . it is given at the start as an impulsion, not placed at the end as an attraction." [5]

The conflict between unity and multiplicity is not new. It is clear that if you wish to represent unity then multiplicity you have only to tip the triangle upside down. This was a tendency, however, that even the most primitive religions seem to have reckoned with and

[5] Bergson's "Creative Evolution."

tried strenuously to prevent. The history of the triangle is the history of man. And Life never looked fair nor perfect to the ancients except as they visioned it through the equilateral triangle accurately placed on its base and uniting towards the heavens above. All the great religions of life were founded on the family group idea of divergence then unity on a higher level. This was also a part of race development carried on like the octave on an ever ascending scale.

The triangle, whatever else it may have expressed, was, from the remotest periods of which we have any knowledge the pre-eminent symbol of the Trinity in Unity. Other symbols typified a section, a part of life. The equilateral triangle symbolised the completed whole of life. Simple, complex—clear, mysterious, it contained all the moral law and the prophets.

It is presumable that man was conscious almost from the very first that there was a part of himself higher than the body or the mind, and that he looked upon the divine in himself as a spark from the Divine Fire, the Light of Lights, the Unknown and Unknowable Source of All Life. In all his religions one finds this reaching out toward something higher. Man seems to have realised intuitively that in responding to the divine in himself he was fulfilling the Divine Will or Primal Cause, and to have feared instinctively the disintegrating influence of multiplicity unless enclosed by a surmounting, overtopping singleness of purpose.

His religions are strewn with totems and magic, fetiches, taboos and sacrifices which represent man's heroic efforts to harness nature and himself, to subdue the lower to the higher.

Eternal conflict and the desire to propitiate or subdue are a part of man's inheritance.

The Hindu religion perhaps more nearly realises the triumph of renunciation.

While recognising the three qualities they, too, emphasise the need of subduing the lower to the higher. They call the three qualities *sattva,* light or truth, *rajas,* passion or desire, and *tamas,* darkness or indifference. "These are the powers born of nature; they bind . . . the eternal lord of the body within the body."

Thus the history of man reflects his age long struggle with the triangle. Again and again he has revolted against the eternal over lordship of the soul, rebelled against the triangle, tried the parallel—the feminine principle adores the parallel—only to discover that Nature will not tolerate anything so dull as two straight lines; he has tried to repeat himself, to rest, to lie down, only to find that Nature objects to resting, or sameness, or standing still. He has attempted to abandon it to escape from the "Plain of Truth"; he has gone off on tangents of experimentation with only one side of his nature; he has taken up cults of phallicism, stoicism, epicureanism, asceticism and a thousand others with the avowed purpose of realising life; he has sprawled on the bottom with the serpent of materialism and sensuality; invented the French triangle; tipped it in every possible way that he could think of, dragged it about with him like a chain and ball——

He couldn't live with it, and he couldn't live without it, for it was himself, his family, his universe, his gods, his all. And one may not unfairly ascribe the swift rush of decadence that has occurred again and again in history to these times of rebellion against the demands of the whole nature, to the fact that man had lost his sense of proportion, lost his conception of himself as 'three in one.'

Now comes the most interesting and illuminating as it was the most daring of all religions. The highest, the most poignantly beautiful conception—the Christian religion—may be called the absolute revolt of the soul. Heretofore, in all his religions of life, man had reckoned with his three-fold nature.

It was reserved for the Christians to give an unexampled twist to the symbol. Like all other religions it was a new presentation of an ancient idea—something built out of the old, a part of the ever flowing stream of life. The Church Fathers discarded, codified, retained many of the old solar myths under a new form, retained the Eucharist, created a magnificent, "comprehensive system where under the shadow of a great epic . . . a place was found for as many religious instincts and as many religious traditions as possible."

The Church naturally and inevitably took over all the old symbols of life that have figured in every religion. The cross became the symbol of Life Everlasting and the triangle was as usual the highest symbol of all—the symbol of the Trinity now realised in one God —Father, Son and Holy Ghost.

The history of Christianity may be regarded as a prolonged and hectic combat with the triangle.

Mankind, ever amenable to suggestion, soul sick of everything that other religions were offering, ready to try anything that was the exact reverse to a degenerate and corrupt paganism—the early Christian typifies the inspiration of the impossible. While accepting the symbol, he resolutely rejected the base, cut away the foundations of his own being, and, poised on the peak of the triangle endeavoured to live in the soul alone.

Nothing more sublime nor more pathetic was ever attempted.

He believed that the world was coming to an end, that the second coming of Christ was near, that the hereafter was all.[6] He welcomed torture. Death was a sweet punishment that proved his faith. When he couldn't die for his belief, he mortified the flesh, wore hair shirts, inflicted flagellations upon his quivering body. He renounced the world, took to the desert—and wherever he went, whatever he did the triangle came to disturb him. No amount of blinding himself as to ultimate values, no denials, no affirmations of what constituted the highest expression of life could change its proportion, nor lessen its power as an irresistible force that soon or late must be reckoned with—soon or late would demand its toll.

He himself had been formed by the union of two. The three in one of which the triangle was the potent emblem was himself, his universe, his God. Yet as realised in himself he despised it. He gave up family. He became a monk—transcendental, mystic. He *would* live on a point above everything earthly without visible means of support. And to his credit, be it said, the early Christian has given us the highest proof of sincerity and the most exquisitely beautiful religion the world has yet known.

The trouble was, of course, the triangle.

[6] It has been shown how essential and integral a part of the Jewish belief in the Messiah was this expectation of the final completion of his mission in the dissolution of the world, and the restoration of a paradisiacal state in which the descendants of Abraham were to receive their destined inheritance. . . . This appears to have been the last Jewish illusion from which the minds of the Apostles themselves were disenchanted. And there can be no doubt that many of the early Christians almost hourly expected the final dissolution of the world, and that this opinion awed many timid believers into professions of Christianity and kept them in trembling subjection to its authority."—Milman's "History of Christianity."

Men married still—common men—not men with religion as their avowed purpose in life—loved and married, for there is no doubt that, in spite of its manifold faults, there is something very lovable about the feminine principle. In this new religion the "notion of woman as the ally and satellite of Satan" which harked back to the Hebrew version of the Fall of Man was intensified by the "institution of sacerdotal celibacy." The fact that woman was now regarded openly as an influence to be fought against and resisted put her in the irresistible and pleasurable category of the forbidden. Not that she wished to be there. On the contrary, taking her colour as usual from the prevailing mode of thought, she wished ardently to be a nun.

She was a nun—and a thoroughly good nun at that. And if man had stayed a good monk, no doubt the problems of our modern civilisation would have been spared us—for there would have been no civilisation—the Christian materialistic one, I mean. There would have been no fundamentalists or modernists. We would have been dead long ago. We would have died out in purity and sanctity—the soul triumphant over the body.

But it was not to be. It wasn't in man to be a monk too long. Life is too strong to permit so simple a solution. Because he had placed himself a bit too high, though, in the beginning, one can understand why, in yielding to the inexorable need of his nature, he did so with a feeling that he was falling and that sex was a shameful thing. Consciously or unconsciously this attitude has pervaded the Christian religion ever since. In truth, the Christian had many things, many discrepancies, many wide gaps between his professions and what he really was to trouble him. Demons and wild beasts in the jungle were nothing to the tortures that were inflicted by his own alert and chastening soul. Nor was that all. He was sore beset, not only by the triangle of himself—his three-fold nature—but by the triangle as an emblem of the Trinity.

Believing the Christian religion to be a direct emanation from God, the position of the symbol became a torment to the theologians. To reverse it meant multiplicity instead of ultimate union with the Most High. To keep it as it was suggested the old days of pantheism, the divine in everything merging in the One above All.

Controversy raged in the Middle Ages over the interpretation of the Trinity by the equilateral triangle. The Trinity became a metaphysical subtlety—a source of acute contention to the keen intellects of the thirteenth century who "cared little to comprehend anything but the incomprehensible."

The attempt to change the whole nature of man in order to make it fit into an idealised, dogmatic, denying religion—or conception of Life—became like a strait jacket to the normal minded, thin ecstasy and emotionalism to the dreamer and an uneasy ghost to the logician, who is rarely concerned with the essence of things—and religion is the essence of life. It was at this period when discussion of the Trinity ran highest—especially in France that the Church stepped in. It poured oil upon the troubled waters. It diverted, disarmed, soothed. The Church saw with alarm that instead of a religion it had a debating society on its hands, that its whole system which was to have been above body and mind was now lodged firmly in the mind, and was becoming as a consequence coldly, arrogantly intellectual—a lop-sided development into the soaring and unfettered masculine, which might lead anywhere under the shining sun—anywhere except to unity. There was but one brake that could be applied successfully to this intellectual runaway called the masculine principle.

The Church applied it, deftly, artfully, delightfully. It exalted the feminine. The Church became the Mother Church. And the divine Mother of Christ the second Eve, the Mother of all the world, the Virgin of Virgins. In devotional pictures she was crowned as the Queen of Heaven and was given the sceptre. Attended by adoring angels she was the Queen of Angels. Weeping or holding the crown of thorns, she is our Lady of Sorrow (*Mater Dolorosa*). She is the Madonna, the Blessed Virgin, the *Santa Maria Virgine*. She was called *Stella Maris* 'Star of the Sea.' She was the woman of the Apocalypse "clothed with the sun, having the moon under her feet, and on her head a crown of twelve stars" and was portrayed in art with the glory of the sun about her and the crescent moon under her feet. She was the Virgin of all the old nature myths with a fatherless son, and was given all the old symbols—the *fleur de lis,* the palm, cypress, olive, rose, pomegranate, dove, apple, globe. The serpent was depicted under her feet in allusion to the prophecy 'she shall bruise thy head,' and seven doves typifying the gifts of the spirit, when she is depicted as the Mother of Wisdom (*Mater Sapientiæ*). In the days of chivalry the Virgin was given the title of Our Lady—*Notre Dame, La Madonna.* She became the Virgin of Mercy—Our Lady of Succour and appeared as intercessor. Her most popular representation in art, however, was as *Mater Amabilis* or the Virgin and Child where she is depicted simply as the Mother. Raphael's pictures of her in this character have never been surpassed.

The Church succeeded beyond its hopes. Worship

of the Virgin became a passion, sweeping intellect aside, before, with it, engulfing it.

Henry Adams devotes a characteristically amusing chapter to this in *Mont Saint Michel and Chartres.* He says "Not only was the Son absorbed in the Mother but the Father followed, and the Holy Ghost fared no better. The poets regarded the Virgin as the Templum Trinitatis. . . . The Trinity was absorbed in her. . . . This is a delicate subject in the Church and you must feel it with delicacy without brutally insisting on its necessary contradiction."

This graceful assumption could not last, however. Still maintaining the idea of a direct and definite revelation that broke with tradition, as she gradually incorporated into her religion the accumulated wisdom of all the ages back of her, enemies within and without accused the Church of subterfuge. The Catholic Church knew, if her critics did not, that she could do no other and remain a religion of life. The Church realised but too well that it could have no real and vital religion and no adherents or followers if it broke with Life—and Life was sex, life was three-fold, life was body, mind, soul—father, mother, child.

The triangle spoke irrefutably of this one eternal truth. While adopting the symbol the tenets and dogma of the Church denied by implication its meaning. And it may have been because of this—because of this fundamental difference that no amount of argument or sophistry could reconcile, that bigotry took the place of faith and self-assertiveness of meekness. In spite of all that she believed, all that she stood for the Church's record became one of hypocrisies, compromises, persecutions, intolerance, worldliness. Exalting the Virgin was undoubtedly the most mystically satisfying of all the things that had been adapted from past religions by this most deeply mystical and esoteric religion. In exalting the feminine principle the Church was simply responding to the inexorable need of the human heart, although in doing this she was contradicting the idea upon which Christianity was founded. In this new religion of the soul alone, there could be no soft dalliances, no pleasures that were not deadly sins. The flesh not only was to be subdued, but harshly, ruthlessly sacrificed to the spirit. It was a swing of the pendulum, perhaps, against the dissolute practices of a decadent paganism. Another of man's undying efforts to realise his best. The Christian religion was built up upon the belief that once the soul was satisfied there would be, could be no heart hunger nor physical hunger. Christianity was founded upon the idea that life was of no account—something to be extinguished gloriously in order to win Eternal Life.

'Dying to live' was again the keystone, but living was not renewed annually with the awakening of nature in the Spring, but removed from this world entirely to a remote region of the fancy—a 'new heaven and a new earth' where there 'shall be no more death neither sorrow nor crying . . . for the former things are passed away.' It was in the Holy City of the Apocalypse, its streets paved with pure gold, its walls garnished with precious stones and each gate a pearl. There in the midst of the street of it, on either side of the river—a 'pure river of water of life'—*there* stood "the tree of life which bore twelve manner of fruits and yielded her fruit every month; and the leaves of the tree were for the healing of nations." (Rev. 22: 2.)

To adjust a religion to life that had originated in a magnificent though futile disdain of life required compromise. But no matter how delicately administered nor how deftly inserted, the soul, which had been triumphantly in the ascendant so long, sniffed the danger to itself in the Church's attitude and resented it.

Revolt flamed up again in Luther only to find the last condition worse than the first. Still doing battle gallantly, implacably against our own evil nature we dropped away from the Wise Mother Church which was prone to forgive, prone to deal too kindly with those who failed to sacrifice the flesh to the spirit. We of the protesting religions once more sternly abjured the feminine principle. We refused to regard the Virgin as an object of worship. We discarded myths, symbolism, saints, poetry. The old Covenanters tried to abolish the festivals of Christmas and Easter as heathen celebrations carried over from paganism—as, in fact, they were—but here nature was too strong. Nature and habit together can outwit even a Scotch Presbyterian. Christmas and Easter refused to be banished from the protestant religions. Or, what is more likely we refused to let them go. Most of us retained the Trinity and all of us the belief that Christ was born of a Virgin. We had, in truth, borrowed most of our religion from the Catholics, as the Catholics had borrowed before us, incorporating from the past those things that can never be safely discarded—except, in our zeal to purify and be 'holier than thou,' we had taken a religion founded on love, and again made it an expression of all that was unlovely. And all the time we were trying desperately to be good.

And thus, after vain struggles and acrimonious contentions with the Mother Church, whereby we gained nothing in saintliness of living and the Church grew no worse, perfectly outraged by our own insubordination we landed as inevitably as you please into the dismal and depressing triangle of Calvanism—Original Sin, Depravity and Atonement.

And there we remained, grim, determined—resolved on uprightness for ourselves and others—alas, very much for others! A hard and sterile formalism seized upon the tenderest and most elevated of all religions. We became puritans. We kept the Sabbath. We burned witches—until we couldn't stand our own repressions any longer. We broke up into innumerable sects, each professing to be Christian, and each antagonistic to the other. We had—not a re-birth into joyous living—not yet. We were now quite past being saved or mollified or even distracted by the feminine principle which, left to itself was making ready to enact a new rôle. Siva the god of religious apathy and destruction had become our master, multiplicity our absorption, wars—industrial wars, political wars, sex wars, wars of aggression, wars for greed and power our occupation.

This culminated in 1914, as if in response to some unknown and undreamed of Law, in the greatest war of all history.

The war ended leaving us suddenly, brutally confronted by the fact that we have added enormously to the means of life—the accessories, the non-essentials—have acquired an incredible amount of knowledge as to scientific ways of destroying life, but of Life itself, whence it comes and whither it goes we know no more than the first man of all.

Since the Armistice that left us so far from peace, we have been drifting, appalled by our own complexity, reduced to confessing that so far, as Santayana puts it, mankind has found "no way of uttering the ideal meaning of life."

The ancient Greeks, perhaps, came the nearest. No race has equalled them in joyousness of living, nor left such imperishable records of beauty in drama, art, literature. No race more fully lived. The Greeks developed the whole man. They had such a healthy conception of life, such balance, that everything that they did was done intelligently and beautifully. They believed that all was good—soul, mind, body. In time, however, as their power as a nation weakened, their poetic conception of life became dulled and gross, they lost their sense of balance, of just proportion, and yielding to man's besetting sin, they concentrated upon a part instead of the whole, ended by exalting the human body as the highest and most beautiful of all things—and the Greek civilisation passed out with so many others.

The triangle looks back upon a long, long path. It still holds its inscrutable message of Perfection, of the Unrealised. This immutable symbol in its stark, austere, almost terrifying simplicity suggests an interpretation of life that had it been realised in the physical or family sense alone, must have carried us to the skies.

In witnessing the failure of the soul when it disdains the body—its failure alone to preserve a pure religion of life unsupported by mind and body, one asks, if the old feud between soul and body could be made up—is that it? Had the Greeks paid greater homage to the soul—it is so *exigéant,* the soul—might they not still be the leading race? Has not the soul been a little selfish these past two thousand years—one hesitates to say it—but has it not? Must the soul put itself into everything that the mind conceives and the body performs—

lose itself to find itself—the soul above, but permeating and making divinely beautiful the whole man—is that the message of the triangle?

It is so important! No wonder the ancients debated the position of the triangle. If we hold strictly to the analogy of the trinity, to the unit of three in one, we must conclude that the religion of life holds further possibilities never yet fully realised—possibilities of orderly sequence, orderly progression, going forward with your whole self.

XXII

CONCLUSION: MAINLY CONTROVERSIAL

"Man is a mis-shapen monster with his feet set forward and his face set back. He can make the future luxuriant and gigantic so long as he is thinking about the past . . . to-morrow is the gorgon; a man must only see it mirrored in the shining shield of yesterday. If he sees it directly he is turned to stone."—Chesterton.

XXII

CONCLUSION: MAINLY CONTROVERSIAL

LA FONTAINE, who borrowed from Æsop, from history and mythology, from all the arts and professions as well as the popular customs of the day, composed his fables, one half suspects, for the delight he experienced in tacking on to them a few observations—moral or otherwise—of his own.

As this book is another borrower from the eternal sources of myth, fable and symbolism, I trust that I may be forgiven for following so illustrious an example. Although, I hasten to add, these are hardly conclusions—it is most unsafe to draw conclusions about life—and there is but one moral. The rest is speculative, scarcely more than suggestion, in no sense assertion—the speculations that come unbidden to the mind that seeks without prejudice, bias or partisanship for truth.

Nothing has greater or more enduring interest than to be meeting and overtaking ourselves on the long, brightly checkered path that history makes. It is on the whole an enchanting path—made so by ourselves. It is ours—our record.

When I return from one of these excursions, my mind still full of these ancient, lovely myths and beliefs—physical, mystical, spiritual—each supplementing, supporting, strengthening the other,—I look at man with fresh understanding. I find him a dear—at core quite untouched. I feel like saying joyously as one says to a much loved friend who has been away for ages but has now come back, "Well, here you are! And you don't look a day older than you did before you went away." You see, in the present civilisation we have missed him, he has been away a long time.

Always doing something grandiose, superlative, spectacular—this man! In one age he is obsessed with pyramid building, in another he creates aeroplanes and automobiles and moving pictures. His toys change but he himself remains the same. He is forever busy hitching something together to see how it will work, even "hitching his wagon to a star" if he happens to be Emerson.

Here he is! Impelled by the same forces—the same creature of insensate passions, having the same desires, wants, emotions, the same needs, same longings, same conflict of wills——

Curiosity enormous. . . . .

The same unquenchable love of theorising and prophesying and explaining. . . . .

Pursuing throughout the ages the same path from unity through duality to multiplicity. . . . .

The same losing the way in multiplicity until forced to go back to unity again.

As we survey man's picturesque efforts to change nature and change himself, to understand nature and understand himself, the real wonder is, not that we have lost our way so often, but that in the maze—mostly self-created—we ever find it at all.

In all this maze of ideas, however, two things stand out and they are curiously explicit. One is that we never get away from the swing between the two forces, Spirit and Matter or Form.

The other which is equally emphatic, inescapably so, and will be referred to at some length later on, is the survival of our primal instincts.

Whenever religions past or present lose themselves in subtleties neglecting the substance, or again when they pay greater attention to form or its visible aspect and neglect the invisible spirit they fall into decay.

To keep these forces in equilibrium has been the problem of the ages—the problem of ancient religions.

All symbolism deals with these two principles which merge into the Creative Life Principle. Methods and manifestations change and pass out, the Eternal things remain.

Death has various ways of terminating man's existence on earth. He may meet it now flying or in an automobile accident, where in Roman days it overtook him in the hippodrome or in chariot racing. Yet—Death itself as a force remains unchanged.

Life, ... Death.
Spirit, ... Matter.
Light, ... Darkness.
Heat, ... Cold.
Fire, ... Water.
Order, ... Disorder.
Osiris, ... Set.
Man, ... Woman.

These are the unchangeable forces—the "pair of opposites," that were forever being symbolised in the effort to adjust the equilibrium of harmonious life.

Beyond death man sees life renewed by the same power of progression that brings light again as darkness passes. His desire to prolong either phase, to make day into night, or night into day—to worship either principle exclusively, or to negative both principles and worship their manifestations, may account for his many failures. In spite of failure, however, his idealism persists. That's the beauty of him. No matter how often deceived, nor how many times he deceives himself, *au fond* "man is the born enemy of lies."

The one thing that we cannot afford to lose sight of—cannot let little things crowd out, is the tremendous importance of man and woman since time began.

The potency still of the old religious symbols of the dual principles show how momentously they have impressed themselves upon religion and civilisation. If the father god is worshipped exclusively you have a certain sort of a civilisation. When the pendulum swings and the Mother goddess is exalted you have another kind which eventually and inevitably, it would seem, passes out.

In all religions, as in Life itself, there are the two forces, one non-progressive, inert, becoming static—those who would sit by the tranquil stream of life dreaming that all is known, all has been said—and those who like fire rush on sweeping over and consuming the results of ages of effort, unless checked by the wholesome power of water—or the negative force that binds and restrains. Thus man fails when he drops out of the unhurried movement of life, when he no longer re-acts to change; he also fails disastrously, creating widespread havoc when he rushes headlong, bent only on change and loses the resilient power of coming back. It is this coming back that is so great. And it is here that the feminine or passive principle is of such enormous value. It corrects the excesses of the masculine not by any power of reasoning but simply by the law of its own being.

Whenever the vibration between the two forces Spirit and Matter or Positive and Negative ceases to be normal and creative, there comes conflict, antagonism, dissolution.

The old religions all show this—show poise first, then overbalancing of forces, a weakening of the spirit until the material preponderates; matter or form without the quickening power of the spirit becomes inert, lifeless, unresponsive, corrupt—and religion and civilisation go out together.

Throughout his entire history one finds the tendency to develop one side—never the whole nature of man—to sacrifice and subdue, never to strengthen, which force is to be subdued depending upon which force is in the ascendancy.

The Christian religion, as we have seen, began in a supreme disdain of form. It was the soul's revolt against the corrupt practices of a decadent paganism. And it seems scarcely an exaggeration to say that in Christianity the soul took the bits in its teeth and ran away with religion. It opposed itself relentlessly to nature worship, and quite as relentlessly to the feminine principle, which happened at that time to be the principle that men were worshipping. The soul had again been forgotten, and it exacted penance to the last ounce of flesh. It contrived a religion of expiation for past orgies. Making no attempt to reconcile the dual principles it scorned the body, nature, earth. Instead of illuminating the dark corners of existence the soul was now chiefly concerned in absorbing all life and light for itself.

I confess that the soul troubles me. I think the soul can trouble any one. Having had some experience with *exigéant* souls I believe that there is nothing so unstable as the human soul. I am inclined to think that the soul can be recalcitrant, proud, obstinate, a self-willed shirk. The body automatically rebels, whereas the soul willfully neglects its job. It loves to soar in higher space, to imagine, dream, escape restraint. It is even more insubordinate than the mind, for mind and body are both clay whenever the soul is content to use them to express its purpose.

If you happen to have one of these dodging, soaring, escaping souls, that loves to dwell in the blue ether and doesn't care a bit whether you are symmetrical or not, you will understand what I mean. And I cannot help fancying that you will agree that the abandon to the soul of all religious functions has not improved our minds, our bodies, nor our looks.

The soul cares nothing for the body, however. It is no penance to the soul to mortify the flesh. It adores it. I am perfectly convinced that the early saints took ecstatic and cruel delight in mortifying the poor, quivering, agonising body. It was done as a re-action against a corrupt paganism that had exalted the body above the soul—but was it religion?

Not being at all sure that it was ever intended that the soul should refuse to live at peace with the body, or that it should leave the body before the last flight comes, I ask the question tentatively. Can the soul create, and has it been able to create a workable religion alone? Has not the soul been a rebel in the Christian

Photo. Alinari

PSYCHE

(Museo Nazionale, Naples)

religion enjoying itself hugely at the expense of everything else, sanity included?

If this seems a little harsh, I may add that I am only inimical to the soul that is draped in pretension. There is proof on every hand that there is nothing so easy as to lose yourself in spiritual ecstasy. One can be a spiritual voluptuary as well as a physical voluptuary. And what is far more menacing, spiritual ecstasy has an ominous way of degenerating into the physical. Having a somewhat difficult soul that would soar off on the slightest provocation, the point I would make is this. Whenever the soul attempts to escape from the body, when it loses the protection, the sanity, the form given it by the body does it not, as a rule, fall victim to its mortal enemy the mind—fall prey to a sort of arid, unemotional intellectualism that eventually destroys it? If the soul is the animating force of the body can it afford to neglect the body? Does not the soul also need the body as well as the body the soul?

When the soul rises up undaunted after disaster we hail it joyfully. It represents to us the eternal triumph of life. It may be true as the Catholics say that certain natures are called upon to be high examples of faith and renunciation for all the world to see, but I am always a little afraid when the soul seems to be having too good a time. There is nothing so conducive to one's own inner cheerfulness and every one else's misery as being an acknowledged martyr.

Chesterton describes the death of St. Francis of Assisi on the bare, cold earth, and adds, that in spite of physical suffering he was probably the happiest man in the whole world.

There is not a doubt of it. He had carried the matter consistently through.

If I may be permitted to say so, and without the slightest wish to offend those who look upon the soul as an infallible guide, I think that in the Christian religion, except at brief intervals of recurring sanity, the soul has been having the time of its life.

I was expressing myself in some such way to a Jesuit priest not long ago.

He looked at me keenly, then said thoughtfully "So you think that in the Christian religion the soul went off on a spiritual lark."

As I had been working for months and months with archeologists who make tentative suggestions, rather than positive assertions, I replied cautiously, making use of the time honoured archeological phrase "It may be so."

The point is, however, that much as you may regret it, nothing stays. These revolts against paganism and materialism were necessary, and the body must be put down if the soul was to pursue its high and respected way alone—but was that the intention? Did Life really mean that the soul should ignore the body and go off on spiritual quests alone?

We are enormously amenable to suggestion. Although in mediævalism the Christian religion—having gradually adopted all the old nature ideas that have been interwoven and are a part of every ancient religion—flowered into transcendent beauty, yet after a period the suggestion of penance returned. We had been taught to fear beauty—to fear being naturally, healthily happy. We continued in our cowardly, shrunken, fearing hearts to look upon pleasure as a sin and Nature as an enticing jade unless you worked for her, when she became a remorseless hag. We accepted the feminine principle grudgingly yet we had to bow to form, and never were more beautiful forms created than in the Middle Ages during the time when the two forces were harmoniously united by the far seeing wisdom of the Mother Church.

Nevertheless one must be dull, indeed, who does not detect an undercurrent of protest even when yielding, as if the soul once having tasted the joys of heaven was impatient with everything that had to do with earth. Having once been a runaway, it continued to be a runaway, ready on the slightest provocation to spurn matter. Yet without matter it could create nothing beautiful.

A letter from Ralph Adams Cram expresses admirably the necessity for form. While looking upon Christianity "that is to say explicitly and definitively Catholic Christianity as a divine revelation," he goes on to deplore the passion for the "big thing." "This approaches too closely to that imperialism which is the nemesis of our modern civilisation. Devotion to the 'big thing' means the forgetting of limitations. Your limitations are exactly the greatest gift of God to man. Without them we should be amœba or jelly-fish or indeterminate gases. We must work within our limitations, that is what life is for. Chess is a good example. It would not be a game at all but for its magnificently narrow, and therefore broadening limitations. We have got to see everything in the large, regard life as a whole, but we have got to work within those limitations which are imposed upon us. Forgetfulness of this fact is the nemesis of Unitarianism, New Thought, Christian Science, Pragmatism, all the vague and illusory religious and philosophical delusions of modernism. The greatness of great art is that it works within the hide-bound limitations of its media. So in the case of life, of which art is type and an exponent."

Except for that lovely flowering time in mediævalism never has the contest between spirit and form been more virulent than in the Christian religion. And it is the petering out of the soul when permitted to splash on its own, that is the most startling of all of Life's paradoxes. If we had not been trained for centuries to look upon the soul as sacrosanct we would all see this.

Those who have made a study of the occult declare that it is quite possible under certain conditions for the soul of an Adept to leave the body, but admit that it is an extremely dangerous thing to do, for if anything happens to the deserted body during its absence the soul must wander without a home.

This may explain much that would otherwise be inexplicable. While materialism has been permitted to flourish, crowding out the dreaming, wandering, runaway soul, the soul, wearied by too much freedom, degenerates into revolting charlatanry in its fatigued efforts to present itself in some new and startling form. Its dominance over various nondescript religious cults is really a plea for the materialistic pleasures of life. The soul is now beseeching the kind graces of matter —asking matter to take it in. Yet even now it does it arrogantly, condescendingly, as if it knew all the tricks, as if material things belonged to it, were its to bestow. These cults have nothing to say about martyrdom or sacrifice or crucifixion for the right. Their promise is the material blessings of health and prosperity.

The Egyptian is the oldest conception of a real life hereafter of which we have any record. They said of the dead "they depart not as those who are dead but they depart as those who are living." And they were the first who made happiness in the future life dependent on character.

Decadence set in in that oldest of known civilisations, in precisely the same way, broadly speaking. The High Priests in the Nineteenth Dynasty, corrupted by power and money were anything but religious. One hundred and fifty years later the dethronement of the Pharaohs was brought about by the priests. The kings no longer prayed for character and the blameless life but for the material things which they desired. Breasted in his *History of Egypt* quotes a prayer of Rameses IV to Osiris which might be uttered in any one of the religious cults of the present day.

"And thou shalt give to me health, life long existence and a prolonged reign; endurance to my every member, sight to my eyes, hearing to my ears, pleasure to my heart daily. And thou shalt give to me to eat until I am satisfied, and thou shalt give to me to drink until I am drunk. And thou shalt establish my issue as kings forever and ever. And thou shalt grant me contentment every day, and thou shalt hear my voice in every saying when I shall tell them to thee, and thou shalt give them to me with a loving heart. And thou shalt give to me high and plenteous Niles in order to supply thy divine offerings and to supply the divine offerings of all the gods and goddesses of South and North, in order to preserve alive the divine bulls, in order to preserve alive the people of all thy lands, their cattle and their groves which thy hand has made. For thou art he who has made them all and thou canst not forsake them to carry out other designs with them; for that is not right."

We are a little less naïvely dogmatic—not quite so

dictatorial to the God to whom we say our prayers. It is a democratic age—but we pray for practically the same things, most of us. Nor has the war even scotched the desire for material blessings above everything else.

Religion in its highest form is simply an avowal of faith in the supernal glory of Life—a ritual for expressing the beauty and splendour of Life. Throughout history the soul in its eagerness for flight forgets that this is a three-cornered affair—this life—forgets the mind, forgets the body, forgets that if religion is life, spirit must enter into every phase of life, make strong and upright the body and give animation to the mind. It forgets that to inform form, fill it with life and energy is the purpose. And its very forgetfulness is death to the soul.

Life is not a mood nor is religion static. Each new revelation is built on the old form but renewed as the race is renewed.

The moment a religion has become definitive, believes that it has said all—from that moment it says nothing. It has ceased to grow. And also, whenever it typifies but one side of life, it is thin (spirit), or too heavy (materialism).

In this most thrilling contest between spirit and matter, one finds that neither paganism nor Christianity offers man the slightest support when he permits either force to overbalance the other. His religion is not a support, it is—most unfortunately at times—man's very self. If it is woozy, vaporous, weakly sentimental, has lost the beauty, the essential quality of form, the man is also a sentimentalist. If it is a frigid intellectualism without imagination—thus then we have become.

It seems clear enough that whether man worships nature or worships mammon, whether he is a professing but insincere and perverted pagan or a professing but insincere and perverted Christian his collapse and demoralisation are equally sure.

It is also unmistakably clear that whenever the decadence of a nation's ideals takes place something has gone wrong with the spirit.

Along with the eternal conflict between spirit and matter are certain primal *instincts* that cut their way sharply across the tangled and intricate web of life. The survival of these, our absolute and unfailing loyalty to them and the way they can be played up to now as in the past is almost beyond belief.

The way everything we think, feel, do, have been and are dovetails, making a patterned whole—it is that that ensnares thought and imagination.

It is amazingly significant, too, how true we run to form—to that form assigned to us before history began.

With these inherited instincts either to govern man or to be governed by him, one can see that in all his various religions he has been trying, not only to express his worship for an Unseen Force, but also to express and cope with himself so that he could live at peace with himself. Although his religion may be dressed up in different forms there is always the man underneath, evincing in greater or lesser degree the same tendency to resort to magic, propitiation, sacrifice, the instinct to worship something higher, the instinctive reaching out toward perfection, the same passionate devotion to theories and discoveries, the same deathless desire to know the secrets of life, the instinct to turn to shibboleths as a panacea for human woes—and standing out above everything else is trust! Our worst heartaches come from betrayals of trust. Trust is such a deeply imbedded instinct that it seems to me this in itself negatives Frazer's assertion that most religions were founded on fear. Fear was a weapon in the hands of unscrupulous priests, and by fear they debased life, debased religion. And it is true that nations ruled by fear never rise above savages. It seems a little warped, however, to make the savage mind the touchstone, or to attribute to it the creation of symbolic customs. As far back as we can go we find wise men as well as savages the same as now. We don't any of us really know, do we? But we love to surmise about past, present and future. This is another inherited instinct. We *love* to surmise and sometimes—both doubtless quite wrong—one surmise is as good as another. A woman does not need to be an anthropologist in order to surmise. She does it naturally.

My surmise—I say this humbly but hopefully—as to the ancient mind and the ancient religions is that then as now the mind betrayed the same bent, the same seeking, the same trust, the same ardent desire to know God. The normal man begins his life trusting in Life, with a love for it, belief in it and belief in his fellow man. Anatole France expresses this charmingly. Soliloquising over having arrived *'au milieu du chemis de la vie,'* he speaks of tomorrow. *"Demain! Il fut un temps où ce mot contenait pour moi la plus belle des magies. En le prononçant je voyais des figures inconnues et charmantes me faire signer du doight et murmurer, 'Viens!' J'aimais tant la vie alors! J'avais en elle la belle confiance d'un amoureux . . . Je ne l'accuse pas. Elle ne m'a pas fait les blessures qu' elle a faites à tant d'autres. Elle m'a même quelque fois caressé, par hazard, la grande indifférente! . . . Malgre tout, j'ai, perdue l'esperance . . . je n'ai plus confiance en mon ancienne amie la vie. Mais, je l'aime encore."*

We must conclude that fear is a product of human experience. If experience forces us to part with our beliefs, we do so unwillingly, sadly, with a sense of being cheated. Faith and belief in Life is so strong in us that failing to realise it here on earth we transfer it to the skies.

We will trust and we will worship.

The instinct to worship is also a part of our inheritance, not only to worship an Unknown God but to demand a visible image that shall embody our ideas of what is great and noble and fine. Before this image we prostrate ourselves as much as in the days of old. Now, however, instead of an idol of wood or stone we have substituted human beings. Denied the 'graven image' to worship we endow some man of heroic proportion with all the god-like qualities. He becomes our symbol of greatness.

"Now as always the great mass of men look for the master-man who can form in definite shape the aspirations and the instincts that in them are formless and amorphous; that can lead where they are more than willing to follow, but themselves cannot mark the way. . . . It is perhaps not so much that men now reject all leadership as it is that they blindly accept the inferior type, the specious demagogue, the unscrupulous master of effrontery. Men follow to-day as they always have and always will, the difference lies in the quality of those that are followed." [1]

In other words we are born hero-worshippers, sheep

[1] "The Nemesis of Mediocrity," Ralph Adams Cram.

who must have a leader who, if not vouchsafed to us from on high we create for ourselves. We must worship something near as well as remote.

Bayley comments upon the recondite knowledge of the ancients. And one must admit that whether derived from the long lessons which tradition enforces, or from a flash of divine inspiration carried on by tradition, the ancients showed in many ways a deeper understanding of life than the moderns. Here, at least, they seemed to have understood human nature when they provided images of the gods for man to worship.

The truth is, although you yourself may remain loyal to your human god and spend time and strength in keeping him propped up on the pedestal that your faith and adoration has supplied, when he deliberately steps down and out, what are you going to do? You may still vociferate your belief, go out of your way to assure the world that your hero still occupies the high pedestal of greatness—if you are a true hero worshipper you will not admit even to yourself that he ever side stepped or slipped down from his niche, but the public's eyes are sharp. Elevating and worshipping human gods is a hazardous and heartrending business.

One has only to reflect upon how torn we were in the United States in very recent times by our adoration of two ex-presidents. Men who were the exact antitheses of each other, who typified opposing forces, responded to different needs and cravings. Each brought disappointment and heart burnings. Each suffered, too, from misunderstandings and abuse. Each brought that human unpredicable quality that keeps worshippers who say "He is that!" on tenterhooks.

If he only would be "that"—your human god—but alas! more times than not he isn't, and at last even you are forced to say wistfully, apologetically "Ah, well! After all he's only human." But that isn't why you worshipped him. You wanted the superhuman.

Having experienced the shattering of faith following the Great War, having seen this ineradicable human tendency exemplified in the worship extended to various political leaders who have none of them stood up—except Mussolini who still stands and who is the one great leader in the world to-day—having seen and experienced disillusion where we looked for greatness, I am thoroughly convinced that the ancients aimed to make life placid and gently amusing, and above all to permit us to keep our faith when they encouraged us to worship images of greatness. One can scarcely doubt that they knew quite well what they were about, that they had discounted everything that seems to us new. They knew—one may be sure of it—that worshipping a 'graven image' was a mild and innocuous diversion compared to worshipping a human image.

I am not at all sure that we did well to permit the Jewish mind to guide us about the 'graven image'—not a bit sure that the graven image is an abomination, but I like his scapegoat. Any one who has been the family scapegoat will look back longingly to the ancient Jewish way of rendering harmless a peculiarly deep-rooted instinct in the human race.

In Judaism there was the "one great annual *piaculum* the Day of Atonement and the first sin offering in which the temple and altar are expiated. The second and characteristic feature of the ceremony follows. The high priest lays his hands on the head of a goat and confesses over it all the sins and iniquities of the children of Israel and all their transgressions; the sins of the people in the year past having thus been laid upon its head, the scapegoat bearing all their iniquities is led away into an uninhabited region and there let go. In later times, at least, to make sure that the goat with his burden of sin did not wander back to the abodes of men, he was pushed over a precipice. . . . Such methods of ridding the community of evils by loading them upon man or beast and driving the beast out or putting him to death are found among many peoples." [2]

In reading this description of an abandoned custom, one must agree that the ancient Jew not only showed an understanding of human nature, but that deeper knowledge of life which involves making human nature safe to live with.

In other races sometimes the burden bearer was one of themselves who was chosen by lot for a year as in the Beltane fires.

This, too, is one of the ineradicable instincts. We are more casual. We do it with less form. We don't let a high priest choose the victim. We select him ourselves. Thus scapegoats like brothers have multiplied. We load our sins upon the handiest person—one whom we conceive to be weaker than ourselves, more yielding and unselfish, therefore a convenient burden bearer, and then to be sure that the poor scapegoat—usually a friend or relative—does not wander back into the abodes of men carrying our load of sin exposed on his quivering back, we push him over a precipice and congratulate ourselves that at last we are without sin.

The ancient custom of dealing with man's desire

[2] Moore's "History of Religions."

to evade consequences was considerate both for him and ultimately for the goat, inasmuch as it made one goat do for a multitude, thereby lessening the number of scapegoats that are now sent heedlessly dashing over precipices.

As I said before, one who has been the family scapegoat does not need to be told that without a scapegoat upon whom to cast the burden of sin we are lost, humiliated, discomfited—unable to hold up our heads. The scapegoat found, on we go gaily. Human nature demands that some one offer himself as a sacrifice for the sins of others.

Nor does one need to be told that in politics, too, this instinct still prevails in even more than its old time liveliness and vigour. Hardly any one who is now in politics can hope to escape being a scapegoat. Instead of the blind leading the blind, it is scapegoats driving scapegoats. At the brink of the precipice even the driving ones balk and the merry chase goes on back somehow into power. The only requirement is a volatile nature, the ability to leap from crag to crag—and that, of course, a political scapegoat unblindfolded has.

There is still sacrifice, but it is useless, unfocussed, without direction.

We have the scapegoat, he is everywhere, but he escapes consequences.

One finds in the modern man as in the old the same unquenchable desire to discover the secrets of nature—a sort of highly developed curiosity that turns us to religion in one age and science in another.

I have commented in *Woman and Man's Inventions* upon man's passionate invention of theories. He was born 750,000,000 years ago—I believe that is as far back at present as we are able to go—loving theories. When not trying to be something that nature never intended him to be, he is busying himself in inventing some plausible reason or excuse for his being at all. His theories are almost as wasteful of human energy as his inventions of modern armament.

Knowing their unaccommodating nature, that they refuse to grow or expand, for very love of them man accommodates himself to theory. He would slice off arms and legs—even his own—if by so doing he could contrive to fit into a theory. He worships them—one at a time.

It is probably true, after many disconcerting, not to say upsetting experiences with Life that scientists feel more at home, so to speak, with bones and fossils and quite dead things. Bones and fossils are serious things and conversely being serious might mean being a fossil. Now, you may take a lot of credit to yourself for knowing about fossils but you will never like to be called a fossil even though you be one.

Thus we are made, preferring life to fossils.

The old religions sought to know from nature the secret of life. Science seeks the secret from the dead. The ancient studied nature seeking the supernatural. Science measures skulls.

At the moment science is working in a peculiarly complicated and contradictory way. Not satisfied with its inevitable advent according to natural processes, it seeks to produce death on a gigantic scale. Nevertheless, while constantly engaged in inventing new and more devastating methods for destroying life, it is equally busy in discovering ways for prolonging life.

"Can Old Age be Deferred?" is the scientific quest of the hour.

Here, too, the monkey proves invaluable. Once our Father, now he is our Saviour. Having enthroned the monkey as man's progenitor, science now falls upon the monkey gland as man's restorer.

One might refer the monkey glanders to the saying "Those that love truth die young whatever their age"—but one must not deprive science of its little pleasures.

One finds, too, as you look into this curious nature of ours that the desire for perfection is a fire that dies down but never goes out. In spite of what cavillers and dreary pessimists are saying, I venture to affirm that never has it burned with such ardour, such intensity—one might say with such consuming ferocity as now.

There is the same instinct, the same desire for perfectioning, but, the race no longer the objective, we have become deeply concerned with the welfare of the world, perfectioning and reforming *en bloc.*

In the very early days of Christianity "a kind of sublime selfishness excluded all subordinate considerations."

With everyone busy saving his own immortal soul you can see that it might become a selfish world. With everyone busy saving his neighbour's immortal soul, it becomes a world of bedlamite unrest—a world that sways with hasty exits.

True, we began by being vaguely altruistic. Having decided that it was our duty to save humanity we went about it loftily, majestically—preferring causes and issues to individuals. Thus it came about that to the conscious possessor of a seerlike quality of mind modern life offers a continuous flow of vicissitude. He has the old undying instinct to preach and prophesy and perfection others. Democracy invites reformation. It also permits it. Anyone can be a reformer. All may prophesy freely and inconclusively. Prophecy and reformation have become the pre-occupations of democracy. Having abandoned family admonishments the modern seer feels that he must mount a soap box or die. Alas, everyone mounts the soap box, preaching has become an affair of the mob. Nor is talking all. The same spirit of mob prophecy, mob ethics has invaded literature. The same spirit of too much.

In order to give new vent to our instinct, and also to give it a certain lawful abandon which had the sanction of our 'holier-than-thou' instinct—another persistent one, by the way—we were obliged to invent another catchword.

Nothing so well shows the growth of ideas, nor the spell of a phrase, nor incidentally, the way we can be mentally baited and intrigued by words.

We had given much time and a great deal of money toward benefitting humanity. Philanthropy had become our hobby. Nevertheless, humanity kept oozing away from us into the vague and illusory. Humanity somehow refused to play up.

It was necessary to visualise again, to have a definite symbol, a form upon which we could lavish our perfectioning instinct.

We called it the Brotherhood of Man.

Although draped pretentiously, even deceitfully, any one with brothers and sisters needs only a moment's reflection to perceive that here is a phrase of something more than soft linguistic possibilities—that behind the seeming beauty of the words there lurks the dynamic, not to say explosive.

Once brotherhood is assured an intimacy follows that far exceeds the wildest dreams of democracy. The moment you look upon your neighbour as a brother perfectioning becomes an urgent family affair.

It is interesting to follow the peculiar gyrations—up in the air usually—of this instinct when denied its legitimate direction.

To regard your neighbour with the true brotherly, corrective eye is, I repeat, more than democratic. If he resists, baffled only for a moment, the altruistic urge returns with cumulative frenzy when you reflect that this is the Age of the Brotherhood of Man.

In a land where all are given equal opportunity to follow the pleasantest pursuits known to man, we are left in no manner of doubt that the most agreeable pursuit yet devised, the one of all others that gives zest and flavour to life is the pursuit of each other.

"What must I do to be saved?" is no longer heard. The cry is, and it is a full-throated one, like hounds at bay, "How may I pluck my brother as a brand from the burning?"

We are very much concerned, very much in earnest about this brother of ours. The quiet, easy street of personal salvation—not the blatant, pushing Main Street of the present day—but the old delightful shaded street bordered by sweeping lawns, dignified homes, the pleasant village life, not too intimate and not too formal—prayers before breakfast, grace at meals, Church of a Sunday—all this is abandoned. Forgetting that where all would reform there are none left to be reformed, we have become such insistent pluckers of each other from more or less perilous but pleasant descents, that we are forced to make a mad rush to the intricacies of city life to lose each other. Here, not to be balked, we form societies and movements and leagues and employ secret agents for rescuing each other. We enact a federal amendment with the sole aim of controlling and reforming the 'other fellow.'

"To come to cypress groves exceedingly tall and fair and to green meadows where we may compose ourselves and converse" is no longer the objective. Fear possesses us. All feel pursued. It becomes a part of crowd psychology to prefer strangers. We have not a famine but a plethora of prophets and perfectionists. Where all are would-be haranguers the instinct is to get away from those we know in the hope of finding someone whom we ourselves may safely harangue. We trample on each other ruthlessly, heedless of the maledictions of the injured in our haste to stay the man who is fleeing and escape from the one behind. We dare not pause. On we go, wave upon wave, rushing pell-mell, headed nowhere, seeking and repelling each other.

Symonds speaking of the Renaissance says: "The strange caprices of the later Renaissance too often betrayed a double mind disloyal alike to paganism and Christianity in their effort to combine divergent forces." Four centuries later instead of the "double mind of the Renaissance" we are perilously near, except at spasmodic intervals, to having no minds at all. This is so true that governments are adopting the idea of thinking for us on even the most trivial, not to say intimate and private subjects. We are too wholly absorbed in the thrilling complexities of baffling and controlling each other to consider anything else—to consider what this means.

One notes the paradox, too. The more we concern ourselves with each other the less we love each other.

Interest intensifies and love diminishes. As the pace quickens there comes over us a curious combination of the sullenly inimical and the apathetically hostile and indifferent. We cling to nothing but our ideas. We are beginning to hate the object of our chase. The truth is, we are getting tired. Perfectioning our brother is a serious matter. We would like to slacken speed, to pause, to rest. We dare not do so. Greater than our desire for rest is our fear and loathing of the man —our brother also—who is sweeping on to dispense his wisdom to us from behind.

Our dissatisfaction with life grows. Many of us have retired to our study, not for the sake of peace, of a tranquil withdrawal from the busy hum of modern life. Not at all. We make the study a vantage point from which we continue the combat. We pelt our brother with books. We pour out our vitriolic and our sentimental views in books. The Younger Generation have adopted books as a means to shock as well as attack.

The colleges foster this. Each year they turn out droves of young things perfectly trained in the technic of writing—having every equipment except possibly that of having something to say. Their writings must necessarily be autobiographical—autobiographical before life has begun, or prophetic—dealing solely with the future. One bars out from this the few who really have imagination.

Prophecy without roots in the common experience —which ultimately interprets itself in terms of the universal or the accumulated wisdom of the race—degenerates into radicalism.

And here again comes in the "Brotherhood of Man." Much that seems almost whimsically disheartening in the present day attitude toward life may be accounted for by the fact that the moment you regard all men as brothers differentiations cease. You no longer have proportion. Humour passes out.

Universal dead-level-dom is a desperately serious affair. Its adherents take it most seriously.

One sees at once the complications that may ensue from a too close following of any idea. Trained by the age he lives in, it is only natural that the modern should come to feel himself self-begotten, self-created. On the other hand, fathers having also become brothers forget that they have sons. One can understand why the Younger Generation alternately abuse and plead with the Older Generation to move on. Science, too, has much to answer for in this topsy-turvy condition, by devising ways to kill off the young and preserve the old. Aided by science and the dentists, the old seem only too willing to forget that the world revolves by an orderly system of displacement. Without this constant displacement there comes what we are seeing now, congestion, lack of proportion, a furious clash of egos.

It helps one to understand, too, why the modern, discarding the past, having gone from nothing sees nothing ahead but himself and his own personal reactions to life. A book that came out a year or so ago, Ludwig Lewisohn's *Up Stream* is a striking example of this modern tendency.

When Chesterton undertakes to tell us *What is Wrong with the World* he does it wittily, enjoyingly. He convinces us that we have strayed away from the Eternal Verities. He does not remove the Eternal Verities.

Lewisohn's prophetic vision sees nothing beyond chaos, nothing beyond the present moment, nothing beyond self. After you have commended his exquisite literary style you are impressed by the intense personal egotism, and the strange binding narrowness of outlook. It isn't even bleak, for bleakness implies wide though barren spaces. He is not witty. He is not grateful. He is not tolerant. He does not instruct. He does not amuse.

It may be that this book does not accurately represent the modern, but is rather the result of an inbred racial instinct. We cannot ignore the fact, however, and it is very well worth noting, that it is this spirit that is beginning to dominate, not only in literature but is giving us through every available channel its own arid and peculiarly uninspiring interpretation of life.

There is such a thing as brotherly hate. The spirit that is beginning to dominate is the perfectioning instinct that, standing aloof disdains to affiliate with any but those whose minds run along with its own.

According to some of the more expert diagnosticians and psychologists the same radical tendencies that are so apparent in the social organism may be observed in the human organism. In other words, bolshevism has struck in.

You have to spend only a little time in contemplating the working parts of your own machinery—which you have believed up to now that you dominate—to ask yourself if you do dominate. Is not your throne trembling, too? You begin to be conscious that here, too, the head is despised. The labouring classes are up in arms striking for higher pay and shorter hours and all clamouring for self-expression. You understand why the human race is becoming stunted. The way modern doctors and specialists treat disease invites the belief that lungs, heart, liver, kidneys—all the various organs of your body are bent on growing little legs of their own so that they, too, may go off on a wild, howling, independent prance of uproarious, social equality freedom. The heart rebels at pumping blood through the lungs. It would like to live for its own heart throbs. The lungs have a wild longing to breathe something besides air. They remind you constantly and pettishly that they are sick of work. Each organ magnifies itself into a separate unit jealously resentful of the ignominy of working with or for any other part. Forced by the inscrutable law of being to jog along together in the narrow confines of the body they wreak their spite on each other. The true spirit of perfectioning, of Calvinistic reformation has entered in. The tonsils attack the knees. The teeth menace the whole body. The former master of his own domain is growing tired, too. Mind, the king is weakening. The parts are greater than the whole. Aided by the counsels of mental healers who have sprung up mushroom-wise to assist in the restoration of the old dominance of the mind, we are trying to think ourselves into states of consciousness comparable to that idyllic state when the organism was composed of silent, willing, obedient members. The very effort defeats itself. We are doing consciously the things that can only be well done unconsciously.

There is an amusing side to all this. When our breath wheezes and our heart jumps and neuritis sets into our arms and sciatica into our legs and we have indigestion most vilely—we used to say that we had lost our health. Now, we are assured by Freud—and rather gravely, too,—one finds no suggestion of irony—that what ails us is suppressed desires. Whatever it is that afflicts us, this modern attitude towards the parts of the human body furnishes a not inapt illustration of our attitude as individuals toward society.

Such is the marvellous potency of a phrase, however, and its soothing, soporific effect upon the mind, that the advocates of the theory of Brotherhood and Internationalism carried over from pre-war days will tell you even now with a seraphic smile that we are all brothers. After listening to them talk, however, you find that they are demanding your sympathy for the criminal, nor do they hesitate to pour out splenetic fault-findings with the victims of the criminal who surely are brothers, too.

Thus do we spend ourselves in our eager love of perfectioning—thus do we still make fetiches as in the days of old—slaves to our ideas.

Even in modernism there are the same persistent instincts but turned in, not out. There is the same quest—productivity, but production of the unimporant, production that creates artificial desires. The striving for unity displays itself in the effort to build up a huge industrial machine. There is sacrifice, too, but it is the sacrifice of all joy or interest in work. Massed production necessarily robs the workman of the joy of creation, of viewing the finished product as something that he has carried through from the beginning to its completion. Naturally no amount of wages can compensate for having driven the creative spirit out of labour, for making machines of men. Yet one must believe that this was done without intention, in blindest ignorance of what would be the result. Man was simply in the grip of one of his ideas. His soul having gone off on one of its long flights, he sees nothing in life but amusement and material gain. In his industrial madness, man uses up womanhood as remorselessly as he makes machines of men.

No religious cult of the most savage tribes could have demanded a greater sacrifice, or a greater number of victims. This is a sacrifice not to a God but to the "big idea"—the sacrifice of manhood and womanhood, of the joy of life for the material things of life.

The primal, energising force called man hasn't a notion of this. Having lost his reverence for life, he has lost his sense of direction and the power to think except in the groove defined by his one idea. In his business life as in his religious and social life it is the spirit that has weakened, that becomes remiss or vagrant, that wanders away or sinks into sluggishness and inertia, preferring listlessness and stupefaction to life. This goes on in this three in one creature called man until mind usurps the place formerly dominated by the soul. And mind uninformed by the spirit gives us a crude, hard capitalism on the one side and a crude, striving, getting proletariat on the other. Gentleness, grace, beauty, repose ooze out of existence and in their place we have the antics and the grimaces of the arch exponent of materialism—the Jew. Remaining in the ghetto so long as society is strong, upright, inspired, harmonious—only to come forth again with vigour unabated, climbing into power as society weakens and the materialistic spirit prevails, espousing every idea that subverts or breaks with the traditions of the past, pushing his way in where beauty is and by his presence he crowds out beauty—and then vilifies the ruin of all loveliness that his entrance makes—he is more than materialistic—he is the vulture that picks the bones of every dying civilisation. He is pathetic, too, for he had hoped to pick it alive.

He always appears when choas threatens. That is his rôle, the part he plays in this world drama. More than all else, perhaps, it is the impotent and arid striving of the mind, that throughout history has been so strikingly exemplified by the Jew—that brilliantly intellectual race that is the same yesterday, to-day and to-morrow, that knows not the blending and growing processes of nature, that demands entrance, speaks of the melting pot, loves the phrase, then stands outside the melting pot, throws stones at it, and jeers and curses all that it has produced. A sad, dissatisfied race, that like the mind alone uninformed by the spirit, throws down and destroys wherever it goes.

And along with modernism as with religion there is the pathetic picture of the wandering, homeless soul trying to break through and create some form for itself in socialism, or various welfare cults organised for society's good. Step by step with modernism go these ineffectual and sublimely sentimental organisations that the errant soul creates.

And step by step, encroaching somewhat, gaining ominously in strength comes feminism, and this brings us to Sex.

If, as I suspect, religion is life, then it comes back to the interplay of the two forces that create life—and here we have the problem of sex—the old problem of Man and Woman—the forces that create religions, civilisations, life.

The ancients, who faced nature and themselves unabashed, seemed thoroughly aware of this and of the enormous importance, the dangerous importance of sex. Their religious symbolism was built upon it. If we look at life cosmically instead of in detached fragments we find that the Divine principle of life differentiates more and more the higher the evolution. The ancients never lost sight of this. As we have seen on the foregoing pages everything sinuous, curving was a symbol of woman. Whatever was pointed, direct was a symbol of man. Their entire history has been one of conflict, of union and disunion, the marriage of forces that refuse to stay married—that keep up a state of continual oscillation, unless they follow the law that nature has mercifully provided and lose themselves in the race.

Without this thought of a future in which duality merges into unity, without the culmination which results in the child, religions vibrate between recognising sex as all, or denying it *in toto* as a shameful thing. And by religion here, of course, one means our conception, our ritual, our manual of life.

The problem is not new. Each civilisation has been confronted with it. Whenever these forces cease to co-operate, they attempt to supplant or duplicate each other, become inimical or too fond—until the question arises—and it is a very serious one—are we to do without curves or are we to be all curves with nothing straight or direct about us—or can we really be a curve and a straight line at one and the same time?

In this connection one must bear in mind that throughout the ancient religions it is the masculine and feminine principles and not man and woman as individuals that are symbolised. There are all sorts of men and women—all sorts of days, dull, grey, dark, gloomy days, but the principles day and night, light and darkness, active and passive, masculine and feminine never alter.

The Egyptians saw eternal conflict between Light and Darkness. They made it dramatic, poetic, inspiring. The sun rose victorious after a night spent in battling with darkness. Light prevailed. Good had conquered evil. The issue was a square one. It was a splendid, heartening contest.

The conflict between man and woman is wholly tragic, for love, attraction, repulsion, disillusionment, disappointment enter in. Both are good and both are evil. Neither can conquer the other without disaster. In these sporadic attempts to break down the eternal order of things, there is battle but the issue is not clear. The forces are not so much opposites as they are opposing—something of the Kilkenny cat variety. The soul, too, is again away from it all on one of its protracted journeys.

I can hardly hope to be agreed with, nevertheless, in spite of the painful efforts of those well meaning but deeply harassed early Christians to convince themselves and others that woman was an ally of Satan—backed up by symbolism I am ready to maintain that man as the active agent—although he has a marvellously ingenious mind for making excuses for himself, can never honestly squirm out of his responsibility for decadence in the past, modernism in the present—and shall it be decadence or a re-birth into a higher and finer civilisation in the future? His will be all the credit in either case.

There was a time when I dreamed that woman was the spiritual leader. Before and even during the war I used to hold her to blame as man is so fond of doing. I no longer do so. It seems more nearly true that she takes her entire cue from man. It may be that she out Herod's Herod, but that is her nature. In this respect she resembles the Jew. She carries everything to an extreme. She is diffuse, expansive, negative. She is water, earth, sky.

In the legend of Isis and Osiris, it is worth recalling that it was Osiris, not Isis whom Set the spirit of evil persuades to lay himself down in the box which Set has prepared for him. Nor does Isis go up and down the earth searching for Osiris *until after he has been overcome by evil.*

The significance of this applies equally well to conditions of the present day. As I have suggested, it is more than probable that man is the one who first leaves the "Eternal circle from Goodness through Goodness to Goodness"—the circle which encloses and bounds him and which is woman, and equally probable that woman would always remain quiescent and passive if man himself kept within proper bounds.

Throughout the ages when man works with nature —with the earth, woman is important. There is some indissoluble, mystical connection here. Whenever he leaves nature and creates an artificial life woman becomes negligible. He either makes a toy of her, or tries to fit her into the artificial conditions with which he has surrounded himself. In either case life, the race, is the sacrifice.

He is an interesting study—this man. Activity is his essence. He tires of the circle, tires even of woman. Yet having broken through he reflects upon her eternal usefulness. Here, one cannot be quite sure. It may be a stab of conscience or a gracious act of condescension, or possibly he feels the need of a companion in iniquity and invites woman to abandon the circle, too—or, perhaps he refrains from all gesture knowing that the barriers broken she will inevitably follow.

In any case, obediently out she comes, leaves the circle, and tries to make herself into a straight line. She becomes an office assistant, a factory hand. She enters man's business life to become a thing apart—the most atrocious punishment a woman can have. Or she goes alone and embarks on a career. In all these activities she is outside a centre—but there is probably a meaning for this. Frequently she combines marriage and a career—attempts to be a curve and a straight line.

The change in the relationship of these forces comes about gradually, insidiously. The effect is cumulative, startling.

The active force called man rather flatters himself that he is giving woman greater freedom. And so he is. He would give her anything if she would let him alone, except to work for him on the lines he has chosen to exploit in the pursuit of his "big idea"—and to amuse him when he needs relaxation.

Plutarch describes Isis as the "power in matter which becomes everything and receives everything as light and darkness, fire and water, day and night, life and death, beginning and end . . . therefore called by Plato the nurse and all receiver, but by the common people the many sided, the goddess with ten thousand names—because under the influence of reason she receives all forms. And she has an inborn affection for the first principle of all things—which is the same as good—and she longs for it and pursues it. On the other hand she flees the evil principle and thrusts it away, although she is space and matter for both. However, she always inclines to the better and freely offers herself to it . . . for the reproduction of its likenesses in which she rejoices."

If in spite of her new freedom, and much vaunted power to vote—to be the equal of man, she is a bit cynical, a bit heavy hearted—no longer worshipping man or anything else, for that matter; if one finds her a 'bit dullish' or too terrifyingly brilliant, it is due to disillusion, perhaps. She is torn by her desire to follow him, her desire to guard, protect, care for—and her resentment over his indifference, his casualness, his absorption with occupations that once were hers—doing everything that she once did, too much, too well—and paradoxically not so well.

Although her power is in many ways almost unlimited, although it is again making its ominously historic mark, she really does not like a feminised world—a feminised world is an effeminate world, a corrupt world. Nor does she like to be loved as man loves her now. She is wearied with sex.

When man chooses evil he denies himself. He is untrue to himself.

Woman is without choice, she is the acted upon—with strange, inexplicable periods of violence, of terrific resentments. When she finally emerges from the esoteric and manifests herself in the open it is as devastating to civilisation and the orderly scheme of things as a flood or an earthquake. She is nature first, last and all the time.

There is no doubt that woman has broken through the circle. The truth is, they are both outside the eternal circle as much as Adam and Eve ever were.

By the most strenuous and emphatic exertions of the male they have both managed to get outside their 'hide bound limitations.' The advocates of the New Freedom have written tomes on the subject. Much eloquence has been expended upon the joys that waited upon this perfect freedom and equality for both sexes. Yet even they could hardly describe their convulsive flops and gaspings as convulsions of ecstatic joy. Society was built up on the ideal of *noblesse oblige*. In the New

Freedom it is the trampling of a stampeding herd that is the ideal. Even the most hardened war profiteer who breaks his way, like the famous bull, into society, finds it much like the strata he had hoped to leave behind. Without form there are no social stratas.

All sorts of things can happen when you abandon form. The advocates of freedom and perfect social equality object to many if not most of nature's laws. They find nature tiresome not to say irksome. Take the feet for instance. It is quite wrong that the feet should support the body, thus putting the head necessarily on a higher altitude. (We have referred before to the ignominy attached to having any head.) Having decided that the position of the body politic must be altered for a change, feet are now waving frantically in the air—mostly masculine, it must be admitted, largely encouraged by the feminine principle. As for the head—the masculine head—you can't see it. It is buried like the ostrich. There is a far fetched reasonableness about this, too. It is the head unguided by the spirit that has got us into this mess. The feet, however, are wildly evident aimlessly kicking the air. Every movement is a protest. You can't believe that they are enjoying themselves, that they wouldn't prefer resting upon the solid earth. However, the head is being punished and there is something in that. It is difficult to say whether the Jew or woman is the more responsible for the absurd situation. To the modernist—either the capitalist who asks only to be left alone, or the reformer who believes that topsy-turvey-dom creates a New Heaven and a New Earth—the picture is not a happy one.

One cannot deny that the feminine principle has been doing everything possible to bring this condition about. It has been intent on power. Once outside the circle the two forces left form and co-operation behind. They have lost creative desire, sex is all and the struggle for sex supremacy is a bitter one.

Once more, in spite of the early Christian effort to put down and trample upon the feminine principle, "The gods die but the goddess is undecaying." The feminine principle dominates modern society in a so-called Christian civilisation as ruthlessly, as *sans gène* as in the dying days of a corrupt paganism.

The Jew and the feminine principle are apparently working together. Yet it is the feminine principle that ultimately defeats the Jew. He is intent on subverting, on changing, on getting everything in his own hands. She is slowly, consistently, implacably bent on breaking down. He is bent on destroying truth, honour, patriotism—everything that stands in the way of a purely materialistic conception of life. She is bent on destroying materialism, destroying a civilisation that no longer represents beauty, love, livingness, Life.

It is dangerous in a man made world to teach woman to think. In a divinely ordered world she does not need to think.

In the grip of multiplicity, of a multitude of ideas and enterprises that ramified to the uttermost parts of the earth, enterprises of such magnitude, requiring such intense pre-occupation that religion had almost ceased to be even a Sunday affair, nothing but a smash could stop this soaring, vaulting masculine principle.

It is not too fantastic to regard the Great War as a crash head on between these antagonistic forces—we called them in the beginning autocracy and democracy—the final and awful conflict between the active and passive principles, the culmination of a long and bitter sex warfare, each having reached the *nth* degree of perversion, each representing the climax of wilful, unloving selfishness. And again it is the race that suffers. It is the young that make the magnificent sacrifice.

Although democracy won the war, the analogy holds good in the chaos that follows the triumph of the feminine or negative principle. There is nothing more extraordinary in the legend of Isis and Osiris than when with evil conquered and given to her to guard, Isis lets it go. Nothing more clearly indicates the feminisation of the force opposed to the Germans than its hesitations, its indecisions, its willingness to let evil escape its just punishment, its lack of vision, its absolute inability to deal with the situation.

It has been said that the great masters in any field whether of art or finance or government make use of precisely three forces—investigation, elimination, concentration. Democracy investigates, rarely eliminates, never concentrates. It is expansive, diffuse, feminine.

If there is chaos again, one cannot blame woman too much. She is used to being held responsible for things she has never done. Absolutely pliant to a certain point, history shows that there comes a time when she balks. And whenever she does this, that particular apple cart of a civilisation is upset.

These forces repay our interest in them. It may be that the Chinese philosophy has the true conception when it calls them the two Regulating Powers which balance, counteract and discipline each other. The Two Regulating Powers *Yang* and *Yin* create by their co-operation all that takes place in nature. "These two Regulators who, mutually extinguishing and giving way to each other, keep at work a ceaseless process of revolution which produces all the phenomena of existence. . . . The struggle between and different admixtures of these two contrasting, elementary forces make all the conditions that prevail."

Once upon a time, this was also in the Christian era, I believe, the masculine intellect proved conclusively that women have no souls.

This may or may not be so. There is no doubt, however, about the feminine mind—that it moves circuitously. It swoops around logic in one glorious circle and arrives unerringly at the starting point. The feminine principle describes a circle—but if that circle invariably leads back to truth?—

The war showed the magnificence of man. If returning youth sulks, it is only because it believes that it has failed to release beauty and honour and unselfishness, because science is still trying to interfere with orderly progression, because darkness and chaos still control. On the other hand, there is little doubt that chaos is the result of the feminine principle's hatred of substitutes and semblances and imitations—the thousand and one useless things that man has created on his own initiative. The corsetless girls, the short, tight skirts are a drive back to nature which shows itself in the final analysis through sex. All this that the pious or censorous regard as depravity is the surging rebellion of the young pushed to the last extreme by modern futilities and artificialities. The war, betraying the impotence of the older generation, has given them the right, they think, to give the final kick to a craven, irresolute, pusillanimous, rotten state of affairs. They are not responsible for the wretched upheaval. They detest the falsity, the insincerities, the opportunism, the hatreds that brought it about. It is the natural revulsion.

Life—this alluring, tingling, bracing thing called life is again back to the older, the finer struggle, the primeval struggle between Light and Darkness. As much as the Egyptians of old we are anxious spectators looking on at the solar drama. There is no doubt of our longing to see day triumph over night. We are sun worshippers all, we adore the masculine principle. Even the feminine principle, that strange, smouldering, unfathomable compound of brooding tenderness, unreasoning jealousies, cloud burst tendencies—that encompassing, enfolding, loving, gently nurturing feminine principle that is earth, water, sky—is never satisfied until the sun is restored to power.

At the moment all eyes are on Mussolini. He stands out, not so much as a man but as a world force, the recrudescence of the masculine principle at its best. He represents purpose, concentration, unity. He is direct, awe inspiring, convincing. He says to the feet, that were waving even more frantically in the air in Italy than elsewhere, "To the ground!"

To the ground the feet go joyfully—and very much relieved, if the truth were known, to feel the solid earth under them. It was all the fault of the idiotic reformers anyway. Mussolini says "Talking is imbecile." How well we know the futility of words. Have we had anything else for five weary years? Even though man becomes secretive again—if only he will be strong!

He tells Italy that the one thing that carries a race forward in the struggle for existence is "*Lavorare e Obbedire.*" The very sound of the old half-forgotten words evokes boundless enthusiasm. The feet are indeed travelling on sure ground. The response is instantaneous. The Italians are working and obeying as never before. He offers his followers, what? Sacrifice—*sacrifice of self* and they accept the terms joyously. And all the world watches and rejoices. There is no doubt about it. The masculine principle is tremendously popular. Even the feminine principle bows in admiration before the masculine principle when it shows itself. Is it not the Sun, Heaven, Light, Good?

In Italy one begins to see the mystery and glory of light emerging from darkness. The eternal process from chaos to order repeating itself from the first myths to the chaotic present—which must in turn give way to order. Mussolini as a leader is appealing to the beautiful, the soul inspiring thing that is in the nature of man—his love of order, of obedience, of work, of sacrifice for the carrying out of an ideal.

He appeals to youth. He commands obedience.[3]

Even as I write of the symbols of these marvellous creative forces that have played such a part in religion —those Two Regulating Powers that "create by their co-operation everything that takes place in nature," of the cross, creative energy; the circle, perfection; the

[3] The sinister murder of Matteotti has occurred since writing the above. In New York at the time and struck by the attitude of the newspapers there toward Mussolini, all seeming consciously or unconsciously to reflect the attitude of Moscow, I sent one to a friend in Italy. He replied July 10, 1924. "The N. Y. newspaper you sent me with articles on the Italian situation makes statements of which there are *absolutely no proof whatever.* It would be literally quite as justifiable to say that the Communists slew Matteotti in order to put the blame on Mussolini and Fascismo and so divert public opionion from the imminent trial of the Communistic people accused of the murders at Empoli. There is *no proof as yet available* either for the one or the other and it is an iniquity to declare either presumption to be true. Everything else is merest surmise."

serpent the means of combining creative energy and perfection; the triangle, the result, the ultimate realisation of multiplicity in unity, of three in one—and all the other life symbols, the poetic and imaginative interpretations of this mysterious Life Force by those wise and understanding ancients—and of the trouble the soul makes, and the mind makes, until finally the exasperated feminine principle makes trouble all around——even as I write—as if there were not enough to bother us, word comes that the mind is trying to stir up things again.

You would hardly believe it possible, but that is the extraordinary thing about life that it is the same battle again and again between the two forces, masculine and feminine, then comes the recalcitrant soul, the usurping mind, the body spurned or made use of—always made to pay the price—then sex—an orgy of it—and then the avenging Great Mother—the great nature goddess.

And then Life—living that is true again.

While I am writing of these things word comes that the clash between the fundamentalists and modernists in the Episcopal Church is approaching a crisis. Not long ago the rector of one of the most fashionable churches in New York City doffed his priestly vestments, donned the gown of a doctor of theology, entered the pulpit and denied the doctrine of the Virgin Birth, questioned the Holy Resurrection and defied his bishop to try him for heresy. On the same Sunday another rector in another Episcopal Church in New York who had been called to account by the bishop for introducing classical dancing in his church was preaching a sermon on the "Necessity of Paganism" in religion.

Guthrie's symbolic dancing is not so much a question

of taste, but of whether you can force yourself and others arbitrarily back into the necessary state of mind to make such exhibitions real. Julian the Apostate tried it, but even then the austerities of the early Christian had made an indelible impress upon the hearts and souls of men—or, perhaps more truthfully, pure joy had gone out of the sophisticated pagan before Christianity came in. The mistake, if mistake it be, in going back to the pagan festivities is in believing that in a decadent, soul-less age we can recapture the early pagan child-like joyousness, the spirit of innocent abandon and faith that made them such a lovely expression of life.

This same entertaining clergyman—and very entertaining he is—also experimented, I believe, or permitted the experiment to be tried—of superinducing emotion by an arrangement of different coloured lights streaming in on his Church audience. I don't recall the combination, but under a blue light say—you were supposed to respond by feeling religious—if anyone knows what that means. Apparently, in his eagerness to share with others his own abounding joy in life, poetry, art, he momentarily lost sight of the fact that the old colourists who produced the marvels of stained glass were not working to superinduce emotion in others, but to express emotion—express themselves. A subtle but powerful difference that distinguishes the one who creates because he must express his own soul, his own consciousness of life, beauty, art—from the charlatan who would play upon the soul of others.

The heart of a child which made these old nature festivities lovely cannot be dealt out to us by some beneficent being who would like to make everyone happy. To recapture it in a world that man has made unspeakably stereotyped and ugly requires more than coloured lights or effectively staged dances.

When the great question religion is forever propounding is Life—how to live well—the soul winces over the pifflingness of these modern devices—of these far-fetched doubts.

The modernist who believes that the Bible should be interpreted in the light of modern science may interpret it—but he will never change it.

I sometimes think that religion is to the mind what a bull dog is to a collie. The bull dog seems small and the collie large. The collie can never resist the attack even though he comes home limping—as he always does.

The modernist attitude is simply the old story of the difficulties the mind finds and makes when confronted by feeling.

"Le cœur a des raisons que la raison ne connait pas."

One wonders which is happier in this mystical world of mystery, the one who beats his intellectual brains out trying to explain literally the eternal processes of nature, life, religion—or the one who accepts Life as the divine mystery that always eludes the intellect. The one who opposes nature or the one who sees nature as the "living garment of God. . . ."

Steeped in early symbolism, with your head full of the beauty of nature, feeling yourself a part of the "eternal stream of life and power and action which issues from the original source of all life," you feel like saying "How very unimportant this all is—what does it matter really, poor dear old mind! How you do bother yourself—and others—about things that do not concern you, that you were never intended to understand. How little the mind knows, how inane, how stupid it is when it approaches Life!"

The mind which decries the simple lovely things that satisfy imagination and heart, that after making religion a profession—denies—does a futile, a hopelessly irrelevant and unconvincing thing. No one can quite tell how or why, but only the mind suffers defeat. And whatever twists and contortions and elucidations and interpretations priests and theologians have given to religion, whenever these have opposed themselves to nature, life, feeling, they drive religion out of the church doors, it is true, and have nothing but an empty meaningless formalism on their hands. But the amusing thing is, that while the theologian develops a decided limp and the priest's voice has a hollow sound, Life and nature and feeling have a way of appearing around the corner as if quite unaware that the mind had reduced them to a doctrine.

The truth is, you may not believe in the Virgin Birth or the Resurrection—and you may pin your faith on the ape as father—and you may be right, but the fatal thing is, you no longer interest. A religion without imagination is very dull. Life itself offers the strongest protest.

These ancient symbols and customs, these gracious beliefs founded on who knows what inner truth or revelation—the Virgin Birth, the Eucharist, the Resurrection, the Blessed Sacraments—the whole ritual that stretches back so far, opens such wide horizons of thought, gives us such an assurance of continuity—these are the *noli me tangere* of religions. He hazards his own soul who opposes or who attempts to abolish them.

If a Catholic can believe that he literally partakes

of the body and blood of Christ, don't flout it. His is a superb conviction of one of nature's eternal truths.

Belief in the Virgin Birth is a part of the whole myth of existence, going back to the beginning of all things. Having survived every assault of the mind will it not continue to survive?

The Virgin Birth is, perhaps, only the symbol of Oneness that the heart demands. Man creates diversity, plunges into multiplicity, gets bewildered, lost—and back he comes to unity again. Literally the Virgin Birth may or may not have been—mystically, who can doubt?

When you see how important a part the Virgin Birth has played in every myth and every religion who could have the heart to cast it out? Personally I love it, symbolising as it does a conception that is born of love and not of passion.

And so, too, with the resurrection of Jesus Christ. We know intellectually that there were many other twice-born gods that were born on December 25th, and that Easter was a pagan festival in celebration of the awakening of nature to re-newed life in the spring. Freely admitting this, yet we know, too, in some inner, soul-satisfying way that it was inevitably true that Christ should become a part also of the whole system of awakening life; that He would have been out of it, an abstraction if He, too, had not been given to us on the day that had been celebrated with such joy since time immemorial—if the birth into our consciousness of His divine purpose and mission had not been celebrated on December 25th. The Church when it adopted this knew in some mystical way that the more deeply He was associated with the marvellous processes of nature the more reality Christ would have for us.

For some Christ may never have existed. To others He was but a man and not divine. Yet the Life of Christ is eternally true.

Perhaps all of life is myth and fable and Death the only reality—but those who love life think otherwise. The great adventure is life, and death but the thrill of awakening to a new and illimitable Life.

The undying strength of the Catholic Church rests upon two things, the Voice of Authority and these jealously guarded traditions of the race. In spite of its glaring faults, its sins and omissions, its foundations are solidly built on the eternal truths of life. "Catholic dogma is merely the witness, under a special symbolism of the enduring facts of human nature and the universe; it is merely the voice which tells us that man is not the creature of the drawing room and the stock exchange, but a lonely, awful soul confronted by the Source of all Souls."

When we can no longer find the truth in the myths, rituals and symbols so preciously held and guarded, for all generations to puzzle over until finally they come to them as a little child, we are indeed turned to stone and must be broken up to pave the road for others, who pass through the portals of Life, making the quest more gladly and joyously than we who would live in the mind alone.

These, that I have gathered for you here beseech your interest, your tender love and faith. Perhaps they are only myths, only symbols of a forgotten past —but how beautiful, how heartening they are—and how truly they proclaim the long, long contest between light and darkness, good and evil, order and disorder and that light follows darkness as day follows night.

Here they are, a nosegay for you—all these imperishable records and imaginings that the mind uninformed by the spirit seeks to destroy.

Are they not lovely—worthy of our love?

And don't they make you feel that at the very heart of us man and woman are the nicest things that ever happened—the most important and beautiful things that ever happened—except the child?

And still Life goes on—pulsating, vitalising life—the same life that revealed itself to the eager, speculative eyes of the ancient seers in trees, flowers, animals, sun, moon, stars and most of all in man himself—the same great, unfathomed mystery.

Perhaps that is the true function of the life symbols, the reason why they endure though civilisations crumble, to take us back to the glorious days of wonder, to pull us out of apathy and despair—to make us once more tremendously, vitally, wholly alive.

GLOSSARY OF SOME OF THE MORE PROMINENT SYMBOLS AND SYMBOLIC FIGURES FOUND IN EARLY ART

GLOSSARY OF SOME OF THE MORE PROMINENT SYMBOLS AND SYMBOLIC FIGURES FOUND IN EARLY ART

Acacia. A mystical symbol remarkable for its reproductive powers and used by the Egyptians in their capitals and thence borrowed by the Greeks.

Active and Passive, Spirit and Matter. "Between these two poles all things perpetually alternate. What lives is slipping towards death; what is dead is creeping towards life." [1]

Adonis. The mother of Adonis was fabled to have been changed into a tree which at the end of nine months burst and Adonis was born. The story of his being found as an infant by Aphrodite and concealed in a chest which the goddess gave to Persephone who refused to give him up until Zeus, appealed to by Aphrodite commanded that Adonis spend six months with each, is simply a variant of the Babylonian myth of Ishtar and Tammuz. Adonis grows up into a beautiful youth, is the beloved of Aphrodite who shares with him the pleasures of the chase. One legend relates that Ares (Mars) jealous of Aphrodite's love for him transformed himself into a wild boar and killed him. Others represent Adonis as being carried off by Dionysos. Another tells of Aphrodite rushing to the spot where her lover was wounded and sprinkling his blood with nectar from which flowers sprang up. In one myth Aphrodite changes him into a flower. Scarlet anemones were said to have sprung from the blood of Adonis. One of the loveliest myths is that the red rose owes its hue to the death of Adonis. Aphrodite hastening to her wounded lover trod on a bush of white roses. The thorns tore her tender flesh and stained the roses forever red. Worship of Adonis is thought to have originated in Phoenicia spreading from there to Assyria, Egypt, Greece and Italy. In the Asiatic cults Aphrodite is the fructifying principle in nature and Adonis the twice-born god who dies in winter and is revived in the spring. The festivals of Adonis were celebrated in Athens, Alexandria, Byblus and many other places.

[1] "An Introduction to the Study of Chinese Painting," Arthur Waley.

Aegis. The shield of Zeus or Athene with the Gorgon's head in the centre. Later it came to mean the breast plate worn by emperors and others.

Agni, (**ignis**). The god of the moving flame at times beneficent and again destructive.

Almond. A symbol of virginity and self-production, also fruitfulness. The mystical *Vesica Piscis* surrounding the Virgin Mary in some representations in art is derived from the *mandorla*, almond—and is used to convey the same symbolic idea. Candied almonds with a white coating and distributed in boxes to each guest is a part of the ritual of Italian weddings. The almond is also identified with the *yoni* of phallicism. "In Phrygian cosmogony an almond figured as the father of all things perhaps because its delicate lilac blossom is one of the first heralds of spring." (Frazer.)

Ambrosia Vase. In Chinese art this was originally a dish held in the hand of a god to catch the dew of heaven. In the hands of Kwan-yin it is long-necked and used to sprinkle the water of life on worshippers. Sometimes the vase rests on a stand beside the goddess who holds in her hand the willow branch.

Amentet. It was during the journey of the deceased through *Amentet*, the Hidden Place that he came in contact with the gods and "invoked the powers of the amulets with which they were so closely connected."

Ammon or Amen the Hidden One. A sun-god of Thebes whose worship extended until as Amen-Ra he became the national deity of Egypt. He is represented as a man wearing the lofty double plumes and holds the sceptre, the *crux ansata* and sometimes the *Khepesh* or war knife; sometimes he has the head of a hawk with the solar disk and uræus, and before him the *crux ansata* or *ankh* which has been given arms and legs and is offering him lotus flowers; or again he has the head of a ram, crocodile or lion with the disk, plumes and uræi. He has even been represented in the form of the solar goose. He was usually depicted, however, with a ram's head, symbol of creative energy, and was known as the ram-headed god of the sun.

Amorini. A name given to the small Cupids or little love-gods that are frequently found in the decorative art of all ages.

Amphora. A two-handled Greek vase, usually of large size and intended to hold liquids. Some were mounted on a foot, others not. The prize to the victors in the Panathenaic games was an amphora.

Amulet. A word derived from the East and applied to various objects or "charms" which, when worn, were supposed to ward off illnesses and evil influences and bring good luck to the wearer.

Anchor. Symbol of hope. In Japan an emblem of good luck.

Animal Symbolism in Chinese Art. In the art of no other people does the animal occupy so important a place. China has symbolised by animals all the cosmological beliefs that for countless ages have influenced her intellectual, moral and social life. Her art is "symbolical narration." This primitive symbolism based largely upon the zodiacal juxtaposition of certain animals is used again and again to express certain ideas. The twelve animals of the Duodenary Cycle were the dragon, hare, tiger, ox, rat, pig, dog, cock, monkey, goat, horse, serpent. "This zodiac corresponds to the 'Twelve Earthly Branches' which together with the 'Ten Heavenly Stems' form a series of sixty combinations used for naming the year, month, day and hour. . . . Every Chinese knows well under which animal he was born. It is essential that he should do so, for no important step throughout life is undertaken unless under the auspices of his particular animal."[1] . . . As seems to be inevitable with the Chinese the symbolism as it is finally developed resolves itself back *tout simplement* to the *yang* and *yin*. *Yang* is the luminous principle, *yin* is that which is cold, obscure, dark. *Yin* is represented by the north and midnight, *yang* is south and noon day. The morning corresponds to spring, the evening to autumn. The animals belong either to *yin* or *yang*. The *yin* animals are of cold nature, patient, slow, often burrowing into the earth. The *yang* are hot-blooded loving warmth and light. The dragon and tiger represented the two constellations, Scorpio and Orion. The bird and tortoise, emblems respectively of *yang* summer and *yin* winter, only appear after them. The symbolism of the Dragon and Tiger is very old preceding that of *yang* and *yin*. Again one represents spring, the other autumn. The dragon symbolises heaven, the sky, spring, fertility, the tiger, chief of all land animals the earth. The two express the happiness attained when heaven and earth are in accord. Representations of the Cock and Dog also typify the union of the two forces. The cock who announces the rising sun is the symbol of the east and *yang*. The dog who watches over the night symbolises *yin*. These and many other combinations of these fabulous animals are constantly recurring in Chinese art as typifying happiness, prosperity, longevity. Many are in the form of a rebus or homophone.

Anubis or Anpu. The jackal or dog-headed god Anubis is the Egyptian Hermes. He is called the Opener of the Ways. He is the messenger, custodian and servant of the gods, and the conductor of souls to the promised land. Anubis was said to be the son of Osiris and performs the service of watch-

[1] "Symbolism in Chinese Art," W. Percival Yegg.

ing over Isis and Osiris. In the temples he is represented as the guard and protector of the other gods. The place in front of the temple was sacred to Anubis. Again the horizon was called Anubis and depicted in the form of a dog because the dog sees both by day and night. The early Greek writers all testify to the worship of the dog in Egypt and the myth of the dog as companion and assistant to the gods which is found among the Persians and Hindus probably goes back to the worship of Anubis in Egypt. Traces of it are also found in Greece where the "mythical Rhadamanthys of Crete commanded that men should not swear by the gods but by a goose, a dog and a ram." It was said that Socrates swore by the dog as well as the goose. The jackal, a species of wild dog was reputed to hunt up the lion's prey for him. Thus Anubis originally the jackal type is later represented with the dog as emblem. The confusion in term may be attributed to the growth or domestication of an idea. Jackal in Egypt denoted judge and it was probably the jackal god who ministered to Osiris and acted as guide to the nether world.

Anvil. Symbol of the "Primal Furnace," the Force which helped to hammer out the Universe.

Aphrodite, (Venus). The goddess of love and beauty and said by some to have sprung from the foam of the sea. A personification of the generative powers of nature she was called the mother of all living beings. Wife of Hephæstus she does not scruple to have amours with Ares, Poseidon, Dionysos and Hermes among the gods, and inspired by Zeus she also conceived an invincible passion for Anchises a mortal. Her love for Adonis has been interpreted as the myth of the changing seasons. She was reputed to be the mother of Priapus by Dionysos and of Hermaphroditus by Hermes. Aphrodite has a magic girdle which cannot fail to inspire love for those who wear it. The sparrow, swan, swallow, dove, dolphin, hare, tortoise and ram were sacred to her. She was given also the apple, poppy, myrtle and rose. She is associated with the planet Venus and the month of April and the numbers three, four and seven are sacred to her. Sacrifices offered to her were mostly garlands of flowers and incense. The worship of Aphrodite was derived from the East where she is identified with Astarte and the biblical Ashtoreth. As the victorious goddess she has the helmet, shield and sword and sometimes an arrow. She is sometimes draped but in the later period she is nude.

Apis bull. Worshipped by the Egyptians as an incarnation of Osiris. At Memphis it was looked upon as a form of Ptah or the "second life of Ptah," also as the son of Osiris. The bull of Memphis has been called the greatest of gods. The signs by which the newly born bull was recognised as the god Apis have been variously described. As the bull was looked upon by some as sacred to the moon and by others as sacred to the sun or Osiris in whom the sun was worshipped, this may account for the divergent views as to its markings. According to Herodotus the bull was black with a square mark of white on the forehead, the figure of an eagle on the back and a lump like a beetle under the tongue. Pliny described it as having a conspicuous spot of white on the right side shaped like a crescent. Other authorities speak of the mark on the forehead as triangular. It seems reasonable to suppose that, as the triangle was a symbol of divinity, whereas the square denoted the earth, the Egyptians would search for an animal bearing the divine rather than the earthly symbol. "As the birth of Apis filled all Egypt with joy and festivities, so his death threw the whole country into mourning." The bull came to be regarded as a symbol of the astronomical and physical systems of the priests. Under this development there were twenty-nine marks on its body which were known to the priests. The cult of Apis is a very old one and the connection of the bull with Osiris a very obvious one. "Osiris as a water god poured the Nile over the land"; the bull god as the personification of virility and might provided the strength which enabled the Egyptians to plough it up.

Apollo. A Greek god who was identified with Helios or the sun and also with the Egyptian Horus. He is the god of light who at his birth destroys Python, the serpent of darkness. He typified also mental light and presided over knowledge, music, poetry and eloquence. Apollo was the national divinity of the Greeks "reflecting the brightest side of the Greek mind." He is the protector of flocks and herds, the god of the bow and arrows, who punishes and destroys the wicked and wards off evil, he is the god of prophecy and his most famous oracles were at Delos, Delphi, Branchidae, Claros and Patara. The finest temple to Apollo was at Delphi. In art he is represented as the "perfect ideal of youthful manliness." As god of music he holds the lyre and is depicted draped or with long, flowing locks. Again he holds the bow and arrow. His symbols are the wolf, raven, swan, lyre and laurel, etc. The number seven was sacred to him.

Archer. The Assyrian deity Ashur is represented as an archer shooting a three-headed arrow at the enemies of Assyria. Sagittarius is the archer of the zodiac.

Ares, (Mars). Whereas Athene represented wisdom and foresight in the conduct of war, Ares is the god of force who typifies the horrors, tumult, confusion of war. He was one of the lovers of Aphrodite and when she transferred her affections to Adonis, Ares waylaid him in the form of a wild boar and killed him. The wolf, cock and woodpecker are sacred to Ares.

Ariadne. A daughter of Minos, King of Crete. Falling in love with Theseus who had been sent from Athens to Crete to be devoured by the Minotaur, she gave him the string by which he found his way out of the labyrinth. Her legends vary. In one she marries and goes away with Theseus who deserts her, whereupon she takes her own life. In another she is killed by Artemis. In others Dionysos enamoured of her beauty raised her to the rank of the immortals and gave her a crown of seven stars. Ariadne was called a serpent goddess and is frequently represented in art and on ancient coins and gems usually with serpents. Theseus and the labyrinth are interpreted as solar.

Ark. One of the oldest symbols of the feminine principle.

Arrow. A symbol of lightning, rain and fertility as well as war, famine, disease, death. It is associated with the sun, moon and atmospheric gods.

Artemis, (Diana). One of the great divinities of the Greeks known under many aspects. Called by some a daughter of Zeus by Leto and sister ot Apollo, others call her the daughter of Demeter. An Egyptian account makes her the daughter of Dionysos and Isis. As sister of Apollo who was identified with the sun or Helios she becomes a moon goddess and like Apollo is armed with a bow, quiver and arrows and has the power to send plagues and death to men and animals. Like Apollo, too, she is unmarried. She is the 'chaste Diana', the maiden unconquered by love. She is the protector of the young, of flocks and herds and the chase. "She is the huntress among the immortals." As the Arcadian Artemis she is goddess of the nymphs. Hephæstus makes her bow and arrows, and Pan provides her with dogs. Four stags with golden antlers draw her chariot. As a nymph, fish were sacred to her and Artemis and Apollo both have the laurel. Among the symbolic animals of the Greek Artemis were dogs, stags and the boar. In Greek art when depicted as huntress she has the bow and arrows or spear, dogs and stags. As the moon goddess she wears a long robe and has the moon crescent above her head. Sometimes she carries a torch. The Tauri, a people of European Sarmatia, sacrificed all strangers to Artemis. The worship of the goddess was orgiastic and it is believed that this was originally an Asiatic moon goddess whom the Greeks confused with their own Artemis. Aricia was the seat of her worship in Italy where she was known as Diana and also called Trivia when worshipped at cross-ways where her statues were usually placed. The Ephesian Artemis is an

Asiatic goddess of nature whom the Greeks found in Ionia and to whom they gave the name of Artemis. As goddess of fertility she is many breasted, wears a mural crown with disk as emblem of the full moon, her legs are swathed like a mummy, the lower part of her body ending in a point like a pyramid upside down and covered with mystical figures of bees, flowers, bulls and stags. The pine cone was sacred to Artemis, [see pine cone,] also the cypress or fir tree. The symbol of the Ephesian Artemis was a bee.

Asp. A small, venomous, hooded serpent of Egypt and Libya and an Egyptian symbol of dominion.

Ass. In Egypt a form of the sun-god. According to Plutarch the ass, because of its reddish colour, was also given to Set and was looked upon with loathing by the Egyptians.

Athene, (Minerva). One of the great divinities of the Greeks and said to have sprung in full armour from the head of Zeus. She is a goddess in whom "power and wisdom are harmoniously blended" and typified the ethical rather than some physical aspect of nature, thus differing from the great mother goddesses of earth and sky. She is a virgin goddess removed from the passions of love and hate. She is the goddess of wisdom, war and all the liberal arts. She could hurl the thunderbolt, prolong the life of men and bestow the gift of prophecy. As goddess of war and protector of heroes she is usually represented in armour with the aegis and a golden staff. In ancient art she is frequently given a helmet ornamented with ram's heads, griffins, sphinxes and horses, or again with the aegis and sometimes a shield which has in its centre the head of Medusa. The owl, serpent, cock, lance and olive branch are her symbols. The olive in allusion to the fact that she was said to have created the olive tree in her contest with Poseidon for the possession of Attica. She was the Roman Minerva and was also called Pallas and Tritonia.

Axe. A solar symbol of great antiquity. Its use in Egypt for religious or magical purposes "goes back to the neolithic and perhaps palæolithic age." The earliest form was the double axe. The axe was a sacred emblem in Egypt, Scandinavia, Germany, Mexico and Central America. In Egypt the Double Axe typified double power. The sacred Double Axe as a religious symbol of the sun is particularly associated with the island of Crete. Churchward attributes the origin of the Masonic *gavel* and *double-headed gavel* to this source.

Ba. The Egyptians represented the *ba* or soul by a bird, sometimes with a human head. There was also the luminous one or *Khou* which hid itself in the darkest corner of the vault.

Baboon. The cynocephalus or dog-headed ape plays an important part in Egyptian mythology. In the judgment scene the baboon sits upon the standard of the scales and warns Thoth when the pointer reaches the middle of the beam. It's habit of chattering the moment the sun appeared gave it the name of 'Hailer of the Dawn.' The baboon with uplifted paws symbolised wisdom saluting the rising sun. A companion of the moon-god Thoth it is also associated with the sun.

Bacchus. Called by the Greeks Lord of the Palm Tree. [See Dionysos.]

Ball or Tama. A symbol among the Buddhists of the sacred emanations of the gods. It is sometimes surmounted by flames and is called the 'flaming jewel' or 'flaming pearl.' It is the third eye of Buddha, the symbol of transcendent wisdom.

Bamboo. The symbol of gracefulness, constancy, yielding but enduring strength, of high breeding, fastidious taste as opposed to vulgarity. The bamboo is constantly depicted in Chinese and Japanese art with birds and animals, as well as alone or with the plum and pine tree.

Basilisk. A fabulous creature with the body and wings of a dragon, head of a serpent and tail ending in a serpent's head. The glance of its eye would kill. It could only be destroyed by holding a mirror up so that it must see itself, when it would burst asunder with horror of its own appearance. We have here the same thought of the Taoists about evil being made to recognise itself. In sacred art the basilisk was used to symbolise the spirit of evil.

Bast. The goddess is usually depicted in the form of a woman with the head of a cat. Occasionally she is given the head of a lioness surmounted by a snake, in her right hand she has the sistrum and in her left an aegis with the head of a lioness or cat in the centre. Bast is a personification of the power of the sun in its milder aspect. Like Sekhebet she is also a goddess of fire. When given the cat's head she is also identified with the moon. The changing of the cat's eye is likened to the moon. The cat like the lioness and vulture was an Egyptian symbol of maternity.

Bat. Frequently depicted in Chinese art as a symbol of happiness. Five bats no matter how grouped represented the 'five happinesses,' peace, riches, love of virtue, long life and a happy death.

Battle Axe. A symbol similar to the sword, hammer or cross. It frequently had two edges and in this form was the weapon of the Amazons. [See Axe.]

Bau. A Sumerian goddess whose symbol was a falcon on a pole.

Bee. Vishnu when depicted in the form of Krishna was given a blue bee hovering over his head as a symbol of the ether. Carved on ancient tombs the bee symbolised immortality.

The bee was a prominent feature of the Mithra cult. On an altar dedicated to the Persian sun-god was found a gilded bull's head and three hundred golden bees. Napoleon I adopted the bee as an emblem of sovereignty. The sanctity of the bee may be derived from the ancient custom of smearing the bodies of the dead with honey to prevent decomposition.

Beetle or Scarabæus. A symbol of self-existent being and worshipped by the Egyptians as a pre-eminently sacred emblem of the rising sun and eternal life.

Bell. An ancient Eastern symbol used by the priests to summon the Supreme Spirit. Bells were believed to have the power of subduing storms and driving away plagues and demons. Hence the bell is one of the symbols of St. Anthony. The bull Nandi the *nahan* of Siva was always depicted with a bell hanging by a cord or chain around the neck. The ancients often decorated the handle with a flaring three-fold top either three circles, the trefoil or the *fleur-de-lis*. Sometimes the handle was the *vajra* or thunderbolt. The Buddhists attached a similar meaning to the *vajra* and the bell to that of the *linga* and *yoni* of the Hindus. The *vajra* represented Buddha, the creative principle, the *linga*, and the bell Dharma, matter, the feminine principle, the *yoni*. The bell was an old symbol of virginity. The bell was looked upon by the early Christians not only as the "call of Christ but as a sign of Christ Himself." The custom of tolling a bell to announce a death, the number of strokes representing the age of the deceased persisted for ages. Durandus in the *Symbolism of Churches* says, "Moreover the bells ought to be rung when anyone is dying that the people hearing this may pray for him. For a woman indeed they ring twice, because she first caused the bitterness of death; for she first alienated mankind from God, wherefore the second day had no benediction. But for a man they ring three times, because the Trinity was first shown in man." Durandus was born about the year 1220 A.D. when the feminine principle was still somewhat in disrepute.

Bennu. A sort of heron exalted by the Egyptians as a symbol of re-generation typifying the rising of the sun and the return of Osiris. It was said to have sprung from the heart of Osiris. It is also identified with the phoenix.

Bes. One of the oldest Egyptian gods and called by Churchward a primary form of Horus I. Other authorities identify Bes with Set or Typhon. Budge says, "The figure of this god suggests that his home was a place where the dwarf and pigmy were held in high esteem. . . . The knowledge of the god and perhaps figures of him were brought from this region which the Egyptians called the 'Land of the Spirits.' "

According to another legend Bes was a foreigner introduced into Egypt from the land of Punt (the spice land of Arabia). In some aspects he resembles Bacchus and presides over gaiety, music, dancing. As a war god he carries a sword. Representations of him are hideous and grotesque. He is depicted as a squat, crooked dwarf sometimes wearing an animal's skin with the tail hanging down behind. His tongue is frequently extended and often he has a crown of feathers. His sacred animal was the sow. There is a small temple to Bes at Denderah. On one of the royal chariots found in the tomb of Tut-ankh-amen the straps of the harness saddle of the breast harness pass through the mouth of the god Bes.

Bird. Birds symbolised the spirit of the air, the spirit of life. Among the Egyptians the bird symbolised the soul of man. In Christian art the bird was also used to typify the soul.

Bird upon a pedestal or pillar. Placed there to give life to the pillar signifying the union of spirit and matter.

Bird's Wings with Globe. A circle or globe with the extended wings of a bird on either side was the Egyptian symbol of the deity. It was also used in the same way by the Babylonians and Assyrians.

Black. In China and Japan black was associated with the north, *yin* and water. Black horses were the principal sacrifice to the rain god in Japan.

Blue. The Egyptians also Swedenborg made blue the symbol of Truth. Blue is the symbol of the feminine principle, signifying also heaven, fidelity, constancy. In Christian art Christ and the Divine Mother wear the blue mantle typifying heavenly love and heavenly truth. St. John the Evangelist was given the blue tunic and the red mantle.

Bo-tree or bodhi-tree. Each Buddha is believed to have a special tree under which he is born, does penance, preaches and dies. The fig tree is supposed to be the one under which Gautama Buddha attained knowledge, others represent it as the banyan tree.

Buddha. He is said to have been born eleven times as a deer and to have preached his first sermon in a deer park. Thus a gilded wheel between two gazelles or deer found in Buddhist temples symbolises the preaching of Buddha. Other symbols are the circle, swastika, lotus, ûrnâ—the precious gem usually a moon stone or flaming pearl worn on the forehead between the eyes. [See Ûrnâ.] Statues of Buddha represent him in many postures, standing, seated with legs crossed, or recumbent.

Buddha's Eight Familiar Symbols. Also called the "eight lucky emblems." The conch, umbrella, canopy, knot, fish, lotus, jar and wheel of the law.

Buddhist Symbols. Rope, axe, goad or spear, scroll of texts, begging bowl, sacrificial cup, fan, bow and arrow, wheel, incense burner, rosary, lotus, fly brush, hare and moon, cock and the sun, the vase for shrine use, musical instruments and calabash or medicine bottle.

Builder's Square. Used symbolically in the Egyptian Ritual also represented in temples and the Great Pyramid as seats for Osiris and Maat, the goddess of Truth. In the judgment hall Osiris is seated on the Square. This is also a Masonic emblem.

Bull. In ancient religions the bull symbolised the power residing in the sun. It also typified the humid power of nature and was thus given to Osiris. Sacred bulls were worshipped above all other animals because they had "helped the discoverers of corn in sowing the seed and procuring the universal benefits of agriculture." Mithra is depicted in Persian bas-reliefs as a youth with a conical cap "slaying the sacred bull whose sacrifice was supposed to be the origin of terrestrial life."

Bull-roarer. One of the most ancient and wide spread religious symbols in the world resembling the rhombus which figured in the ancient mysteries of Greece. It consists of a slab of wood tied to a piece of string which upon being whirled rapidly round gives forth an unearthly, roaring sound. It was used, it is presumed, as a sacred instrument to evoke the Supreme Spirit who manifested himself in the blasts of the mighty wind. It is still used by the Australians and New Zealanders and is also employed in their religious ceremonies by the natives of Africa, Ceylon and the Malay Peninsula.

Caduceus. The staff of Hermes (Mercury) with which he conducts the souls of the dead is a rod encircled by two serpents surmounted by wings. In its original form the caduceus was a staff—perhaps the sacred tau—terminating in a circle upon which rests a crescent. The name is also given to the staff covered with velvet and topped by the *fleur-de-lis* which was carried in grand ceremonials by the herald or king of arms. It is applied also to a herald's wand, a rod of olive wood covered with garlands. The caduceus of Hermes is described in Homeric hymns by Apollo: "Thereafter will I give thee a lovely wand of wreath and riches, a golden wand with three leaves which shall keep thee ever unharmed."

Canopic Jars. A name given to the vases used by the Egyptians for the viscera which were removed from the body in the process of mummification and treated separately. The jars, four in number were placed near the sarcophagus and were under the special protection of the four gods of the dead, the sons of Horus Hapi, Amset, Duamutef and Kebehsenuf who were represented respectively with the head of a baboon, man, jackal and hawk. After the XVIII dynasty it was customary to put the symbolic heads of these gods on the covers of the jars.

Canopy. A symbol of sovereignty and carried over the heads of Eastern rulers and emperors on state occasions. When placed over the head of Buddha its shelter typified the sacred tree under which he received enlightenment.

Cantharus. A two-handled Greek vase or cup sacred to Dionysos who is frequently represented holding it in his hand.

Cap with Up-turned Horns. A symbol among the Babylonians of divine power. A cap or turban on a seat or altar may have been used to typify the 'world mountain,' the symbol of the chief Babylonian triad Anu, Enlil and Ea.

Cartouche. A name usually given to the oval in which the name of a royal person is inscribed. These ovals bearing hieroglyphic instructions were also placed in the tombs of Egyptian kings. In its oldest form the cartouche was circular, the circle symbolising the course of the sun around the universe. The king's name written inside indicated therefore that he was the representative on earth of the sun-god, that his rule extended over the course of the sun and his name like the sun would endure forever. The cartouche was developed later in the form of scrolls ornamented with foliage or garlands of flowers. In the Gothic period the cartouche was shaped like a bannerolle with the ends rolled up. Those of the Renaissance are considered the most beautiful.

Castor and Pollux. [See Dioscuri.]

Cat. Worshipped in Egypt as a form of the sun-god. When a cat died it was taken to the embalmers, its body treated with drugs and spices and then put to rest in a case carefully prepared for it. Whoever wittingly or unwittingly killed a cat was sentenced to die. According to Plutarch because of its nocturnal habits and the contraction of the pupils of its eyes with the waning of the moon the cat also denoted the moon.

Ceres. [See Demeter.]

Chains. "That excellent and Divine fable of the Golden Chain, namely, that Men were not able to draw Jupiter down to earth; but contrariwise Jupiter was able to draw them up to Heaven." [Bacon.]

Cherub. The head of an angel emerging from two wings and used as an ornament in sculpture and painting.

Cherubim. A term derived from the Assyrian and now used to signify angels or those of the second degree of the nine-fold celestial hierarchy who have the gift of knowledge as the first (the seraphim) have the gift of love. The cherubim in the temple of Jerusalem and Solomon's Palace have been identified with the winged bull of Assyria; from these also came the winged figures that modern art received at the hands of the Greeks. The bird power, associated with the deity by the Egyptians and Assyrians, was humanised by the Greeks in their flying angels of victory.

Chimera. A fabulous, fire-breathing monster with three heads, that of a dragon, a goat and a lion. Homer described it as having the head of a lion, body of a goat and tail of a dragon. It was Bellerophon who, mounted on his winged horse Pegasus succeeded in destroying it. The chimera is frequently represented on ancient Greek coins and various combinations of fantastic animals called chimeræ were used in the Middle Ages as caryatids or supports in pieces of furniture. The term chimerical applied to anything without semblance of truth or reality is derived from the chimera.

Cinquecento. An abbreviation for *mille cinquecento* and applied to the art of Italy in the 16th century.

Cista. The mystic *cist* or chest in which were kept the articles that pertained to the worship of Demeter and Dionysos and belonging to the same class of images as the ark of the Egyptians and the Jews.

Clover Leaf, (St. Patrick's Shamrock). An emblem of the Deity more ancient than Christianity. As the gods were worshipped in triads and the three-fold aspect of life recognised in all its significance the trefoil became a natural emblem of high importance and a widely accepted symbol of the Trinity.

Conch-shell. A symbol of the voice of Buddha or the preaching of Buddha. It is one of the eight familiar symbols of Buddha and also typifies the *yoni* or feminine principle.

Cock. A solar symbol, and in ancient days placed on the summit of churches as an emblem of watchfulness. Frequently the "bird of vigilance" on the top of a church spire becomes a *weathercock*, a vane or pirouette in the form of a cock which turned with the wind.

Cornucopia. In classical art the cornucopia is associated with the gods who preside over the natural world. It is shaped like a horn and filled with fruit and flowers, sometimes the pine cone appears in the centre. It is a symbol of peace, prosperity, plenty.

Cow. Sacred in Egypt to Hathor, Nut, Isis and Nephthys, as well as other nature goddesses and typifying fertility.

Crane. A Chinese symbol of longevity, hence of life. A stork or crane standing on the back of a tortoise forming a candlestick typifies light and life, expressing the Chinese saying "May your days be as long as the tortoise and stork." Cranes and herons when depicted standing in the water symbolised the dawn.

Criophorus. A Greek word which means literally "one who carries a ram." It was a name bestowed upon Hermes by the people of Tanagra because he had saved them from a plague by carrying a ram (thrice?) around the walls of the town. Hermes is frequently represented thus in Greek art.

Crosier. A staff with a crook carried by bishops and abbots as a sign of office. Originally in form like the sacred tau it was not until the seventeenth century that it was given the bent appearance which it has since retained.

Cross. One of the oldest and most wide spread symbols of creative power and life to come.

Cupid. [See Eros.]

Cypress. The ancients worshipped the divine Creator in the form of a pyramid cone, or obelisk. Thus the cypress reaching toward heaven like a pointed flame became a living and arresting symbolic figure. It was an androgynous symbol. Always green it was a symbol of life and was associated with the sun and moon, with Venus and all the other nature goddesses, and with Zeus, Apollo, Hermes and various other gods. There was the cypress of the sun and the cypress of the moon. Two pyramidal cypresses surmounted the one by the sun, the other by the crescent moon are found on Asiatic monuments. It was also a mortuary emblem of high significance.

"Dark Warriors." These are the serpent and the tortoise who together form the Chinese symbol of the North.

Demeter, (Ceres). The Greek goddess of the earth, daughter of Kronos and Rhea and mother of Persephone and Dionysos by Zeus. Aided by Zeus, Pluto carries off Persephone to the lower world. The rape of Persephone and the anger of the goddess mother which results in a famine on earth when nothing is permitted to grow is simply another embodiment of the old nature myth of the winter season when the productive powers of nature or the earth rest or lie concealed. Zeus yielding to her entreaties permits Persephone to spend half the year with her mother and Persephone in whose charge the seed is committed to the earth typified the "fructified flower that returns in the spring" dwelling in the light a portion of the year. Worship of Demeter has been connected with belief in a future life and the Eleusinian mysteries celebrated in her honour were said to have had an ennobling effect. Demeter not only was goddess of the fertility of the earth but of fertility in general and thus was the goddess of marriage. She was worshipped in Attica, Crete, Delos, Sicily and the west coast of Asia. She is the goddess of agriculture, of corn and harvests. Pigs, symbols of fertility were sacrificed to her, also cows, bulls, honey cakes and fruits. In art the goddess is represented draped and with a veil. She frequently wears a garland of ears of corn, in her hand she holds a sceptre, an ear of corn or a poppy and sometimes a torch and the mystic basket. Her expression is one of great dignity.

Diana. [See Artemis.]

Dionysos, (Bacchus). The god of the vintage and the cultivation of the earth was called both by the Greeks and the Romans "Bacchus, the noisy or riotous god." This was originally however merely a surname for Dionysos. The legends of this god are innumerable, his adventures endless. He was said to be a son of Zeus by Semele, he was also called the son of Zeus and Lethe, Zeus and Persephone, Zeus and Demeter as well as many others. The father never varies nor do any of the legends minimise the wrath of the jealous Hera. Zeus was said to have placed him in his thigh and given him to the nymphs of Mount Nysa who brought him up. He was also associated with the Muses and Hermes is somehow mixed up with the early life of the god who is frequently represented as a child carried by Hermes. Dionysos is said to have discovered the cultivation of the vine and wanders over various countries of the earth teaching its uses. One legend tells of his coming to a lake and one of two asses whom he met on the shore carried him safely across. The god placed both animals among the stars and henceforth the ass was sacred to Dionysos. His influence is both benign and evil. He is god of the "productive, overflowing and intoxicating power of nature which carries man away from his usual quiet and sober mode of living." As god of wine he is inspired as well as inspiring and thus has the power of prophecy. He is also a god of healing and as protector of the vine, he becomes protector of trees and thus comes into close relationship with Demeter. Like Apollo he was thought to possess eternal youth. In the earlier period the Graces or Charites were his companions. In later times he was worshipped as androgynous. Afterwards, as his worship changed he was accompanied by bacchantes, wild and dishevelled women, satyrs and centaurs inspired with divine fury and carrying in their hands thyrsus staffs, cymbals, swords and serpents. Dionysos is a twice-born god of vegetation, a promoter of civilisation and lover of peace. He is also god of the drama and protector of theatres. He is depicted in art as an infant with Hermes or being played with by satyrs. As the youthful or Theban Bacchus his body is masculine with firm outlines but with a certain softness and roundness which suggests the feminine. His expression is dreamy and lanquid, the head is crowned by a diadem or wreath of vine leaves or ivy. He is frequently depicted leaning on his comrades, or riding on an ass, lion, tiger or panther. Occasionally, on coins only, he is given the horns of a ram or bull. His attributes are the thyrsus, cantharus or drinking cup and sometimes the basket. The vine, asphodel, laurel, ivy, panther, ass, serpent, tiger and lynx were sacred to him. The ox and ram were sacrificed to him. Dionysos was said to have "loathed the sight of an owl."

The Dioscuri, (Castor and Pollux). The twin horsemen are given white horses. They are also symbolised by twin circles.

Dolphin. Was looked upon by the Greeks as the saviour of the shipwrecked. It is sacred to Poseidon (Neptune) and was supposed to bear the souls of the deceased to the Island of the Blessed. It was a favourite of Apollo. In the heraldry of France the bearing of the dolphin was reserved for the Dauphin or heir to the throne.

Dorjé. A small sceptre used by the lamas of Tibet composed of two or four tridents combined, the outer prongs touching the central one giving the whole something the appearance of a crown.

Dove. The dove with an olive branch was a symbol of Athene or renewed life. The dove is also an attribute of Ishtar and Venus and the symbol of the Holy Ghost. Among the Christians it is pre-eminently the emblem of the soul.

Dragon. Although figuring in nearly every ancient religion as the personification of evil, the dragon among the Chinese and Japanese is a most potent symbol of the blessing, the rain giving power of the gods of water. It is a symbol of power, royalty, sovereignty. The dragon is chief among the four supernatural creatures that play such an important part in Chinese imagery and art. In Japan the dragon is the symbol of the Mikado. In China dragon painting reached its zenith in the thirteenth century.

Eagle. Among the Greeks the eagle was the symbol of supreme spiritual energy.

Eight. The figure 8 typified regeneration. It is one of the symbols of the Egyptian god Thoth who "pours the waters of purification on the heads of the initiated." Swedenborg makes eight correspond to purification.

Ennead. In later times nine gods took the place of the triad in Egypt. The ennead consisted of five gods and four goddesses or four pairs of deities and one supreme god.

Eros, (Cupid). The god of love. Hesiod, the earliest author that mentions him describes him as the cosmogonic Eros. "First . . . there was Chaos, then came Ge, Tartarus and Eros, the fairest among the gods, who rules over the minds and councils of gods and men. . . . Eros was one of the fundamental causes in the formation of the world, inasmuch as he was the uniting power of love which brought order and harmony among the conflicting elements of which Chaos consisted." In accordance with this conception he was called a son of Kronos or a god who came into existence without parentage. It is only among the later poets that he is represented as a wanton boy, sometimes as the son of Aphrodite, sometimes the son of Hermes and Artemis, or again he is given a mother but not a father. In this later aspect he typified the love of the senses which begets disharmony rather than unity. He makes sport of gods and men. He twists the thunderbolts of Zeus, tames lions and takes away his arms from Herakles. He was given a bow and arrows which he carried in a golden quiver, some golden and others blunt and heavy as lead. He has golden wings and is frequently represented blindfolded. He is often depicted with Aphrodite also with Hermes and statues of Hermes and Eros usually stood in the Greek gymnasia. Thespiæ in Bœotia was the chief place of the worship of Eros and where in ancient days he was represented by a rude stone. He was also worshipped in Samos, Sparta and Athens. He was a favourite subject with the Greek sculptors. Praxiteles, who represented him as a full grown youth of great beauty being especially famed for his statues of the god of love. Later the fashion grew to depict him as a winged infant or wanton child. He is thus shown in the illustration of *Ares in Repose.* Wild beasts are sometimes shown tamed by the god. His attributes are the ram, hare, cock and rose.

Eye. A symbol of Horus and Osiris typifying divine omniscience. The same meaning is also attached to it in India. According to St. Matthew the single eye symbolises light. "The light of the body is the eye; if therefore thine eye be single thy whole body shall be full of light." (Matt. 6: 22.)

Fan. An ancient Chinese emblem of power and dominion.

Feather. An attribute of Maat the Egyptian goddess of Truth.

Fig Tree. A sacred tree believed to combine both masculine and feminine attributes and held in especial veneration as an emblem of life. Its tri-lobed leaf suggesting the masculine triad became the symbolic covering in representations of nude figures.

Fire. Pyramids, obelisks and triangles with the point up symbolise fire.

Fish. Used universally as a symbol of fecundity and life, and one of the eight emblems of Buddha. Among the Chinese the fish typified happiness. Two fish were a symbol of marriage. The early Christians used three fish intertwined to symbolise the Trinity.

Foot-prints of Buddha. There are usually seven emblems on the soles of the feet, the swastika, wheel, conch-shell, fish, vajra, crown, vase. The idea was taken over from Vishnu, an earlier god.

Frog. A symbol among the Egyptians of the watery elements or primordial slime which was considered as the basis of created matter in the Egyptian cosmogony. Each of the four primeval gods, Heh, Kek, Nau and Amen were represented with the head of a frog while their feminine counterpart or energy had serpents for heads. The cult of the frog is one of the oldest cults in Egypt.

Ganesha. An Indian god who is invoked by the Hindus as an overcomer of obstacles. He is represented by an elephant or a man with the head of an elephant. Images of Ganesha are found at cross roads and architects place figures of the god at the foundation of buildings.

Gazelle. An animal sacred to Mul-lil, the Akkadian god of storms who was originally the lord (mul) of the dust (lil), that is the husband of the earth, the phallic father or great snake. The oryx, goat, (wild goat or ibex) and the antelope are all the equivalents of the gazelle and are all typhonic, symbols of Set. Horus tramples under foot the gazelle. Horus holding a gazelle typifies his victory over Set. Lunar crescents are associated with gazelles. The association of deer, the ibex or wild goat, oryx, gazelle or antelope with the lotus is symbolic of the sun or moon or both. Deer are given to Diana. The Hindu moon god Chandra rides in a car drawn by antelopes. An antelope is given to Siva who is represented by a moon crescent.

Girdle Tie in Red Carnelian. An Egyptian amulet typifying the blood of Isis and which had the power to wash away the sins of its possessor.

Goose. A solar bird associated with the sun-gods of Egypt, India, Greece and Britain. It was given to Isis and Hera, also to Apollo, Dionysos, Hermes and Eros. It was the emblem of love. In China it was called the Bird of Heaven and looked upon as distinctively a bird of *yang* or the principle of light and masculinity.

Gorgons, The. There were three gorgons with "curls of hissing snakes" instead of hair and whoever gazed upon them was turned to stone. All were immortal except Medusa, whom Perseus encouraged by Athene succeeds in killing and her head was worn henceforth upon the ægis of Athene. Medusa was frequently represented in Greek art. The head seen full face with serpents coiled about it, the face one of horror with parted lips was much used for decorative purposes. Small images of the head of Medusa were also used as charms.

Green Stones. The Egyptians put green stone amulets in their tombs to symbolise youth and immortality. Horus, the young morning sun who typified eternal youth was called 'Prince of the Emerald Stone.'

Griffin, Griffon, Gryphon. Fabulous creatures half-lion, half-eagle symbolising eternal vigilance and wardenship. They were the protectors of the treasured gold of the North from the thieving, one-eyed Arimaspians and are also mentioned as guarding the gold of India.

Grove. Often a mis-translation for the wooden image of Ashtoreth or Astarte the chief goddess of Baalism.

Hathor. The Egyptian goddess of the feminine principle in nature. As goddess of maternity she is given the head of a vulture surmounted by the moon crescent or horns and the solar disk. Again she is represented as the World Cow typifying fertility. "The heads of Hathor were lucky charms. Hathor represented fate, and he who wore her head earned her favour and a happy destiny for himself." She is a cosmic goddess, the mother of light and sometimes represented as a sphinx.

Hawk or Falcon. A solar bird particularly venerated in Egypt and given to all the sun-gods. Horus is the falcon god. The hawk of Horus typified the spirit of the sun. Having the swiftest flight of any bird the hawk was the emblem of divine intelligence and wisdom.

Hekt or Heqet. The Egyptian frog goddess and identified with Hathor. She was the protector of mothers and new born infants and the frog typified re-newed birth.

Hephæstus, (Vulcan). In early Greek art the god of fire is depicted as a dwarfish figure in allusion to his lameness. In the finest period of Greek art he is represented as a full-bearded man of powerful frame. He wears an oval cap and the *chiton* leaving the right arm and shoulder bare. His symbol is the hammer and sometimes he is given the tongs.

Hera, (Juno). The "only really married goddess among the Olympians" and one of the few divinities who are purely Greek. Unlike the other great nature goddesses Hera was not the "Queen of gods and men" but the wife of the Supreme god Zeus and equally reverenced by the other gods. Zeus listens to her counsels and she feels free to censure him when occasion offers. Nevertheless, she is his inferior in power and obliged to obey him. She is represented as obstinate, jealous, quarrelsome and quite ready to resort to cunning and intrigue to compass her ends. Hera personifies the atmosphere, she is "Queen of the Air," the great goddess of nature and is identified with the Roman Juno. Her most celebrated temple was at Mt. Embœa. A colossal sitting statue of Hera of gold and ivory made for her sanctuary was the work of Polycletus. She was often depicted wearing a crown adorned with the Charites and Horae and holding in one hand a pomegranate and in the other a sceptre surmounted by a cuckoo. She was frequently represented veiled. In the earliest form of her worship the goddess was represented by a pillar or possibly the "aniconic image" that was associated with most of the great nature goddesses. The peacock and cuckoo were sacred to her.

Herakles. The most celebrated hero of antiquity and a son of Zeus by Alcmene of Thebes, wife of Amphitryon. His birth arouses the jealous wrath of Hera who sends two snakes to devour him before he was eight months old. The infant Herakles seizes them and crushes them in both his hands. His first great victory was his fight with the lion of Cythæron. Henceforth Herakles wore the lion's skin as his ordinary garment with its head for a helmet. Some accounts give him the lion's skin as an attribute of his victory over the Nemean lion. The subservience of Herakles to Eurystheus was brought about by the strategy of Hera. Zeus having decreed that the one who came into the world last must obey the other has to stand by his word. He makes Hera promise, however, that if Herakles performs twelve great works in the service of Eurystheus he shall become immortal. The latter imposes upon him many and bitter tasks. The Twelve Labours of Herakles are: (1) The fight with the lion of Nemea which Herakles strangled with his own hands, (2) To destroy the Lernean hydra, a monster with nine heads, the middle one immortal. (3) To bring alive and unhurt to Eurystheus, the stag of Ceryneia in Arcadia famous for its incredible swiftness, its golden horns and brazen feet and sacred to Artemis. (4) To bring alive to Eurystheus the wild boar which ravaged the Erymanthian neighbourhood. On this adventure he destroyed the centaurs. (5) The fifth labour was to clean the Augean stables where 3000 oxen had been kept for many years. (6) To kill the Stymphalian birds which infested a lake in Arcadia and fed on human flesh. (7) To bring alive into Peloponnesus the Cretan wild bull. (8) To capture the mares of the Thracian Diomedes that tore and devoured human flesh. (9) To obtain the girdle of the queen of the Amazons. (10) To destroy the monster Geryones and bring his oxen alive to Argos. It was upon this expedition that Herakles erected the two pillars (Calpe and Abyla) on the two sides of the straits of Gibraltar which were thereafter called the Pillars of Herakles. On this journey, too, Herakles, enraged by the heat of the sun shot at Helios who, admiring his boldness, presented him with a golden boat in which he sailed across the ocean to Erytheia. (11) The eleventh labour was to obtain the golden apples from the garden of the Hesperides. It was upon this adventure that Herakles killed the vulture that was consuming the liver of Prometheus and thus saved the Titan, who in return advised him not to go to the garden of the Hesperides but to send Atlas and in the meantime to bear the weight of heaven for Atlas on his own shoulders. Atlas having brought the apples refused to take upon himself again the burden of heaven and declared his intention of carrying the apples to Eurystheus. In this case Herakles employed strategy to obtain the apples and accomplish his mission. (12) The last and most dangerous of his labours was to bring upon earth from the lower world the three-headed dog Cerberus. Having successfully performed these twelve feats of heroism, his life is still one of vicissitude. In the end having been unwittingly poisoned by his wife, leaving him with an incurable distemper Herakles climbs Mount Œta and imploring the protection of Zeus he raises a pile of wood which he mounts and orders to be set on fire. None of his followers would obey him. Finally a shepherd passing by complies and while the pyre is burning a cloud comes down from heaven and amid peals of thunder Zeus bears the hero to Olympus where he becomes one of the immortals. After the apotheosis of Herakles, sacrifices were offered to him as a hero. Later on he was worshipped throughout Greece as a divinity. Herakles, Pan and Dionysos were called the youngest gods. The worship of Herakles spread to Rome and Italy and from there into Gaul, Spain and Germany. The Roman Hercules was looked upon as the giver of health. Representations of Herakles in art cover every phase of his life. Whether depicted as youth, hero or immortal he is always the type of unconquerable strength, energy and resourcefulness. His labours are undertaken for the good of others, never for himself. He is also called a solar god and his twelve labours represent the twelve signs of the zodiac. He is usually depicted wearing the lion's skin or with it over one arm. The animals sacrificed to him were the bull, ram, lamb and boar.

Hermes, (Mercury). He is the god of prudence, commerce, eloquence, skill, of cunning and strategy; he is a thieving god, one who would steal or commit fraud or perjury without a qualm, accomplishing his ends with invincible dexterity and gracefulness. He was the herald and messenger of the gods. In his ministry to Zeus not only was he a herald but also the charioteer and cup bearer. He was said to have been the inventor of the alphabet, numbers, astronomy, gymnastics, the art of warfare and the cultivation of the olive tree. It was Hermes who invented the lyre which he bestowed upon Apollo receiving in exchange the caduceus. As dreams are sent by Zeus, Hermes conducts them to man and thus he has the power of giving or taking away sleep. He was god of the roads and the protector of travellers.

He was the giver of wealth and good luck and thus was the god of gamblers. As the protector of animals he was especially worshipped by shepherds. In the Arcadian religion Hermes was the fertilising god of the earth. One of his most important functions was that of conducting the souls of the dead from the upper to the lower regions. As conductor of the dead he always carries the caduceus with the two emblematic serpents, symbols of life. In the earlier works of art Hermes was depicted with a ram over his shoulder. He was then called Hermes Criophorus. [See Criophorus.] In this aspect he becomes the prototype of Christ as the Shepherd. His usual attributes are the *petasos*—a low wide-rimmed hat sometimes adorned with little wings—winged sandals to denote the swiftness with which he could girdle the universe, the magic staff later developed into the caduceus, and sometimes as god of wealth he holds a purse in his hand. The palm, tortoise, cock, ram, goat, various kinds of fish and the number four were sacred to him. Incense, cakes and honey, lambs, young goats and pigs were sacrificial offerings.

Herms or Hermae. Statues of Hermes, the god of ways, were placed at street corners, cross roads and boundaries. Those placed at three road junctions were called *Trivia.* The name Hermae is given to a peculiar kind of statue consisting of a carefully modelled head or bust set upon a quadrangular pillar tapering toward the base. Sometimes there is a single head or again a double head is set on the pillar. This form of statue is of great antiquity and was highly honoured. To deface the Hermae was looked upon as a serious crime. The Romans used the Hermae in the decoration of gardens or as pillars set at intervals in balustrades or walls. Later, terminal figures of bearded gods or even philosophers were also called Hermae.

Honeysuckle, (Anthemion). An ornament in architecture derived from the young petals of the lotus before they have expanded.

Horns. From time immemorial a symbol of divine power, their use going back to the moon cult. Horns were used as protective amulets against evil forces. Among the mystics the horn typified the call of the spirit.

Horse. "And he took away the horses that the Kings of Judah had given to the sun . . . and burned the chariots of the sun with fire." (II. Kings, 23: 11.) The horse is sacred to the sun. It symbolised the intellect. Bayley suggests that the one-eyed Arimaspians who rode on horses in their attempt to steal the gold guarded by the watchful griffins implied that they were men of intellect only, lacking the eye of Love. Four horses denoted equity, justice. In ancient art the sun was depicted as a charioteer driving a team of four horses across the heavens.

Horus. Prince of Eternity. "I am yesterday, today and to-morrow." Horus is the morning sun, the type of eternal youth. He is given the hawk, sometimes represented as a falcon or hawk. He wears a double diadem as ruler over the North and South. Originally one of the oldest gods of Egypt, he returns as the son of Osiris and Isis.

Ibis. "A bird of deep black colour with legs like a crane, its beak strongly hooked and its size about that of a land rail." It was associated with the moon and Thoth and was deeply venerated in Egypt. Plutarch asserts that the fact that the ibis was wont to stand with straddled legs forming a triangle added greatly to its sacredness. It typified aspiration and perseverance, was a symbol of morning and was reverenced by the Egyptians as a destroyer of serpents.

Incense. Priests burned incense in Egypt to smoke out demons and drive out evil spirits. It was believed also to aid the soul in its last flight. Inspiration was derived from it. The gods were invoked and propitiated by it. In the flood legend the Babylonian Noah burned incense. It is used wherever there is Buddhism as in the Catholic religion of today.

Incense Burners. When made in the form of lions indicate the association of the lion with fire and sun worship. The lion is thus the god and producer of smoke.

Indra. The Hindu god who makes rain. Indra is called the god of 10,000 eyes, or Lord and Watcher of the Stars. His symbol is the *vajra* or thunderbolt.

Isis. The wife of Osiris and mother of Horus has many forms. She symbolises birth, growth, vigour, development; she is a moon goddess, an earth goddess, the "lady of words of power," the greatest goddess of Egypt. She is generally depicted in the form of a woman with the vulture head-dress and in her hand the papyrus sceptre. Above her head is usually the sun disk between a pair of horns, sometimes she wears the double crown of South and North with the feather of Maat attached to the back or, with the horns and disk she will have two plumes. She has the uræus on her forehead and sometimes the ram's horns are given her instead of the horns of Hathor.

Ivy. Denoted eternal life hence placed upon the brow of Bacchus.

Jade. In China it symbolises "all that is supremely excellent," the highest form of human virtue, the "most perfect development of the masculine principle in nature."

Janus. A god who rivalled Jupiter himself among the Romans. Janus releases the dawn, he was also the god of the beginning and end of undertakings. He is represented in art as two-faced and is given the key as a symbol of his power to open and close. In time of war his temple in Rome was open, and closed in times of peace.

'Jewel in the Lotus,' The. At the beginning of the world Adi-Buddha manifested himself as a flame rising from a lotus flower. Sometimes the stalk of the lotus springs from a triangle lying on the seed vessel of an eight leaved lotus, but it is more generally depicted rising from the water. The 'jewel in the lotus' symbolises the union of the two forces fire and water or masculine and feminine.

Jug. One of the eight familiar symbols of Buddha. It gives forth no sound when full, typifying a man full of knowledge.

Juno. [See Hera.]

Jupiter. [See Zeus.]

Ka. This is man's double, a replica of the body but formed of a substance less dense—"an etherealised projection of the individual." The Egyptians pictured the Ka as the vital force which came into the world with the body, passed through life in its company and went with it into the next world. Everything in Egypt was supposed to have a double.

Kalaśa. The Vase which holds the Water of Life. A symbol of the Chinese goddess Kwan-yin.

Keys. Symbol of Janus who flings wide open the portals of the sky and releases the Dawn. Also given to Mithra, the Persian Sun-god, and to St. Peter, prince of the apostles and founder of the Church of Rome.

Khensu. The "wanderer," a moon god and said to be the son of Amen-Ra and Mut and the third of the great Theban triad. He was called a form of Thoth. He is the messenger of the gods, and is usually represented with the head of a hawk or man, has the lunar disk in a crescent, or the sun disk and uræus, and in his hands the usual symbols of life and power. Some times he is given two hawk's heads, four wings and stands upon two crocodiles symbolising the sun-rise and the new moon, and the crocodiles are the two great powers of darkness over which he has conquered.

Khnemu. One of the oldest gods in the Egyptian religion. He was a river god originally known as Qebh and figures as a ram-headed god. He appropriates the attributes of Ra, Osiris, Shu and Seb and is sometimes shown as a man with four ram's heads symbolising fire, air, water, earth. He was called the 'Moulder,' the maker of mankind and when depicted with the four heads he is the type of the "great primeval creative force." He is usually represented as a ram-headed man wearing the White Crown, to which are often attached the disk, plumes and uræi, and holding the sceptre and symbol of life.

Knot. Without beginning or end the mystic sign of Vishnu, typifying the continuity of life and adopted by the Buddhists as one of the eight glorious emblems of Buddha.

Ladder. A favourite symbol of the ascent to the gods. The ladder of Jacob was probably derived from the Egyptian belief that you could mount to heaven on a ladder. Small ladders as amulets were placed in the tombs of Egyptian kings.

Lightning. Symbolised in all nations by a weapon. Thunder and storm gods were given the axe, hammer, pitchfork, trident, the *vajra* or thunderbolt. Sometimes a trident with zigzag branches was used to typify forked lightning.

Lion. Invariably associated with the sun, the lion symbolises the heat of the sun. As the power to modify solar heat is attributed to the sun-god, so he is represented as in the Samson myth as slayer of the lion.

Lioness. In Egypt the lioness, like the vulture and cat, symbolised maternity and was given to the primitive mother goddesses who gave birth to all that exists.

Lituus. A twisted wand something like a bishop's crosier and used by augurs for purposes of divination. When depicted in art it usually takes the form of a spiral.

Lizard. A giant lizard was a symbol of Ahrimanes, the Persian god of evil. A lizard is occasionally depicted upon the breast of Athene. It was thought to conceive through the ear and bring forth through the mouth and was worshipped in Mexico and by the Slav nations as late as the sixteenth century.

Lotus. "I am the pure lotus which springeth up from the divine splendour that belongeth to the nostrils of Ra." From earliest times a symbol of creation, life, immortality, resurrection, fecundity, the feminine principle, re-birth, self-creation. As every Buddha and Bodhisattva was believed to be self-existent he was given the lotus flower support to denote his divine birth. Among the Buddhists the lotus is also the symbol of Nirvana.

Love. Compared to a fire giving warmth; intelligence to a light-giving flame.

Maat. The Egyptian goddess of Truth whose symbol is a feather. Maat is the inseparable companion of Thoth.

Mars. [See Ares.]

Medusa. [See Gorgons].

Meh-urt or Meh-urit. A cow goddess identified with Hathor, Isis and also as a form of Nut, and sometimes depicted as the great cow of the sky. She was the personification of the primeval, feminine creative principle and usually appears as a cow-headed woman with a lotus-entwined sceptre, thus typifying the "great world lotus flower out of which rose the sun for the first time at the Creation."

Menat, or Whip Amulet. Symbolic of strength and supposed to drive away care. The menat is the handle of the whip which was used to keep off evil spirits and as an amulet was frequently surmounted by the head of a goddess. It is also a symbol of pleasure and happiness.

Mercury. [See Hermes.]

Minerva. [See Athene.]

Mirror. One of the symbols of truth. The mirror of self-realisation, the shield which evil dare not face. Concave bronze mirrors are conspicuous among the Taoist symbols, the belief being that "when evil recognises itself it destroys itself." Mirrors were also thought to ward off evil spirits.

Moon. In the moon cult which preceded sun worship the moon was masculine. The Assyrian moon-god was the god of wisdom. In Egypt the moon was identified with Thoth. In the sun cult the moon was associated with the feminine principle. The crescent moon symbolised virginity. Among the Chinese the moon represented the concrete essence of the feminine principle in nature and thus directed everything that belonged to the *yin* principle such as darkness, earth, water, etc. "The Vital essence of the Moon governs Water; and hence when the Moon is at its brightest the tides are high." Chinese and Indian legends agree in making the hare, frog and toad inhabitants of the moon. Eight trees also were said to flourish in the moon. One, the cassia tree Wu Kang, the Man in the Moon was condemned to hew down. The trunk of the tree closed after each blow of the axe. The leaves of the cassia conferred immortality upon those who ate of them.

Moon and Hare. The moon with a hare in it pounding the drug of immortality is frequently represented in Chinese art and is one of the twelve symbols of power. The association of the hare with the moon is very old and has been attributed to the mysterious effect of the moon upon the hare which the primitives could not fail to notice. On clear moonlight nights the hare were wont to gather together in bands and indulge in weird play, silent and bizarre, as if under the influence of some subtle and transforming elixir of life.

Mouse. Sacred to Apollo. "Cinderella's coach was drawn by *mice* which turned magically into white horses, i. e., the golden footed steeds of the Morning." (Bayley.)

Mut. The feminine counterpart of Amen-Ra, the great "world Mother." She is represented as a woman wearing the united crowns of North and South and holding in one hand the *ankh* cross and in the other the papyrus sceptre. Sometimes she has large wings and at her feet is the feather symbol of Maat. Again from each shoulder there projects the head of a vulture. Sometimes she has the head of a man or a woman or a vulture or lioness. When given the phallus and the head of a man it denoted the belief that the goddess was androgynous, or self-produced.

Nazit. A winged serpent goddess in the Delta. The Greeks called her Buto and identified her with their Leto.

Neith, Net or Neit. One of the oldest Egyptian goddesses represented in the form of a woman wearing the crown of the North, with a sceptre in one hand and the *crux ansata* in the other, or a bow and two arrows, her characteristic symbols. She was to goddesses what Ra was to gods. The Egyptians declared she was eternal and self-produced. In other words she was the personification of the eternal feminine principle of life, and is made to say, "I am what has been, what is, and what shall be." She was called the "mighty mother who gave birth to Ra."

Nekhebet. An Egyptian goddess of the South, while Uatchet was goddess of the North. In pre-dynastic times sovereignty of the South and North was represented by the Vulture and Serpent signs. Nekhebet was a vulture goddess and Uatchet a serpent goddess.

Nephthys. Sister of Isis and wife of Set typified death, corruption, diminution, sterility. Although goddess of death she symbolised the coming into existence of the life which springs from death. She is represented as a woman with a pair of horns and the disk.

Neptune. [See Poseidon.]

Nine. In Hebrew the equivalent of Truth because when multiplied it reproduces itself.

Nu. One of the earlier Egyptian gods who personified the watery mass out of which had sprung the germs of life. He is sometimes represented as a man holding a sceptre, again he is given the head of a frog surmounted by a beetle or the head of a serpent.

Nut. The Egyptian sky goddess. She is the feminine counterpart of Nu and looked upon as the primeval mother and later was identified with Neith, Mut and Hathor who are given her attributes. She is represented as a woman sometimes with the head of the uræus surmounted by the solar disk, or again with the head of a cat. Sometimes she is the great cow goddess. As the wife of Seb she is for all practical purposes the same goddess bearing the same titles, and is the type of the great mother. The sycamore tree was her peculiar emblem. "Since the mythological tree of Nut stood at Heliopolis and was a sycamore it may well have served as the archetype of the sycamore tree under which tradition asserts that the Virgin Mary sat and rested during her flight to Egypt." (Budge.)

Obelisk. An ancient symbol of the masculine principle. A pair of obelisks and colossal statues in front of the temples of Egypt with backs to the pylon and facing the city (led up to frequently by long avenues of sphinxes or rams), were to protect the god against evil influences. The obelisk has been called the symbol of Amon-Generator, a ray of light or the finger of the god. Obelisks placed in pairs before Theban temples expressed among other ideas "concepts of generative power and fertility which had belonged to the raised stone from which they partly emanated." (Maspero.)

Orpheus. He is said by some to be a son of Apollo and has been called the inventor of letters and everything that pertains to civilisation. Receiving a lyre from Apollo he charmed the beasts and birds by the magic of his music. Rivers ceased to flow in order to hear him and mountains moved nearer to listen to his song. His love for Eurydice is founded on the old nature myth of death and restoration to life. Upon the death of Eurydice, Orpheus descends to the nether regions searching for her and gains the consent of Pluto that she shall be restored to life and free to accompany him back to earth, if he will refrain from looking at her until after they are beyond the precincts of hell. When in sight of the upper region of light Orpheus turned to gaze upon her and Eurydice melted from his sight. Mourning for his lost love he withdrew into himself. The Thracian women angered by his coldness tore him limb from limb and threw his head in the Hebrus. Orpheus was called the first poet of the Heroic Age. The Orphics were a mystic order founded upon the doctrines and teachings of Orpheus. In early Christian art Christ was depicted as Orpheus surrounded by beasts and birds whom He charmed by His music.

Osiris. A water-god, man-god, solar-god—the god of the sun of yesterday—the great god and judge of the dead—"from first to last Osiris was to the Egyptians the god-man who suffered, and died, and rose again, and reigned eternally in heaven." Osiris is usually depicted in mummy form wearing the White Crown and a *menat* hanging from the back of his neck and holding the crook, sceptre and flail. Sometimes he wears the Atef, the white crown with plumes, sometimes he appears in the form of the tet (tat) pillar.

Osiris, his Amulets. The amulets used in producing the reconstitution of the body of Osiris, torn asunder by Set, were: the four figures of the children of Horus, two bulls, a figure of Horus, four lapis-lazuli tat pillars, two carnelian tat pillars, a figure of Thoth, and two lapis-lazuli *uzats*.

Owl. Sacred to Athene, goddess of wisdom. Owl-headed vases with breasts and the vulva represented by a large circle, the circle sometimes ornamented by an incised cross, were unearthed by Schliemann. These sacred vases were associated with the archaic Greek worship of Athene. Some were found with wings showing their sacred character.

Ox. Symbol of patient renunciation and toil. Eating of an ox was a part of the cult of Dionysos.

Palm. The Greek word for date palm and the phoenix is the same. Thus the tree was fabled to die and then spring up anew like the phoenix. It is one of the most ancient symbols of creative force and the date palm was the symbolic Tree of Life in Chaldea, Assyria and Babylonia. Among the Egyptians the palm tree typified the year because it produces a branch every month. The palm was sacred to Astarte and was also given to Apollo in Delos and Delphi. Among the Christians the palm is a symbol of martyrdom.

Pan. The great god of shepherds, flocks, pastures and forests. He was called a son of Hermes and grandson or great grandson of Kronos (Saturn). He lived in grottoes, wandering about the mountains and valleys and slumbering during the mid-day heat of summer. He was also a hunter and led the dances of the nymphs. As god of the pastoral life he was fond of music and invented the syrinx or shepherd's flute. He exulted in noise and riot and was looked upon as a companion of Cybele and Dionysos. He is represented in art as a short bearded man with the horns, ears and legs of a goat. His attributes are a pipe, crook and the fir tree. Rams, lambs, milk and honey were sacrificed to him. His principal place of worship was Arcadia, thence it spread to other parts of Greece. In Rome he was identified with Faunus and Lupercus. In Egypt the god Pan and a goat were worshipped at Hermopolis, Lycopolis and Mendes. Pan and the goat were both called Mendes and worshipped as gods of fecundity. This is the famous Ram of Mendes whose cult was established in the second dynasty. The ram was distinguished by certain symbolic markings and, like the Apis bull, was searched for diligently and when found led to the city followed by a procession of notables and priests. The cult lasted till the decay of the city.

Panther or Leopard. Because of the eye-like spots on its skin it symbolised the Great Watcher. The Egyptians frequently depicted Osiris as a crouching leopard with above him the open eye symbol. Images of Osiris had suspended near them the spotted skin of the leopard. The panther is also the symbolic animal of the Greek Dionysos. It may have been given to the god of wine and vegetation because of an old superstition that the panther was able to allure men, beasts and cattle by the fragrance of its breath.

Peach Tree. Among the Chinese an emblem of marriage and symbol of longevity.

Peacock. Sacred to Hera (Juno). In early Christian art a symbol of the resurrection.

Phoenix. This fabulous bird is second among the supernatural creatures of the Chinese and like the unicorn was supposed to unite both the masculine and feminine principles. It was looked upon as the essence of fire, is the bird of the sun that burns itself and rises from its own ashes immortally young. It has symbolised life and immortality from remotest times and was taken over by the Christians to express the same symbolic idea. The phoenix was a common device in heraldry for those who would convey the impression of survival. Queen Elizabeth had the phoenix stamped upon her medals and coins, frequently with the motto *Sola phoenix omnis mundi.* "The only phoenix in the world."

Pillar. One of the oldest symbols of creative energy. Two Pillars symbolised the "pair of opposites," or the "twin horsemen" which in early India "seem to have represented father and mother and afterwards day and night." In Egypt two pillars typified the Gateway of Life. The Egyptians symbolised their first Trinity by Three Pillars denoting Wisdom, Strength, Beauty. Three pillars were used by the Mayas, Incas, Hindus and Druids as a symbol of their triune gods. Among the Mayas the vault of heaven was sustained by Four Pillars one on each cardinal point. The Egyptians also had four pillars supporting the sky, each pillar under the care of a god. The pillars were termed the "Four sceptres of the gods."

Pine Cone. A symbol of life among all the semitic races. The "sacred cone" typified an existence united yet distinct and conveyed precisely the same meaning as the *crux ansata* of the Egyptians. It is also a symbol of Venus and Artemis. D'Alviella traces the *cone sacré* to the human silhouette comparing this also to the *crux ansata* which shaped the figures of the early nature goddesses such as Diana of the Ephesians. The combination of the sacred cone and the *crux ansata* penetrated to India where the disk was replaced by an inverted triangle above the tau. The symbol in this form is seen on the foot prints of Buddha.

Pine Tree. Among the Chinese and Japanese a symbol of life and immortality. The god of longevity is usually depicted standing at the foot of a pine while a crane perches on a branch above. Sometimes the bamboo is grouped with the pine and the plum tree. These are all longevity symbols and when grouped together typify good fortune, happiness. The white stag is associated with the god of longevity. Sometimes a stag and stork are shown with the pine each plucking a branch from the tree.

Pomegranate. Used by all semitic nations as a symbol of life and fecundity.

Poseidon, (**Neptune**). The god of the waters and the force and flow of life. Among the Greeks the horse which was likened to a crested sea wave, animated and bridled was sacred to Poseidon. This may refer to the myth of the contest between Athene and Poseidon for supremacy. Preference was to be given by the assembled gods to the one who gave the most useful present to man. Poseidon struck the earth with his trident and a horse sprang forth. Athene produced the olive and was acclaimed the victor. In art Poseidon is generally represented standing on a dolphin or seated in a chariot formed like a shell and drawn by dolphins or sea horses and holding a trident in his hand.

Priapus. The personification of *attraction*. Knight identifies the Greek Bacchus with the First Begotten Love of Orpheus and Hesiod. "In the Orphic Fragments this Deity or First-Begotten Love is said to have been produced together with Ether by Time (Kronos) or Eternity, and Necessity operating upon inert matter. He is described as eternally begetting, the Father of Night, called in later times the lucid or splendid because he first appeared as splendour; of a double nature as possessing the general power of creation and generation, both active and passive, both male and female. Light is his necessary and primary attribute, co-eternal with himself, and with him brought forth from inert matter by Necessity. Hence the purity and sanctity always attributed to light by the Greeks. . . . He is said to pervade the world with the motion of his wings bringing pure light; and thence to be called the splendid, the ruling Priapus, and self-illumined. . . . The self-created mind of the Eternal Father is said to have spread the heavy bond of love through all things in order that they might endure forever." [1] Geese are sacred to Priapus. He is represented as carrying fruit and either a cornucopia or sickle in his hand. The Italians confounded him with various personifications of the fructifying powers of nature and in Greek legends Priapus is associated with beings who are sensual and licentious. He was the god of gardens and the first fruits of gardens, fields and vineyards were sacrificed to him.

Psyche, (breath or soul). Psyche is called the "mythical embodiment of the human soul." The myth shows the helplessness, the unreliability, the tragic suffering of the soul as it passes through the world of experience. Quite without consciousness of anything but beauty and sweetness in life, Psyche excites the jealous wrath of Aphrodite by the elusive, intangible, exquisite quality of her beauty. The myth

[1] "Worship of Priapus," R. P. Knight.

resembles the story of Cinderella. Psyche is beset by the same forces—the jealous goddess or cruel stepmother, the twin sisters of pride and envy and Eros the god of love who, sent by Aphrodite to enchant her with some monster takes her unto himself and thus becomes the Prince Charming of the fairy tale. Eros visits her at night and exacts but one pledge—that she shall never attempt to see him. Psyche, played upon by her envious sisters forgets her promise and "investigates" love, and love, wounded by her distrust, flees from her and comes no more. The rest of the myth shows the soul paying the price for its wavering doubts. Psyche wanders from place to place searching for her lover. Finally she comes to the palace of Aphrodite who recognising and still hating her makes her a slave. Eros finding her there secretly comforts and aids her by his invisible presence. Her humility and patience win at last even the goddess of beauty, and Psyche becomes one of the immortals united forever with Eros. Psyche and Eros are frequently represented together in art. Psyche is often given the wings of a butterfly.

Ptah. The Egyptian Vulcan, the god of fire, Ptah was also regarded as a form of the sun-god and was identified with one of the great primeval gods and called the "father of beginnings and creator of the egg of the sun and moon." As creator Ptah was the embodiment of mind from which all things emerge. "Ptah was the architect and builder of the material world." While Khnemu was fashioning men and animals Ptah was constructing the heavens and the earth. He was represented shaping the egg of the world on a potter's wheel which he worked with his foot. He is usually depicted as a bearded man with a bald head holding the sceptre of power, the *crux ansata* and the tat, symbol of stability.

Ptah-Seker. A personification among the Egyptians of the "union of primeval creative power with a form of the inert powers of darkness or, in other words Ptah-Seker is a form of Osiris, that is to say, of the night sun or dead sun-god." (Budge.)

Ra. The great sun-god of the Egyptians. He is generally depicted with the head of a hawk or again as a hawk. He has the usual emblems of life and power, the solar disk and uræus, the *crux ansata* and sceptre. He is also identified with the ass, cat, bull, ram and crocodile.

Ram of Mendes. [See Pan.]

Rhea. "The name as well as the nature of this ancient divinity is one of the most difficult points in ancient mythology." It is assumed, however, that like Demeter, Rhea is goddess of the earth. Kronos was said to have devoured all his children by Rhea except Zeus whom she concealed giving

Kronos a stone wrapped up as an infant whom the god swallowed. Crete was probably the earliest seat of the worship of Rhea. She was identified with Cybele in Phrygia, was worshipped by the Thracians, under different names she was the great goddess of the Eastern world and was known as the Great Mother, the mother of all the gods. Her priests were the Corybantes who dressed in full armour, with cymbals, horns and drums performed their orgiastic dances on the mountains or in the depths of the forests of Phrygia. Many of the attributes of Rhea were given to her daughter Demeter. The lion was the symbolic animal of the earth goddess because of all the animals known it was the strongest and most important. In works of art she was rarely depicted standing. She is usually represented seated on a throne, wearing a mural crown from which hangs down a veil. Lions crouch on either side of her throne or sometimes she is shown in a chariot drawn by lions. In Greece the oak tree was sacred to Rhea.

Rosaries. Used in ancient days to reckon time. The circle, a line without termination, symbolised perpetual continuity hence circlets of beads. The rosary was used in the religions of the east as an aid in repeating mystical sentences. Different materials were employed by the Buddhists, ivory, jade and crystal beads, also those made from the wood of plum or cherry trees. Originally the beads numbered 108 "corresponding with the number of sins of the flesh."

Sail. The sail springing into movement under the influence of the wind was an Egyptian symbol of the spirit—*spiritus* meaning breath or wind.

Salt. Owing to its incorruptible nature salt was a symbol of immortality. Homer called it divine. Wisdom is personified holding a salt cellar. "The bestowal of *Sal Sapientiæ*, the Salt of Wisdom, is still a formality in the Latin Church." The victims for sacrifice among the ancient Romans were led to death with salt upon their heads. It was considered the worst possible omen should they shake it off. Hence the superstition about spilling salt. Da Vinci uses this same symbolism in the overturned salt cellar by the side of Judas in his "Last Supper."

Sangrael. The Cup of the Holy Grail which according to tradition was used at the Last Supper.

Scarab. An Egyptian amulet that protected against annihilation.

Scarabæus. [See Beetle.]

Sceptre. Derived from the divided pillar and typifying the union of the two forces that create life, and thus from the most ancient days, a symbol of highest power given only to rulers and the gods and goddesses of life. The Buddhists sometimes have a lotus carved on the handle, or it is a short, slightly curving wand of jade or exquisitely carved wood.

Scorpions. Symbol of Selk, the Egyptian goddess of writing and also reverenced by the Babylonians and Assyrians as guardians of the gateway of the sun. Seven scorpions were said to have accompanied Isis when she searched for the remains of Osiris scattered by Set.

Seb. The Egyptian earth god, the son of Shu and Tefnut, brother and husband of Nut and the father of Osiris and Isis, Set and Nephthys. He is represented in human form wearing the crown of the North to which is added the Atef crown or a goose. Seb was believed to have made his way through the air in the form of a goose. It was Seb and Nut who produced the great egg of the world out of which sprang the sun-god in the form of a phoenix.

Sebek. An Egyptian god depicted as a crocodile-headed man.

Sekhebet, Sekhmet or Sekhet. An Egyptian goddess representing the power of the sun. She is the second person of the Memphis triad and worshipped as the consort of Ptah. She is depicted with the head of a lioness or a cat, with the solar disk and uræus. She is also called a vulture goddess. Later Sekhet and Bast were identified with Hathor and called goddesses of the West and East. Each had the head of a lioness but Sekhet wears a red garment and Bast is given a green. Sekhet typified the scorching heat of the sun.

Serapeum. The famous tomb of the Apis bulls at Sakkara. Above stood the great temple of the Serapeum.

Serapis. The Egyptians believed that the soul of Apis united itself with Osiris after death and thus became the dual god Asar-Hapi or Osiris-Apis. The Greeks attributed to Asar-Hapi the same qualities of their god Hades and gave it the name of Serapis. Serapis was accepted both by the Greeks and the Egyptians as their principal object of worship and after 250 B.C. it seems to have been looked upon as the male counterpart of Isis. Bronze figures of Apis have a triangular piece of silver in the forehead, a disk and the uræus serpent between the horns, and on the sides of the body the outlined figures of vultures with outstretched wings.

Serpent. The Great Serpent is depicted by the Egyptians and Mayas as blue with yellow scales. Used as a symbol to figure the heavens or the principle of motion the serpent was depicted of an azure colour, studded with stars and devouring his tail, that is, re-entering into himself by continuous windings like the revolutions of the spheres. Three kinds of serpents are represented in the Egyptian monuments: the cobra di capello (the uræus of the ancient Egyptians and the "basilisk" of the Greeks), which was the symbol of royal and divine authority and appears on the heads of gods and kings, the asp or *cerastes*, and the great *coluber*, the serpent Apep, the symbol of Set or Typhon.

Set or Typhon. In the primitive Egyptian religions Set was not the god of evil but the personification of natural darkness. He was said to be the son of Nut (the sky) and Seb (the earth) and brother of Osiris and Isis. He married his sister Nephthys. In an earlier form he is opposed to Horus the elder. In the second form the combat is between Ra and Set and Set assumes the form of a huge serpent. The third form is Osiris and Set and the fourth is the battle between Horus, son of Osiris and Set. Besides the serpent Apep Set was given the crocodile, pig, turtle, ass and hippopotamus, and animals with reddish brown skins or even red-haired men were supposed to be under his influence and were held in especial aversion. Antelopes and black pigs were sacrificed to him.

Seven Buddhist Jewels, The The golden wheel or disk. Lovely female consorts. Horses. Elephants. Divine guardians of the treasury. Ministers in command of armies. The wonder working pearl. These are the seven gems of a *Chakravarti* or universal monarch. Seven precious jewels also belonged to Brahmanism and are referred to in the Rig-veda.

Seven Precious Things. In China and Japan gold, silver, rubies, emeralds, crystal, amber (or coral or the diamond) and agate.

Seven Wise Ones, The These came forth from the eye of Ra and taking the form of seven hawks flew upwards and together with Asten, a form of Thoth, presided over learning. Ptah as master architect carried out the designs of Thoth and his Seven Wise Ones.

Shu and Tefnut. The twin lion-gods of Egypt "who made their own bodies." Shu is represented in human form wearing on his head one, two or four feathers. As god of space he is sometimes depicted holding up the sky with both hands. The goddess Tefnut often appears with the head of a lioness or in the form of a lioness. The four pillars which held up the sky at the four cardinal points were called the "pillars of Shu."

Sin. The Assyrian moon-god was called the "mighty Steer whose horns are strong, whose limbs are perfect."

Solomon's Seal. Two equilateral triangles forming a six pointed star. This figure also embodied the ancient androgynous notion of the deity, the pyramid with apex upward typifying the masculine, and with apex downward the feminine principle. Here the analogy is perfect for two triangles thus arranged also symbolised fire which mounts upwards and water which flows down. In Rome it was a part of the marriage ceremony for the bride to touch fire and water, the two forces of creation and productivity.

Sphinx. Among the Egyptians a symbol of royal dignity, of the power of the Pharaohs. Believing that the gates of morning and evening were guarded by lion-gods they sometimes gave heads of men and women to these lion guardians which then typified the union of strength and intellect. It was the Greeks who gave the name of "sphinxes" to these figures. The oldest is the famous sphinx at Gizeh. Its age is unknown, but it existed in the time of Khephren who built the Second Pyramid (c. 4000 B.C.) and was probably very old even then. It is supposed to be a symbol of the sun-god Ra-Temu-Khepera-Herukhuti, and the guardian and protector of the tombs about it. In building it the Egyptians were providing a "colossal abode for the spirit of the sun-god which they expected to dwell therein and protect their dead; it faced the rising sun of which it was a mighty symbol." The lion statue with a human head was called the androsphinx, with a ram's head the crio-sphinx. With the Greeks the sphinx was only represented in feminine form with wings and typified the pestilential heat of summer.

Stag. Owing to its antipathy to the serpent which it invariably attacks and destroys the stag typified the victory of the spirit. A white Stag was an attribute of the Chinese and Japanese gods of longevity.

Stele. A term used to denote ancient monoliths or monuments placed vertically upon which were inscribed historic events or tributes to the memory of the dead. *Stelæ* upon which are sculptured the likeness of a departed hero or king form some of the most interesting examples of early Greek and Roman art. In Egypt the stelæ were originally identical with the "false doors" of the mastabas and represented the entrance into the nether world. They indicated also the place to which the friends were to turn when they brought their offerings.

Stones. The Egyptians called precious stones "hard stones of truth." Swedenborg made precious stones the symbol of spiritual truths. "All knowledge and all truth are absolute and infinite waiting not to be created but to be found." Primitive temples consisted of circles of stones in the centre of which was kindled the sacred fire. This circular area was sometimes enclosed in a square one. A *square stone* was a primitive symbol of Venus among Arabians and Greeks. It has been assumed that the twelve stones carried by the Children of Israel from the river Jordon to "a spot called Gilgal" were placed in the form of a circle.

Stupa, (*lit.* **"precious tower"**). A diagram symbolising the elements used in the East by the Buddhists and by the mediæval alchemists of Europe.

Suméru or Mt. Méru. The highest peak of the Himalayas and supposed to be the centre of the universe. This is the sacred mountain where dwelt the Hindu Triad Brahma, Vishnu and Siva. Mounts or Holy Hills were usually three in number. Mt. Méru had three peaks of gold, silver and iron.

Sun. To the Chinese it represented the concrete essence of the masculine principle in nature and was the source of all brightness, from it emanate the five colours. The sun was worshipped by the ancients as the material symbol of God, or the abode of the Supreme Spirit.

Sun disk with outspread wings of a hawk. The Egyptian symbol of the Deity, and constantly depicted in Egyptian art.

Sun with a three-legged raven in it. Frequently depicted in Chinese art and one of the twelve symbols of power. According to Chinese tradition a three-legged raven lives in the sun and the raven or crow is often painted with the sun as back ground. It is a favourite bird in Japan. In Egypt the raven is a symbol of destruction.

Surya-mani. A sun disk surmounted by a trident is called *surya-mani* or sun jewel. Issuing from the lotus it represents Adi-Buddha at the creation of the world.

Swastika or Fylfot Cross. One of the most widespread of all the mystic emblems of the sun and supposed among the many meanings attributed to it to typify solar energy, motion.

Tai-Kih or Ta-Ki. The Great Ultimate Principle of the Chinese is symbolised by a third line from above added to the Chinese monad of opposites. "The *yin* or feminine principle was generated by the 'Rest' of the Ta-Ki or Great All. The other, the *yang* or masculine principle was generated by the 'Motion' of the Great All."

Tat, Tet or Zad. An Egyptian amulet that has been variously interpreted as symbolising the pole that measured the Nile, as the tree trunk which enclosed the body of Osiris, or as the back bone of Osiris, and the setting up of the tat was an important religious feature in connection with the worship of the god. The tat pole has been called an Egyptian type of the "pole or pillar that sustained the universe." The tat like the Buckle amulet of Isis had to be dipped in water in which *ankham* flowers had lain and was hung around the mummy's neck for its protection. The word denotes stability, firmness, preservation.

Ta-urt, (The Greek Theuris). The consort of Set and goddess of childbirth. Ta-urt is depicted with the head of a hippopotamus and is sometimes shown leaning on the girdle tie symbolising the blood of Isis. The cult of Ta-urt was probably co-eval with Egyptian civilisation. As the feminine counterpart of Set she was the mother of the sun-god.

She also figures with the god Bes in a royal birth scene in a relief in the famous temple of Hatshepset, and later appears with Horus holding a crocodile which Horus is about to spear. Although at an early period looked upon with aversion as a creature of malignant power, Ta-urt was venerated in the later religions as a beneficent goddess.

Tefnut. The female counterpart of Shu. [See Shu and Tefnut.]

Thet or Buckle amulet of Isis. This represents a girdle made of carnelian, red jasper or red glass and is also called the "carnelian girdle tie of Isis." It brought to the deceased the protection of Isis giving him access, moreover, to every place in the world of shades.

Thor's Hammer. This symbol has been likened to the Fylfot Cross, the *crux ansata* and the Chinese Y. In Scandinavian mythology the tau cross was known as Thor's hammer. Like the thunderbolt in the hands of the Assyrian storm gods it was a weapon of divine power.

Thoth, Thot, Thaut or Tehuti. The Egyptian god of learning, the scribe, the "pathfinder and awakener of sleeping minds." He is a moon-god and his symbol the ibis. He is frequently depicted with the head of an ibis. The baboon was also sacred to Thoth.

Thrones. Three thrones surmounted by royal caps symbolised the great Babylonian triad Anu, Enlil and Ea. Thrones who support the seat of the Most High belong to the ninefold celestial hierarchy of the early Christians. These were symbolised as fiery wheels surrounded by wings and the wings filled with eyes.

Thyrsus. A staff entwined with ivy or vine branches or sometimes with a knot of ribbon and surmounted by a pine cone the symbol of life. Bacchus and his followers carry the thyrsus. It was also used in their religious ceremonies by the Egyptians, Phœnicians, Greeks and Jews.

Tiger. A mount for the gods, immortals and exorcists. An animal symbolising for the Chinese superhuman powers. The Taoist god of wealth rides on a tiger who watches over the magic money chest. The tiger was honoured by gamblers who burned incense before images of it holding money in its forepaws. It is frequently depicted with the dragon as a symbol of power. When the tiger and bamboo are depicted together it symbolises the bamboo jungle which protects the tiger from the elephant.

Torii. The temple gateway in Japan consisting of two upright and two horizontal beams of bronze, copper or stone, symbolising peace and rest or the Gateway of Life. It is said in Japan that the sun-goddess frequently descends to earth in the form of the "heavenly phoenix" making the *torii* her perch.

Tortoise. One of the four supernatural creatures of the Chinese and a favourite symbol of longevity and supposed to live a thousand years. Sometimes it is represented in art with a long bushy tail which it is said to have acquired at the age of ten thousand years. The tortoise was used in divination and was believed to hold the secrets of life and death. It is also a symbol of fecundity. In Greek art Aphrodite is sometimes depicted standing on a tortoise.

Triangle. The equilateral triangle is one of the oldest symbols of the Trinity or the tri-une conception; it is also the emblem of fire. In Egypt the form that signified the feminine principle or maternity was the hieroglyph of the moon, and is often depicted with the sacred baboon. Sometimes the triangle surmounts a pillar with the baboon before it in an attitude of worship.

Three double triangles surrounded by concentric circles. An Egyptian hieroglyphic for the Khui land or Land of the Spirits.

Triangle enclosed by a circle. "The area within this triangle is the common hearth of them all and is named the 'Plain of Truth' in which the Reason, the forms and the patterns of all things that have been, and that shall be, are stored up not to be disturbed; and as Eternity dwells around them, from thence time like a stream from a fountain flows down upon the worlds." (Plutarch's *On the Cessation of Oracles.*)

Trilobe or Trefoil. A form much used in mullions and arcades of the Gothic architecture and derived from the cloverleaf or the outer rim of three circles, one above two, both of which were ancient symbols of the Trinity.

"Trimurti." The Hindu triad, Brahma the Creator, Vishnu the Preserver and Siva the Destroyer or Apathy.

Triquetra. A mystical three-pointed ornament derived from three elongated circles without beginning or end and forming a symbolical *motif* in architectural decoration.

Tri-ratna. The "three precious jewels," Buddha, Dharma and Sangha whose symbols are the trisula, the syllable a.u.m. and the triangle.

Trisula. A three-forked flame resembling a trident. A buddhistic emblem and called "the invocation of the 'highest.' "

Uatchet. [See Nekhebet.]

Umbrella or Parasol. An emblem of royalty universally adopted by Eastern nations and carried over the head of a king in times of peace and sometimes in war. Like the halo it is derived from the solar wheel and is placed over the head of Buddha as a symbol of power.

Unicorn. In all countries from pre-historic days the unicorn has been the symbol of purity, strength of body and virtue of mind—"the emblem of perfect good." It is one of the four supernatural divinely constituted beasts of the Chinese and was supposed to combine both the masculine and feminine principles. It appears in the earliest examples in Chinese art where it closely resembles the dragon-horse. It seems to be a popular Chinese idea that the unicorn is the size of a goat with a horn in the centre of its forehead. The unicorn is sometimes depicted with a parrot on its back, the unicorn typifying dumb justice and the parrot the vociferous advocate of truth. The early Christians adopted the unicorn as a symbol of chastity and it was thus given to St. Justina. Chemists also used the unicorn as a trademark to indicate the purity of their goods. In the Renaissance, when the imagination broke away from the rigid control of the Church, it seems to have been a matter of instinct with the artists to make use of all the typical figures that belonged to the rich florescence of the mythic past. Thus we see the lion and the unicorn in the famous tapestries in the Musée Cluny, where the unicorn is the symbol of incorruptibility or the nobility of the robe, and the lion is the symbol of force or the nobility of the sword.

Unicorn's Horn. The belief that the unicorn typified purity and virtue led to the further belief that the horn of the animal had the power of revealing treasons and was an antidote against poisons. In the Middle Ages the smallest piece of anything that purported to be this rare horn commanded a price ten times more than its weight in gold. The unicorn's horn now in the Musée Cluny, Paris (in reality a narwhal's tusk) was presented to Charlemagne by the Sultan Haroun-al-Raschid in 807, deposited by the emperor in the imperial treasury at Aix-la-Chapelle, and afterwards placed by his grandson Charles the Bald in the treasury of the abbey church of St. Denis where it was jealously guarded for 950 years as a potent means of protecting the French kings against poisoning. It bears the scars of various notches.

Uræus Serpent. The uræus was an Egyptian symbol of royalty and power and worn on the king's crown was supposed to spit venom on the king's enemies.

Ûrnâ. The shining spot in Buddha's forehead, the sign of spiritual consciousness, symbol of the "eye divine" and later developed as the third eye of Siva.

Uzat. The mystic eye. An Egyptian amulet which, when worn by a cord around the neck, was a protection against malice, envy, evil. The Uzat or Eye of Horus was also a charm against the evil eye, which was as greatly feared in Egypt as in Italy. [See Eye.]

Vajra or Thunderbolt. The Chaldeans figured the thunderbolt by a trident. In Nimroud it is held in the left hand of a god who holds an axe in the right. As the axe symbolised the sun, and the trident is given to the gods of storm and water, we have here again the powerful union of fire and water. The *Vajra* appears in Mesopotamia as a double trident. Marduk holds the double trident in each hand in fighting with the monster Tiamat. A trident with zigzag branches representing lightning is frequently shown in the hands of Assyrian gods.

Venus. [See Aphrodite.]

Vishnu. His Three Strides are his position at dawn, at noon and in the evening. The garuda bird half-giant, half-eagle was his vehicle and his symbol, the discus, is identified with the Wheel of the Law.

Vulcan. [See Hephæstus.]

Vulture. An Egyptian symbol of purification, also of maternity owing to its devotion to its young. Mut, Neith, Nekhebet and various other mother goddesses were given the vulture.

Wheel. One of the oldest symbols of the occult power of the sun. It is given to all the sun-gods as a symbol of universal dominion. Among the Hindus and Buddhists the turning of the wheel represented re-birth. The spokes in the Buddhist wheels were generally multiples of four. The connection between the wheel and thunderbolt is a very curious one. The Buddhist praying wheels turn in the direction in which the sun moves and, while the wheel is turned in the right hand, the dorjé or thunderbolt is held in the left. The discus of Vishnu is identified with the wheel of the law. The rays of the wheel uniting in a common centre symbolised divine unity.

Willow Branch. With it Kwan-yin the Chinese goddess of mercy sprinkles about her the divine nectar of life. The willow branch is sometimes depicted in a vase.

Wood. Swedenborg makes wood a symbol of "celestial goodness in its lowest corporeal plane."

Zen. The absolute is immanent in every man's heart. There is no use seeking Buddha outside your own nature—no Buddha but your own thoughts. Zen means "for a man to behold his own fundamental nature." Buddha is thought.

Zeus, (Jupiter). In Greek art Zeus is always represented as a bearded man of noble and majestic mien. His attributes are the eagle, the sceptre and the thunderbolt. The thunderbolt in his hand typifies that he is the origin, beginning, middle and end of all things. He is heaven, earth, fire, water, day and night. His eyes are the sun and moon. He is space and eternity, the essence and life of all beings. He is sometimes represented in sitting posture in allusion to his immutable essence, the upper part of his body uncovered, typifying the upper regions of the universe, and covered from the waist down because in terrestrial things he is more secret and concealed. He holds the sceptre in the left hand because the heart is on the left side and the heart is the seat of understanding.

INDEX

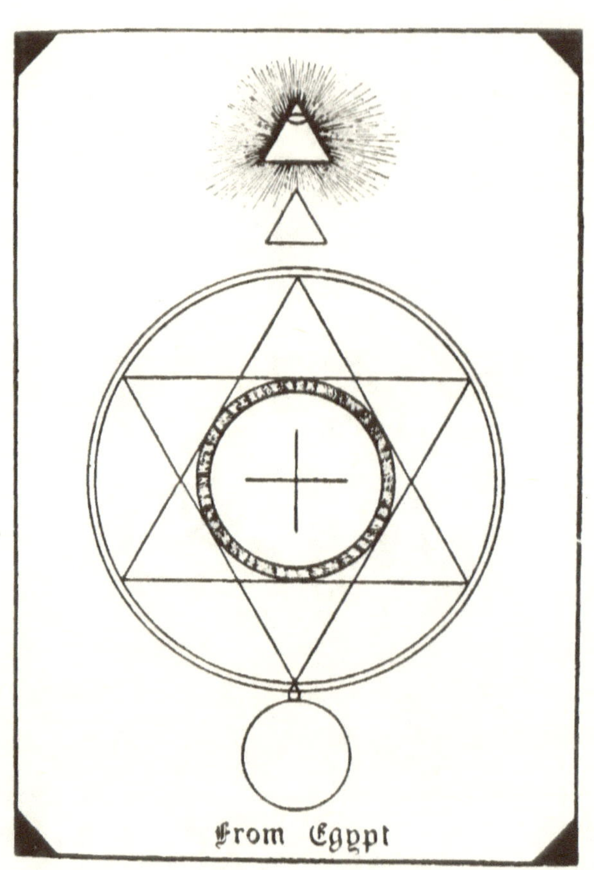

From Egypt

www.ingramcontent.com/pod-product-compliance
Lightning Source LLC
Chambersburg PA
CBHW022014120726
47902CB00012B/37

* 9 7 8 1 7 8 1 0 7 1 8 8 5 *